True Spirit

JESSICA WATSON

True Spirit

THE AUSSIE GIRL WHO TOOK ON THE WORLD

hachette
AUSTRALIA

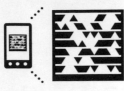

Get the free mobile app at
http://gettag.mobi

Publisher's note

Throughout *True Spirit* owners of smartphones can scan the six tags within the pages to connect with Jessica's video diary entries.

Download the free Microsoft Tag app at http://gettag.mobi Then hold your phone's camera about ten centimetres away from the tag images placed throughout the book, and it will play videos filmed by Jessica Watson while she sailed around the world.

If you don't have a smartphone you can still access the videos by visiting Jessica Watson's YouTube channel at www.youtube.com/ jessicawatsonvideo

hachette
AUSTRALIA

Published in Australia and New Zealand in 2010
by Hachette Australia
(an imprint of Hachette Australia Pty Limited)
Level 17, 207 Kent Street, Sydney NSW 2000
www.hachette.com.au

10 9 8 7 6 5 4

National Library of Australia
Cataloguing-in-Publication data

Watson, Jessica, 1993–.

True spirit: the Aussie girl who took on the world / Jessica Watson.

978 0 7336 2497 1 (pbk.)

Watson, Jessica, 1993–.
Women sailors – Australia – Biography.
Sailing – Records – Australia.
Yachting – Australia.
Voyages around the world.
Ocean travel.

910.41092

Cover, internal and picture section design by Christabella Designs
Front and back cover and inside cover photographs courtesy of Newspix
Cover portrait of Jessica Watson courtesy of Steven Chee
Map and boat guides by Christabella Designs
Typeset in 11.5/18 pt Sabon LT Std by Bookhouse, Sydney
Printed and bound in Australia by Griffin Press, Adelaide, an accredited ISO AS/NZS 14001:2004 Environmental Management System printer

The paper this book is printed on is certified by the Programme for the Endorsement of Forest Certification scheme. Griffin Press holds PEFC chain of custody SGS - PEFC/COC-0594. PEFC promotes environmentally responsible, socially beneficial and economically viable management of the world's forests.

To everyone who followed and shared the voyage
with me, thank you.

And to Mum . . .

A note from the author

Thanks to all the people who have followed my blog. When I was putting this book together with my publisher I started to rewrite the story of the voyage in a more traditional way, but it didn't work. I lost something doing this. Instead, I decided to include the blogs (though they have been edited sometimes) and then expand on them to reveal things I wasn't quite ready to talk about when I was at sea and to pass on things I have learnt since. I hope you enjoy reading about my *whole* journey, not just my 210 days on the ocean.

It can get a bit confusing, but throughout this book I have used kilometres to measure distances on land, and nautical miles to measure distances at sea.

1 nautical mile = 1.852 kilometres

Interestingly, a nautical mile is longer than a normal mile (1.6 kilometres).

I have also used feet and inches when referring to the length of vessels, but metres and centimetres for everything else.

1 foot = 0.3048 metres

All temperatures are given in degrees Celsius.

I've tried to explain the sailing terms as I go, but I have also included a glossary at the back of the book – I hope you find it helpful.

Jessica Watson, 2010

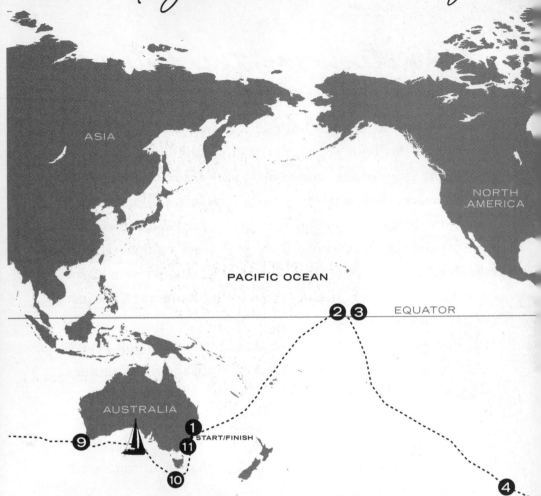

1. Departed from Sydney, 18 October 2009
2. Crossed the equator, 19 November 2009
3. Caught my first (and only) fish,
   23 November 2009
4. Christmas at Point Nemo – the furthest
   point from any land
5. Rounded Cape Horn, 13 January 2010
6. Experienced four knockdowns in the
   South Atlantic Ocean, 23 January 2010

7. Passed south of Cape Town and Cape Agulhas, 23 February 2010
8. Roughly halfway between Cape Agulhas and Cape Leeuwin, 19 March 2010
9. Sailed under Cape Leeuwin, back in Australian waters, 11 April 2010
10. Wild seas rounding Tasmania, 2 May 2010
11. Arrived back in Sydney Harbour, 15 May 2010

Contents

What is it in the sea life which is so powerful in its influence? . . . it whispers in the wind of the veldt, it hums in the music of the tropical night . . . above all it is there to the man who holds the night watch alone at sea. It is the sense of things done, of things endured, of meanings not understood; the secret of the Deep Silence, which is of eternity, which the heart cannot speak.

From Mast and Sail in Europe and Asia
by H. Warington Smyth (1867–1943)

A half-moon had risen, giving the sea a silvery sheen above the darkness below. After sunset, the still, glassy conditions of the afternoon had been blown away by a light wind from the west and *Ella's Pink Lady* was making good time under full sail with the mainsail, staysail and headsail set. I couldn't have asked for better conditions for my first night out. Watching *Ella's Pink Lady* sail along at a steady 4 knots, I felt extremely proud of my cute little pink yacht. Finally being on my way was a big relief, and I contemplated the next few days sailing and the huge adventure that I'd soon be setting off on. It was a beautiful night and the thought of something going wrong was the furthest from my mind.

I'd left Mooloolaba with an escort of boats and helicopters at around ten that morning, and after fifteen hours at sea and weeks of full-time preparation I was feeling tired and slightly queasy. It normally took me a few days to find my sea legs. Confident that everything was fine, I decided to put my head down for a few minutes and have a catnap.

Ella's Pink Lady and I were about 15 nautical miles east of North Stradbroke Island by this point. I'd have liked to have been further offshore, away from the local fishing fleets and possible shipping, however the current and earlier light winds meant I hadn't sailed very far since leaving. After scanning the horizon, checking the radar and AIS (Alarm Indication System) and setting my alarms, I climbed into my bunk, still wearing my life jacket and harness.

A horrible bone-shuddering explosion of noise woke me as *Ella's Pink Lady* was suddenly stopped in her tracks and violently spun around. Jumping up as the awful grinding noise continued, a quick glance up through the companionway told me that we'd collided with something huge, a ship. The sky was a wall of black steel, obscuring the stars and towering over me. The roar of engines filled my head and my whole world.

Leaning out into the cockpit, I grabbed at the tiller, flicked off the autopilot and tried to steer us. It was hopeless. There was nowhere to go, nothing I could do. Shuddering and screeching, we were being swept down the ship's hull. Another glance told me that the ship's stern, with its bridges protruding, was fast approaching. The noises were getting louder and, knowing that the mast and rigging were about to come down, I rushed back below hoping for some protection.

With my hands over my head I sat on my bunk as a whole new and far more terrible set of noises began. A few short seconds passed but to me they felt like hours. The cupboard next to me ripped apart as the chainplate behind the bulkhead splintered it into a million pieces. The boat heeled to one side then suddenly sprung upright with the loudest explosion yet as the entangled rigging suddenly freed itself and crashed to the deck.

When the boat steadied and the roar of the engines started to fade I went back on deck. It was a mess. There was rigging, lines and huge rusty flakes of black paint and slivers of metal from the ship's hull everywhere. Beyond *Ella's Pink Lady* I could see the dark outline of the huge ship's stern slipping away unaffected, leaving us at a stop in the foaming white slipstream.

Shocked and disbelieving, my head still reeling, I desperately tried to come to grips with what had happened while checking the bilges for water and the hull for damage. All I could think was 'my poor boat', and while flicking switches to see what equipment still worked it became a sort of chant – 'my poor boat, my poor, poor boat'. I was numb and still shaking off the last remnants of sleep; being scared hadn't crossed my mind. My only thoughts were for *Ella's Pink Lady*.

Taking deep breaths to calm my shaking hands, I picked up the radio to call the ship and then grabbed the phone to tell Dad what had happened. 'I'm okay,' I told him. 'I'm fine, perfectly okay, but we've been hit by a ship, we've been dismasted,' I finished in a rush.

Back on deck, alone and miles from land, it took me over two hours to slowly clear the deck, lash the broken rigging in place and cut the tangled headsail away. I had to pause frequently to lean over the side and throw up as my earlier queasiness had turned into full-on seasickness. Finally, I turned on the engine to motor the six hours to the Gold Coast.

How quickly everything had changed.

Ahead of me lay at least 23,000 nautical miles of empty ocean, furious gales and the threat of multiple knockdowns. But on that day, I doubted that anything I was to face in my months alone at sea would be as difficult as holding my head high as I steered a crippled *Ella's Pink Lady* between the Gold Coast breakwaters and saw the crowds lining the river, the fleet of spectator boats and the scrum of waiting media.

I didn't know if the crowd was there to show their support or to witness what many thought was my early defeat. I had to force myself to ignore negative thoughts and to concentrate only on guiding us up the river, throwing the occasional wave and half-hearted smile to nearby boats.

I knew that in one horrifying incident I had given fuel to anyone who had criticised me and my parents for what I was trying to do. In their eyes I had proven exactly why I shouldn't ever be permitted to sail alone. However, in that same moment, I had proven to myself that I had the ability to achieve my dream. Any doubts about whether I could cope mentally vanished. I realised my inner strength.

In the coming months, when *Ella's Pink Lady* was thrown violently about by the wind and waves, or when home felt a million miles away as we drifted, becalmed, and the days ran into each other in slow motion, I was able to look back on that day after the collision with the 63,000 tonne bulk carrier *Silver Yang* and draw strength from knowing I'd held myself together when all I'd really wanted to do was fall apart. As the saying goes, what doesn't kill you makes you stronger. That tanker could have killed me but it didn't. And in its wake I was stronger, more determined and ready for whatever came my way . . . almost.

PART ONE

The Starting Point

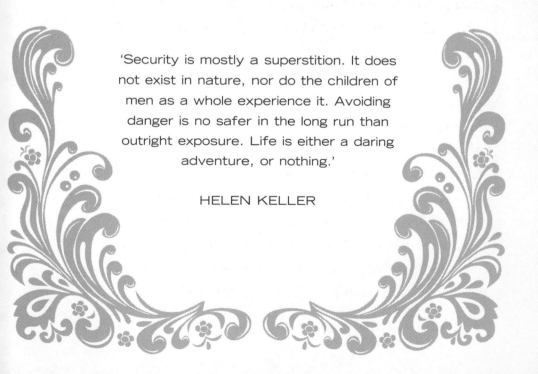

'Security is mostly a superstition. It does
not exist in nature, nor do the children of
men as a whole experience it. Avoiding
danger is no safer in the long run than
outright exposure. Life is either a daring
adventure, or nothing.'

HELEN KELLER

When I was young I was pretty much afraid of everything. I'm not sure when that changed, but Mum tells a story about a day at a family gathering when I was playing with my cousins and my elder sister. They were all holding hands and jumping into a swimming pool, and Mum was watching me closely because I was afraid of water and couldn't swim. I was five years old.

I obviously got sick of only watching the game, because as everyone lined up to hold hands for another leap I joined in. Mum says she kept waiting for me to let go, but I didn't. I jumped with everyone else, shrieking and giggling until we hit the water. I sank to the bottom and my uncle rushed to pull me out.

I wish I could say when it was that I went from being that quiet little girl, tagging along behind the others, to the girl who set off to sail around the world believing completely that with enough dedication she could achieve anything she set her mind to. Somewhere along the way I learnt that if you truly want to live life you have to get involved, pursue your passions and dream big. I don't know when that was, and I don't remember jumping into the pool that day, it's just a story my mum tells. But somewhere between that moment and sailing out of Sydney Harbour on *Ella's Pink Lady*, I came to understand what Helen Keller said far better than I can – 'Life is either a daring adventure, or nothing.'

To tell you about myself and why I wanted to sail around the world, I have to start by telling you about my parents. As Dad likes to remind me, I wouldn't be here without them, and it's only with the support of my family that I've been able to follow my dream.

My mum, Julie, and dad, Roger, are both from New Zealand. They married there in 1986 and in 1987 flew to Sydney, bought themselves an old station wagon from a car dealer on Parramatta Road and drove up the coast to Queensland. Apparently, once they hit the Pacific Highway and started to go a bit faster, they noticed the car had a terrible diff whine that they hadn't picked up on before. Mum laughs about it now and says the dealer must have thought, 'Look at these Kiwis just off the boat, I'll sell them this lemon.' Luckily, the car made it to the Gold Coast and Mum and Dad set about making a new life for themselves.

Mum found work as an occupational therapist but Dad decided to give away boiler-making and try something different. Before he got into real estate he had a business hiring televisions, and it can't be a coincidence that we never had a television when I was growing up. I think Dad saw how dependent people became on them and how they restricted the lives of their owners – keeping them inside and inactive – and he decided he didn't ever want to be like that.

I don't think my parents planned to stay in Australia forever but then my elder sister, Emily, was born in 1992, I was born in 1993, my brother, Tom, was born in 1995 and my younger sister, Hannah, came along in 1997. And so, with four young kids, they were too busy to think about moving back to New Zealand.

Apart from not having a television (which definitely put us in the minority) my childhood was very normal. Mum and Dad were never sailors, in their early days together the closest they got to a boat was fishing in a tinny back in Whangarei. They were big on camping trips and we would get away as often as we could. Dad would give us the choice of either going to one of the local Gold Coast theme parks for the day or spending the same amount of money to head off camping for a week at our favourite spot. Camping always won. Then, when I was in Year Four, Mum put us into a summer holiday sailing camp run by the Southport Yacht Club. I have a feeling she thought Tom would get the most out of it, even though he was only six, but Emily and I were also part of the action. Hannah was too young so she preferred to stay on the beach with Mum. From that camp the three of us moved on to the weekend beginners' sailing class and then to club racing. John Murphy, our instructor, was great, although I'm sure his voice was permanently damaged from yelling across the water at us to 'Pull that sheet in!'

I wasn't exactly thrilled by sailing at first. I was frightened to be out on the Broadwater and so far from shore, but I never felt pressure to keep sailing from Mum or Dad or anyone else. On the windy days when I decided not to sail, I had to sit on the beach with Hannah and I felt very left out. Watching everyone pull their boats up the beach at the end of the day – smiling and full of stories – was hard and I knew I was letting fear stop me from being part of the fun. Emily was really good. She picked up everything quickly and made it look effortless. I could see how much she loved it and I wanted to be like my elder sister. It's a bit like that day jumping into the pool. I didn't want to be left on the beach, waiting for everyone to come back bragging about a race. I wanted to be in the thick of it. On the days when it was windy and the Broadwater was covered in small whitecaps, I didn't have enough strength to handle my boat and was always somewhere at the back of the fleet, struggling. But on the quiet days, when being strong and quick didn't matter, I found that, with a bit of planning, using tactics and a lot of patience, I could be right among the pack and competing for positions. As I got better at sailing my confidence increased and I began enjoying it more and more.

Mum asked me once if I felt pushed into sailing. I didn't. It was just something we did. It became our family thing and, if anything, we kids pushed Mum and Dad into sailing. We didn't play netball or soccer or do nippers, we went sailing. The sailing facility at Southport Yacht Club, at Hollywell, was a friendly, family sort of place separate from the licensed club. It didn't take long for the whole family to be spending all our weekends at the yacht club with us kids taking lessons, racing or crewing on bigger boats, and Mum and Dad driving or manning the rescue boats.

My best friend, Pamela Fredric, and her family were also part of the sailing club, and had the no-television thing going on too, so if we weren't outside we'd be busy making something or playing games. Winter school holidays were the exception. Sometimes

Mum and Dad would hire a television and a video player and we would curl up and watch documentaries and movies together as a holiday treat. Our family favourite was a documentary by Sir Edmund Hilary on his climb of Everest. My parents are very normal people but things like not having a television were seen by many as strange, so that was probably an early indication that they were not going to make certain lifestyle choices just because everyone else did. As we got older, decisions were always made with input from all the family. When tying the dinghies on the roof of the car after a long weekend on the water, Emily and I were trusted and expected to do just as good a job as any adult. I never felt like a dismissed kid who was seen and not heard, but rather as a person with my own valued opinions.

By the time I was in school, Dad had long since left television hire behind and had established a thriving real estate business. Then, out of the blue, he had an offer from someone who wanted to buy the business and, though he didn't accept it, the proposition started Mum and Dad thinking about what they could do if they weren't so tied down. Like anyone, they initially found it hard to contemplate breaking out of their settled life, especially with four kids, but they started to dream and one of the things they discussed was travelling around Australia. About a year later another offer came along and this time Dad accepted. Dad had always said that if he was going to travel he wanted to do it as a family. He didn't want to wait until we had all left home and become a grey nomad. Who knew what could happen in the future?

So, the plan was to buy and modify a bus that we could travel around Australia in before we were too old to want to do it together. I was at the start of Year Five when Mum and Dad sold our house in 2004, and while they were getting the bus ready to travel with all six of us they bought a 52-foot motorboat for us to live on. It was called *Home Abroad*. We had gotten rid of a lot of stuff when we moved out of the house but we made sure our pet cockatiel, Maggie, came along with us. I think the plan was to spend some time on the boat and then head off in the bus on the great adventure, but we ended up on the boat for over five and a half years, cruising up and down the Queensland coast and making the occasional trip on the bus to inland Australia. We left school when we moved onto the boat and the four of us started distance education with Mum 'boat' or 'bus' schooling us.

Right from the start we learnt that boats come with endless breakdowns and maintenance issues. It took a while before we had everything shipshape enough to spend more time out at sea and at anchorages than in the safety of marinas and the necessary boat yards. We slowly learnt how to handle the boat as a family, becoming more confident as we went. Emily and I sat in while Mum and Dad studied navigation and also when they went for their radio licences. It didn't take us long to establish a routine for docking and leaving a harbour. We all had jobs and were all an important part of the crew.

When the boat was sorted and we had the knowledge we needed (and our docking had improved to the point where half the marina stopped putting out extra fenders to protect their boats every time we came and went!) we started cruising further north up the east coast of Australia. This new life gave us kids an amazing freedom. We'd stop at islands where we'd be the only boat in the anchorage. We'd swim, snorkel, collect shells and explore beaches, islands and waterways. There would be walks up to lighthouses, down gullies and to find waterfalls. There was always something particularly special about a place when you had it all to yourself.

We visited some incredible areas, but I think we'd all agree that Lizard Island was the best of all. It was a breathtaking tropical paradise of palm-lined beaches and coral reefs. The main anchorage at Lizard Island is always full of yachts and boats and everyone anchored there would come ashore at sunset to meet up on the beach. It was a very relaxed and friendly environment and as the grown-ups chatted about their comings and goings, the kids would be off exploring on their own. Sometimes we'd meet up with other families on yachts, get to know them and travel with them for a time. There would be fires on the beach, water fights and all sorts of expeditions across islands and up mountains. But most of the time we travelled alone, just us, and because of that Emily, Tom, Hannah and I became very close.

It wasn't all idyllic sunshine, smooth seas and clear skies though. There were family quarrels, sibling fights and teasing, grumpy moods and the need to stop in various ports to wait for bad weather to pass and to stock up on provisions. We'd often fill three or four shopping trolleys at the local supermarket – Tom and I became experts at sneaking in a little extra chocolate! When the weather kept us in one place too long we'd all get impatient (probably when most of the fights and grumpiness flared up), wanting to be on the move again. Mum and Dad used these stops to make us catch up on our schoolwork so we were always pleased when the good weather returned.

One of the only times that we hit any *really* bad weather while cruising is a memory that's pretty embarrassing and, looking back, kind of hilarious, too. We hadn't been living on the boat all that long at the time so we were all still learning the ins and outs.

I was eleven. It was one of those afternoon storms that seem to whip up out of nowhere and turn nasty very quickly. There was terrible visibility, 40-knot winds and a steep messy sea. I spent all my time, when I wasn't needed on deck as a look-out, hiding under the saloon table pretending to comfort Maggie!

Living on the water also meant that we met all sorts of characters and old salts who inevitably hang around yacht clubs, marinas and boat yards; it was fascinating and often inspiring to hear about their sailing and boating experiences. Though, I have to admit it annoyed me heaps when I was dismissed because I was a girl – and a 'scrawny young thing' as well. When you live on the water, it's an unwritten law that when another boat is pulling in you stop to give a hand and take their lines. Being a 'little girl' meant that more often than not, my offer of help would be completely ignored, while the line was passed to the fully grown man next to me. It was incredibly frustrating to have this happen. I was just as capable of handling the lines as anyone else. I hated being judged by my appearance and other people's expectations of what a 'little girl' was capable of.

Dismissals like this may have made some people give up on sailing altogether, but I just got fired up. Maybe part of it was because I knew what I could do and so, even though I was young, I wasn't going to let other people knock my confidence. For a long time I had struggled with reading and spelling (actually, I still have big problems with spelling) but I was lucky because Mum and the teachers at school recognised early on that I was dyslexic. Dyslexia is a neurologically based language disorder that means a person has difficulty recognising and learning the connection between sounds and words. It's one particular form of learning disability that can make reading, spelling and sometimes maths difficult to understand. For some, this can really put a dent in your self-esteem, but I was lucky because no one ever made a huge deal about it with me. I never felt labelled and was never made to feel stupid because I couldn't read properly, which I know can happen to some kids. Mum just kept plugging away, encouraging my love of books by reading to all of us. She supported me and gave me time to find my own way.

Mum always said that one day a light would come on in my brain and my struggles with reading would fade. She was right. My favourite book was *The Little White Horse* and I would pester Mum to read it to me all the time. One day she said, 'Jess, you practically know it off by heart. Why don't you read it to yourself?' So I did. I faltered at first but after that I moved on to other stories and new books. Once I had the hang of it I could escape into another world whenever I liked. I am now a big reader, but I'm not sure my spelling's ever going to be much good. Despite that, I've always been able to get good grades in English (well, I would be able to if they didn't deduct points for it arriving so late) by putting in more time and effort. Luckily, I have someone who checks my blogs before they go up so I don't have to worry too much. Still, I'm sure there's a lot of giggling behind my back at some of my more amusing mistakes!

Getting ready for the trip meant I wrote all the time. I wrote to people for advice, to try and chase up sponsors and I made list after list of what I would need. Writing my blog has also helped my confidence and taught me more than any weekly spelling test ever did. And writing this book has been another challenge but, trust me, it will have been decoded (proofread) before it gets to you!

Dealing with this type of learning difficulty perhaps made me a stronger person, so coping with small knockbacks – from some sailor overlooking my offer of help to tie up a boat, to people saying I didn't have what it takes to sail around the world – never caused me to doubt myself, or rarely ever. Overcoming dyslexia has certainly been a great lesson, showing me what you can achieve with some extra effort, despite whatever setbacks or handicaps stand in your way.

Living on the water on the family's motorboat, surrounded by all things nautical, meant sailing and boating had become a big part of my life. But until the day Mum started to read us Jesse Martin's *Lionheart,* I'd never even considered that I could one day become an adventurer. I'd always thought of adventurers as grey-haired men with beards who climbed mountains or flew old aeroplanes across wide expanses of ocean. Hearing about Jesse made me think differently. It was as if something clicked in my mind. This guy wasn't a superhero, he wasn't privileged in any way, he didn't have a beard and he definitely wasn't old. Jesse was a normal, everyday person who had a dream and decided to make it happen. He was someone I could relate to and it made me wonder . . . Could I do it? Could I sail around the world on my own?

I didn't tell anyone at first what was going through my head. I started reading everything I could about solo sailing. I made lists of what I'd need and collected articles about boats and rigging and long-lasting food. Mum says she knew something was going on because I started putting pictures of huge Southern

Ocean waves and storms above my berth. I was visualising myself dealing with the wild seas and fierce winds before I even knew what visualisation was.

Once the seed was planted and I started dreaming of sailing around the world, the first thing that hooked me in was a curiosity about whether or not it was something I could do. It wasn't so much the action-packed and adrenaline-fuelled nature of it that appealed to me, it wasn't the thought of knockdowns and 12-metre waves, it was all about putting a plan in place and getting the details right so that the risks were minimised as much as possible. I knew I was a young girl and that I didn't have the physical strength of a fully grown man so I had to work out ways to do things that suited me and my body. To me, sailing is not about strength, it is about knowledge, and I spent all my spare time learning about sailing by doing it or talking to really great sailors and listening to what they had to say. I would rather be sailing than anywhere else and I love the challenge of making my own decisions and overcoming the problems thrown at me. When I am on the water reefing a sail or tacking in response to the wind and the waves, everything becomes really simple. It was only after a long time spent visualising what it would be like in the Southern Ocean, mentally putting myself through different situations, imagining how I would feel at different times and constantly asking myself whether I could do it, and whether I really wanted to do it, that I came to the conclusion that I could and I did.

I thought about it a lot, made more lists and read heaps more books, among them was Joshua Slocum's *Sailing Alone Around the World*. He was the first person to sail around the world singlehanded. Slocum left Boston, Massachusetts, in April 1895 and he sailed his boat, *Spray*, into Newport, Rhode Island, in June 1898. It took him three years, two months and two days to achieve his astonishing feat. I read anything I could find on solo circumnavigations and learnt about people like Francis Chichester, who was the first person to sail around the world solo west to east via the great capes. Kay Cottee was the first woman to sail solo, unassisted and non-stop around the world and I read her book, *First Lady*, over and over. I was fascinated to read about Ellen MacArthur, who in 2001 was the youngest person ever to complete the Vendée Globe round-the-world non-stop yacht race and went on to set a new world record for a solo, non-stop circumnavigation of the world. I loved reading about Robin Lee Graham and his five-year journey to sail around the world in his boat, *Dove*. I also read *Lionheart* again and again and finally got up the courage to share what I was thinking with my sister Emily. It was just another one of our discussions about our hopes for the future, so it didn't seem like all that much of a big deal.

Telling Mum and Dad was really hard. I was twelve and we'd just come back from a season's cruising and were having a pretty serious family discussion about what our plans were from there. It was the perfect time to bring up my dream, but if it hadn't been for Emily dropping hints and forcing me to explain I would have chickened out and kept quiet. I knew that Mum and Dad wouldn't tell me I wasn't allowed to go but I was still incredibly nervous.

I had to be able to imagine myself out there on my own, and after a while I could. I'd done enough research to know it was possible, that in theory I could do this. You can never *really* know what's going to happen, the ocean is powerful and completely unpredictable, but I believed if I made the effort, had the right boat, prepared myself physically and mentally, developed my sailing skills and sought out the knowledge a solo sailor needs, that I'd have as much chance as anyone to sail around the world. When I finally brought up my plans with Mum and Dad I might have been telling not asking but, of course, I wasn't going to be able to go without their blessing (until after I was eighteen anyway!). And if they'd had any reasonable objections to my plan I wasn't going to lightly brush them aside. I would listen and absorb theirs – and anyone else's – well-informed advice.

Finally getting the words out was quite a relief. I couldn't have explained what I wanted to do any more seriously (tears and all!). I'm not really sure that Mum and Dad believed me right away or maybe they chose not to, hoping that I'd forget about it and move on to something else. Mum says when six months had passed and I was still totally focused on making this dream a reality, she started to believe I would achieve my goal. She threw her support behind me. Dad didn't get behind the idea till much later. After me constantly pestering, talking, getting him to teach me all he knew about engines, asking him to phone sailors I'd been getting advice from and cluttering up the boat with folders full of cuttings from magazines and pictures of yachts for sale, it was getting harder for him to ignore my dedication.

At the end of *Lionheart*, Jesse Martin says:

We need to encourage and help those around us, particularly our youth, with whatever their dreams may be, and then we'll start to see great things happen. I was just a normal kid with a dream who was serious about what I wanted to do. But without the support of my family, I would never have made it . . . There are people out there dreaming of great things, and it's a good chance that your son, daughter, brother, sister or friend is one of them.

Believe and encourage them so they won't lose one of humanity's most prized assets – the ability to dream.

My parents had always encouraged me to dream and, with their help, I was going to do everything I could to make my dream come true. Thanks to sailors like Jesse Martin, Kay Cottee, David Dicks and Tania Aebi I knew that normal people could do extraordinary things. I wanted to be one of them.

At the end of our second year on *Home Abroad* we headed back to the marina at Mooloolaba for Christmas on the Sunshine Coast. As we got older, Emily and I were finding it tougher to live in such a confined space and not being able to get away from each other or the rest of the family. Being at the marina was great because it meant we could spread out a bit, give each other a little more room and do our own things. The marina is barely 100 metres from the beach, so we spent a great deal of the summer hanging out there with the Rawlings family, who we'd met while cruising the Whitsundays. They were also spending Christmas at Mooloolaba.

Like us, there were four kids in the Rawlings family. Their eldest, Nick, and Emily were around the same age and they hit it off right from the start. Anna, the Rawlings' second child, and I bonded complaining about the annoying behaviour of our older siblings! The four of us hung out together and we'd go sailing in the bay and muck about in dinghies while the youngest two

Rawlings kids, Mikayla and Eric, played around the marina with Hannah and Tom.

After being used to the freedom we had when we were cruising, it didn't take long for our Mooloolaba day trips to be pushed further. We talked our parents into letting us go camping. One time we headed up one of the local rivers in an over-loaded dinghy. We were perched on top of all our camping gear, complete with a 12-volt fridge and a solar panel so we could charge our iPods. We drew some funny looks from the canoeists as we passed by with our little two-horsepower engine *putt-putt-putting* away!

We'd often be out of phone range on our adventures and we learnt fast that it was up to us to get out of any trouble we got into. Being the eldest, Nick was the leader; my role was the parental negotiator, because there was often a lot of persuasion needed to talk the parents into letting us go off somewhere. Despite the fact we weren't drinking, partying hard or taking drugs, Mum and Dad were criticised by other parents around the yacht club for giving us so much independence. They always knew where we were going and they never let us go anywhere without a well-stocked first-aid kit and insisting we take all the necessary precautions. Yes, bad things can happen, but bad things can happen anywhere and wrapping us in cottonwool was not necessarily going to keep us safe. My parents made a purposeful choice to let us have space to explore and they trusted us to do the right thing. No matter what, in their minds, that was the right way and the only way for them to parent their children, and it makes me angry when they are judged.

People often ask me how I talked Mum and Dad into allowing me to sail around the world. The truth is I put in the groundwork and gained their trust with these smaller adventures. It's true that any big thing starts with a few small steps. Nick, Emily, Anna and I always did our research, planned thoroughly, and if all else failed, there was always some persistent and determined nagging. The same principles applied to sailing around the world – actually, less nagging and heaps more planning, but you get the idea.

One particular trip was meant to be an easy weekend's sailing with Emily and Nick on a 23-foot yacht that Nick owned with another guy from the marina. At the time Nick was fifteen, Emily was fourteen and I was thirteen. We'd checked the weather forecasts, bought our provisions, charged our radios and left at first light to sail the 35 nautical miles down to Moreton Bay where we planned to spend the night before returning the next day. To start with, things went smoothly. The sail down was perfect and we pulled into the anchorage in time to have a swim before it got dark.

Things started going downhill in the evening when Nick, who'd had a slight cold, took a turn for the worse and was feeling really unwell. Then the wind changed direction during the night and many of the boats, including ours, started dragging anchor. We didn't manage to get much sleep as we spent the night avoiding other boats and trying not to get blown away. Daybreak was more promising and after a cooked breakfast we were looking forward to the sail home.

Once we'd left the more sheltered water of the bay, the wind started rising and then shifted unexpectedly from the north, the direction we were trying to sail. By mid afternoon we were making no progress in a pretty steep sea and increasing wind. Emily was severely seasick, leaving me and Nick to sail the boat and handle the worried phone calls from our parents. We weren't in any serious danger as we were not far off the coast and only a radio call away from help but, with the wind picking up again and nightfall approaching, things weren't looking great.

Up until then I would have been the first person to go to pieces in a situation like this (and end up under a saloon table) but at the tiller, as Nick navigated, I realised that if we were going to get out of this safely I had to pull my weight. If I had any hope of ever sailing around the world I was going to have to start proving myself. All of a sudden it wasn't Nick calling the shots as he normally would; we were making the decisions together with Nick even taking my lead. Drenched and exhausted as I was, everything suddenly looked different. Wrestling with the tiller became fun. Realising that I could do this, that I could do more than just let the conditions get the better of us, was the most exhilarating feeling. Looking back, I'd say that was the moment that sailing solo around the world became more than just a distant dream. During that drama I found my confidence and discovered that I really could influence how things turned out.

After weighing up our options, and phoning our parents to let them know what we were doing, we turned around and surfed into a safe anchorage. We spent another night dragging anchor before setting off once again the next day when the weather settled down. We started the sail home feeling more than a little apprehensive, but it turned out to be a perfect day. Any triumphant return was spoiled by the rudder suddenly falling off just a few kilometres from home, but we eventually made it back to the marina in a dramatic finish to a full-on weekend of sailing.

Mum and Dad hadn't given up on seeing some of Australia by land and in early 2006 we all packed up for a trip in the bus down the coast, then inland to Adelaide and up the Birdsville Track to experience the outback. It was very different from travelling together on the boat because we couldn't take off and explore by ourselves as much. It was great to see other parts of Australia but we all missed the freedom we had living on the water. And if we thought things could get cramped on a boat, it was even worse in a bus.

The novelty was enough to keep us excited at first and it was good for Mum. She has a bit of a thing for lighthouses, so all down the coast we'd stop at just about every lighthouse and the six of us would have to climb up the almost-always steep path to the top of a headland to check out the buildings and the view. The best one for me was the Wilsons Promontory Lighthouse at the southernmost point of mainland Australia. Built by convicts in the mid-1800s, the tower is made of the local granite and it sits on a cliff that looks out over the often wild Bass Strait. There is no vehicle access to the lighthouse, so it was a full day's walk to get to it, but well worth it. The views when you get there are stunning and it is definitely on my list of places to revisit so I can explore a bit more.

Caravan parks are expensive and because we were completely self-sufficient in the bus, we rarely used them. We'd make the most of truck stops, showgrounds and just about anywhere else you could park a bus and not be moved on. The bus was an impressive vehicle. It was huge, bulky and painted gold with a big red stripe down the side so it really stood out (we came to seriously regret the bold paint job!). It would have been a great bus for a touring rock band. One of the few times we stopped at a caravan park to catch up on a bit of schoolwork during a couple of rainy days, a group of curious campers got together and elected a leader who marched up to the door of the bus and knocked. We were all working away at the table and heard them ask Mum what time would be best for them to be given a tour of the inside. To their credit, they'd decided that if we showed them all through the bus at the one time it would be less inconvenient for us. Just another reason why we avoided caravan parks!

We spent my thirteenth birthday in a car park on the Great Ocean Road looking out at the Twelve Apostles. (Not that there were twelve to count. The ocean and wind keeps taking their toll on these limestone stacks and so there were only eight left when we were there.) I can almost map our trip by marking out the car parks. There was one at Charlotte Pass, in the heart of the New South Wales Snowy Mountains, where we had to wait for the snow to stop so we could bike to the top of Mt Kosciuszko – it says a lot that you can bike almost right to the top of Australia's tallest mountain!

Another time we spent the night on top of a sand dune overlooking Lake Eyre in South Australia. This campsite was made even more interesting because it was at the end of a 100 kilometre boggy, sandy, four-wheel-drive access road. The bus wasn't designed for off-roading, so we got some strange looks from the locals when we set off up the deserted track. Dad was always prepared for any disaster and before we drove off he made inquiries at a nearby town to make sure there was a tractor in the area big enough to pull us out if we did happen to get bogged.

That wasn't the only time we headed off-road. For me, the highlight of the whole trip was when we set off to travel along the Birdsville Track, a 520-kilometre old stock route which runs from Marree in South Australia to Birdsville in Queensland. It is a really beautiful area and the desert stretches out into miles and miles of flat nothingness, broken up only by the odd sand dune. It has a reputation as one of the harshest areas of Australia and can be tough to drive on. Though most of the year it is very dry and dust storms are common, when it rains it can become impassable and flash flooding can happen. We weren't too concerned as we were there in the dry season. We'd stop the bus at the odd water hole and the occasional ruin of an old sheep station to stretch our legs and explore. With the red earth, scarce water and gnarly vegetation it was a stark contrast to the lush rainforests and blue waters of the coast that we were used to.

We soon learnt how the track got its reputation when first one tyre went and then two together. Changing a tyre on the bus was a bit more of a challenge than on a normal family sedan, because everything is just so huge and you can only carry a certain amount of spare parts. The first time, everything went smoothly thanks to the help we got from some people in passing four-wheel drives. The second time wasn't so easy. For a start, we didn't have enough tyres left, so we just had to stop in the middle of the track for the night. Dad called for help on the sat-phone and we waited until some new tyres could be brought out to us. I'll always remember that night. I walked away from the lights of the bus, out into the desert to look at the stars. They seemed endless and were so clear and absolutely incredible! I've seen some pretty spectacular starry nights while out at sea, but there's something even more breathtaking about the sky in the outback.

We had a lot of fun on the road trip and I was glad Mum and Dad gave us the chance to see different parts of Australia, but I think we all knew when we finished that trip that our days touring on the bus as a family were over. We were getting too old for it and we were all keen to get back to the boat. If I wanted to improve my sailing skills I needed to be near the ocean.

By 2007 it was looking likely that we'd be based at the Mooloolaba Marina on the Sunshine Coast for a while, so Mum and Dad enrolled us in local schools. I lasted only a term at Maroochydore High before going back to distance education. Because I half-expected we'd be on the move again sooner rather than later, I didn't get involved in any sport or any other school activities and I didn't really attempt to make friends either. If I was going to sail around the world I needed to put my full effort into making it happen, so going back to distance education gave me more flexibility. I found a job washing dishes at Fish on Parkyn, one of the Sunshine Coast's leading restaurants. I needed to earn money because if I wanted to get some ocean sailing experience I had to be able to pay for airfares to get myself to a yacht. It was tough enough to persuade people that I would be up for crewing for them, but I also had to persuade Mum and Dad that it would be safe for me onboard, and working long hours to pay for my airfare was another way I could show them I was deadly serious about making this happen. You have to be dedicated to keep turning up to wash dishes until one in the morning . . . it isn't fun.

For me, the hardest part of this whole adventure was getting people to take me seriously and working out how to make it all happen. By this time Mum was behind me 100 per cent because she recognised how serious I was. I would use her as my sounding board to bounce ideas off about attracting sponsorship or gathering knowledge. I'd constantly ask her, 'How do we make this happen? What's the next step?'

I started by talking to people, telling them what I was hoping to do. I didn't have the money to do this by myself and I needed to let people know what I was planning. I visited boat yards, marinas and workshops, talked to whoever would listen and asked tonnes of questions. I wrote letters to anyone I could think of who might support me in some way; I even sent a letter to the Queensland Premier, Anna Bligh, to find out if there were any grants available to young adventurers. One of her policy advisers replied on her behalf to let me know there wasn't anything they could do to support individual efforts, but passed on information about the Duke of Edinburgh Awards and also a few websites that might be useful. I contacted newspapers and sent emails to reporters and editors to put my dream out there in the hope that someone might read about me and help me with sponsorship. By the time I turned fourteen I had spent almost three years learning everything I could and researching the best equipment to use. I had to get cracking if I wanted to achieve my goal and one of the main things I had to do was get a boat. Even if my parents had the money (which they didn't) they wouldn't have bought me a boat. At this point, they may have come around to the idea and were helping me where they could, but this was my thing, I had to put it together and show them I had what it took if I had any hope of their continued support.

There were so many people who supported me and helped me get out on the water, but one person who was crucial in getting me ready for this trip was Bruce Arms. Bruce has been sailing all his life, starting off in small dinghies and skiffs, then moving onto keel boats and multi-hulls. He is a solo sailor who has competed in three solo Tasman races and two Tasmanian Three Peaks races, and he won the 2007 and 2010 Solo Tasman Yacht Race from New Plymouth, New Zealand, to Mooloolaba, Queensland. Bruce has a huge amount of sailing experience and he is also a boat-builder, which makes him the perfect person to learn from. Bruce and his wife Suzanne are friends with Pat and Judy Gannon, a couple we met when we were cruising Lizard Island on the family boat. We stayed in touch with Pat and Judy and when they heard about my proposed trip they organised for me to meet Bruce in mid 2008.

At first, Bruce labelled me a little girl with a big scheme, but once we met he decided I had what it took to pull off this trip. Before he did anything he met up with Mum and Dad to make sure I was doing this for the right reasons and that I wasn't a puppet for my parents. It didn't take long for Bruce to see Dad was definitely not behind this and that Mum was supportive but not living her dream vicariously through me.

Bruce and I are very different. Bruce is a very methodical man who thinks things over and goes through the processes to be sure. He was the perfect mentor for me because, early on, I could go too quickly through something and not see the best way – my family call it being a bit blonde. I have learnt to slow myself down and be more measured and a lot of that is thanks to Bruce. After discussing it, Bruce and Suzanne decided they would do what they could to help me out. It was a big call for them and a number of Bruce's friends were worried that, should something go wrong on the trip, he could be held responsible in some way. Bruce knew there was criticism of me and my parents for what I was trying to do and was aware that anyone who agreed to help me would also become a target. He didn't care. Bruce could see something in me that he could relate to and he wasn't going to let others stop him from giving me all the assistance he could.

Bruce and Suzanne own a Chamberlin 46-foot multi-hull catamaran called *Big Wave Rider*. It is a beautiful boat to sail and once Bruce made up his mind to help me out he was a man of his word. He took me on a number of voyages to bolster my experience and to gauge if I had what it took to sail around the world. One trip was from Mooloolaba to Hobart and when Mum asked Bruce for his impression of my abilities he said, 'She has a talent for sailing and is a quick learner.'

If you ask Bruce what it takes to be a solo sailor he'll tell you a person has to be mentally strong, an all-round sailor and able to do everything themselves – cooking, sailing, electrical or engine repair, plumbing, rigging, weather watch, the list can be endless. What he doesn't add is an age or a gender, and from the moment we met I never felt judged or inadequate because I was a teenager and a girl. The sailing world is very male-dominated but for Bruce, and the many other fabulous supporters I have had, it has all come down to my ability, my focus and my dedication. Unlike the sailors who failed to pass me their line to tie up their boat, the fact I am a teenage girl is irrelevant to them. I do wonder if the outrage about me attempting to sail around the world would have been as full-on if I was a teenage boy. I know Jesse Martin and his mum and dad had to deal with a lot of criticism when he was setting off, so perhaps it would have been.

It was pretty clear the first thing I needed to do (besides find a boat) was to get some serious offshore sailing experience, not an easy task when you're a fourteen-year-old girl. Let's just say I wasn't going to be a skipper's first choice. I was already sailing once, and sometimes twice, a week with a local boat *Soraya* and I was also working casually at the local sailing school as an assistant, teaching kids and adults to sail in dinghies. Teaching kids to sail was good fun but I found that some of the adults didn't like being told what to do by someone so much younger than them, which more often than not ended with us all getting wet! This sort of attitude made me more and more determined to make my dream happen.

When I got the job as a dishy at Fish on Parkyn I don't think anyone there expected I would last long. It was hard work and meant a lot of late nights, but I loved the challenge of it, and if I was having a bad night, well, the restaurant made a really good sticky date pudding and someone had to eat the ones that didn't quite turn out! The money I earned went towards flights and things like wet-weather gear.

I can't tell you how excited I was when all my hard work looked like it was paying off. I lined up my first ocean passage from Vanuatu to Brisbane on the 42-foot *Elegant Gypsy*. We'd met the yacht's owners, Sharon and Chris, and their two young boys, Hugo and Max, when we'd been cruising up north, and had kept in touch since. They had just finished a season in Vanuatu. Sharon and the boys were going to fly back to Australia and Chris needed crew to help sail back.

Before Mum and Dad gave the okay, all the voyage details had to be double-checked, there was personal safety equipment to buy and Dad insisted on getting me a personal EPIRB (emergency position indication radio beacon). Mum and Dad nervously drove me down to the airport to see me off, still clearly worried about agreeing to let me go. Their confidence was not helped by the confusion at the check-in desk, where I was told, 'Sorry, there's no booking for anyone under the name of Watson.' Luckily the problem was sorted when it was discovered that I had somehow managed to book myself in under the name 'Ms Mooloolaba'. I still haven't lived that one down!

On the plane over to Vanuatu I met my fellow crew member, Martin, and while practically bouncing with excitement I desperately tried to act completely grown up. In the end the passage was very straightforward, in fact we didn't tack or gybe (change direction) once during the 1107-nautical-mile voyage, which has to be some kind of record. It definitely wasn't the high-action passage I'd been hoping for, but it did give me a taste of offshore sailing and, more than anything, I found that I loved the simple day-to-day life of long-distance sailing.

Maybe Mum and Dad were hoping that once I finished this first passage I would have had enough and would forget all about this solo sail idea. I didn't. I was ready for more.

Back at home again, I did my coastal skipper's course with the local sailing school. The theory side meant a week of learning about navigation, passage planning and interpreting weather charts. The practical side of the course meant sailing up the New South Wales coast from Coffs Harbour back to Mooloolaba on the school's 37-foot yacht. We had very mixed conditions during the sail and I learnt a lot.

I had written to many people for advice over the years and Bruce suggested I contact Don McIntyre. Don is one of the world's great adventurers and one of Australia's most experienced sailors. He has competed in the BOC Challenge Single-handed Around the World Yacht Race and made many Antarctic sailing expeditions. He and his wife, Margie, even lived in Antarctica for a year. Don made a documentary called *Knockdown* about his solo sail around the world in 1990 and I was keen to watch it. I was told Don was a supporter of young adventurers so I felt okay to email him. He sent me a copy of his film and from then on we kept in touch often.

Don was great with advice and contacts and I was feeling things were finally, if slowly, starting to happen. But the crunch came when I got an email from Don that basically said, 'You can't do this without a boat . . . and you don't have a boat!' You might think my total belief that I would be able to pull the necessary support together at that point was part madness, part teenage foolishness, but Don's email really hit a nerve as I'd been thinking and fretting over the exact same thing.

By that time I had a few local sponsors, such as Ullman Sails and Fleming Windvanes, and many suppliers had pledged their support but hesitated at making the final commitment until I had something solid behind me – a boat. It was a strange sort of juggle: I needed the small sponsors to prove that I was serious to get the funding for a boat, but without a boat only a few people were willing to commit themselves.

I didn't know it then, but Don and Margie had talked about me at length and had decided that they would buy a boat that I could use for my circumnavigation. Supporting young people in this way goes to the heart of Don's belief in the power of adventure to inspire. He has said:

Adventure is something that can be a swear word to a lot of people. As soon as you say adventure, they say rescue, and there's a lot of people who sort of question the values of it, but the bottom line is if we keep wrapping up our society and our young kids in cottonwool, which is what we're doing, we're changing the culture of Australia. Australia needs heroes, Australia needs adventurers, and there's a lot of real, serious positive benefits for anyone who's getting out there and having a go, and chasing their dreams and really pushing themselves to the limit.

I had proved to Don that I was doing this trip for all the right reasons and after meeting Mum and Dad he knew that I was driving this. There was no way that I was being pushed and manipulated by fame-seeking parents. Just writing that makes me laugh because my mum and dad are the complete opposite. He also knew there were people, like Bruce, who were ready to put in the hard work to get any boat I had ready for the trip.

Not knowing what Don had planned, I didn't dwell on the negatives and just kept doing everything I could to get experience. I found out about an international organisation called OceansWatch, which works closely with the world's yachting community to undertake marine conservation projects and to deliver humanitarian aid to developing countries. The organisation uses volunteers to crew their boats and help drive their projects and I could see this was a way to gain more sailing experience and also to give something back to the environment. I made contact with Chris Bone, who is the CEO and Project Leader for the Asia–Pacific arm of OceansWatch. Chris has been an environmentalist for many years and was once a skipper for Greenpeace.

I managed to convince Chris I was serious about sailing and very serious about making a solo circumnavigation. He listened, and despite my age he was prepared to give me a chance as crew but made me get my parents to call him so he knew they were aware of my scheme. With Chris's help I made a number of ocean passages on *Magic Roundabout*. My first passage was from Whangarei, New Zealand, to Vanuatu with Melinda Taylor and James Pitman. My kitchen-hand job gave me enough money to fly to places like Vanuatu or New Zealand to meet a yacht and, though the passage was free on an OceansWatch journey, I had to pay twelve dollars a day for expenses. For a five-week trip that adds up.

My next offshore passage was from Vanuatu to Brisbane. I was supposed to be flying home after getting off *Magic Roundabout* but I heard that a yacht called *Serannity* needed a crew to sail back to Brisbane. Perfect for me to get more practice and increase my ocean sailing knowledge while saving me an airfare. I had to call Mum and Dad and persuade them it was a good idea and, after asking Chris Bone to check out the owners, who was going to be onboard and whether the yacht was ocean-safe, they agreed.

My next big voyage was as an unofficial skipper on *Magic Roundabout* from Brisbane back to Whangarei. I was still too young to have a boat licence so Jim Hawke – who had spent years training people young and old to sail – was the official skipper and Ricki Colston was also onboard as crew. Jim agreed to let me skipper the boat and said he would only step in if needed so I could get an idea of what it took to call the shots. He was fantastic because he never once overruled what I decided, just asked me constantly why I was doing things the way I was. He helped teach me to trust my instincts and his questioning was the perfect training to encourage me to think things through carefully and logically.

Of course Mum and Dad asked Jim to give them feedback about my abilities and I was very pleased to find out he told them that, in his opinion, I was in the top ten per cent in my sailing ability and in the top two to three per cent for guts. It was nice to get this assessment from such an experienced sailor and I am sure it helped reassure Mum and Dad.

My Aunty Wendy helped set up another huge highlight for me. She had worked at Campbell Island, one of New Zealand's sub-Antarctic Islands, for the New Zealand Meteorological Service and was able to organise for me to crew on *Evohe*, an 82-foot steel yacht that had been built in the De Wachter Shipyard in Antwerp, the Netherlands, and was designed specifically for the harsh Arctic and Antarctic conditions. The boat was sailing from Bluff, on the southern tip of New Zealand's South Island, to Auckland Island and then on to the Campbell Island Group, which is a World Heritage area. I was especially pleased to get this passage as it meant I could get some Southern Ocean experience. I was crewing with a team of meteorological service personnel and engineers and so it was the perfect setting to ask lots of questions and learn a great deal about the volatile weather patterns that can develop in this region.

When I wasn't sailing or washing dishes, all my energy was directed towards making my trip a reality. As I clocked up the hours at sea, more and more people were helping me, but I still had to use the media to get the message out that I was looking for sponsorship. There wasn't any other way for me to go, but as soon as I did this I opened myself and my family up for criticism. I was hoping the media would be interested and a number of newspapers and television stations started to follow my progress, but the exposure proved a double-edged sword. There was no way I could make the trip without sponsors and there was no way that Mum and Dad would let me go if I compromised in any way on my preparation or equipment. But I was not expecting the negative comments and the way Mum and Dad's parenting was attacked whenever a story or article appeared.

Having people like Don McIntyre behind me helped a lot. Don is no fool and he could see we were doing everything we could to be as safe as possible. I'd been talking to Don for about a year and every time things got nasty he would send a message to me and my family that helped offset the negativity.

I talked to heaps of people about what sort of boat I should use for the trip and Bruce and Don were two of many. They had some great advice. When I had first started putting my dream list of boats together I had pictured using a Sparkman & Stephens 34 (S&S 34). It had been tested in global circumnavigation conditions by Jon Sanders, David Dicks and Jesse Martin and had proved to be a tough little boat. Then I started to think I needed a faster boat and thought about all sorts of different designs. I ended up coming full circle back to the S&S 34. There have been more than fifty S&S 34 yachts built in the United Kingdom and over 160 built in Australia since the mid-sixties. They are still being built in Western Australia. Apparently, every S&S 34 ever built is still sailing. That is incredible. I couldn't go against the boat's established reputation. It was very important that I had a boat I could handle well alone and there was no way I was going to take a risk with an unproven boat, even if it could possibly get me round faster.

When Don and Margie offered to provide me with a boat I was thrilled, but was very careful not to let myself get too excited until everything had been finalised. Knowing that someone believed in me enough to sponsor me with a yacht, and then to have it be someone like Don who knew what it took to make the trip, was amazing. It just didn't seem real at first. In March 2009, I was away in New Zealand when Don went to check out a suitable boat we'd found, and I remember pacing back and forth all day as I waited to hear the results of the surveyor's report. *Shanty*, as the boat was called then, had been built in 1984. In Don's words it 'had a new engine, was in reasonable condition, had a solid mast and an asking price of $68,000'. He negotiated that down to the mid-fifties and did the deal.

What I had hoped and dreamed of for so long was really starting to come together. With the boat sorted, the pace picked up a notch or two and a few times I had to pinch myself to make sure it was all real.

Once we had the boat I spent a few weeks cleaning and polishing her up for a press conference to announce my intentions to sail solo, unassisted and non-stop around the world. I needed to do this to try to drum up some serious sponsorship. At the same time I was also kept busy in the classroom, this time doing a yachtmaster ocean course and learning to use a sextant. I'd had lessons from my instructor, John Bankart, and we'd make trips to the beach to take sextant bearings off Venus, followed by a series of sun sights. It was really satisfying to plot our position on a chart within 4 nautical miles using only the sun, planets, sextant, almanac . . . and a lot of help from John.

Don flew up from Tasmania to help with the media plans and preparations and check out the boat and he brought Mike Perham with him. Mike had set off in his Open 50 high-performance racing yacht, *Totallymoney.com,* from Portsmouth, England on 15 November 2008 in an attempt to become the youngest person to sail solo, unassisted and non-stop around the world (sound familiar?). Sadly, persistent problems with his autopilot and then the rudder meant he ended up having to make lengthy stopovers for repairs in Lisbon, the Canary Islands, Cape Town, Hobart and Auckland and so he was forced to revise his goal and aim to be the youngest person to sail solo around the world. I'd been following Mike's progress over the internet and was totally thrilled to meet him.

Spending time with Don and Mike going sailing, talking about the route, going through the ins and outs of preparation and listening to Mike describe the awesome experience of being alone at sea made me appreciate how very special what I was about to do really was. Though hearing about riding 15-metre waves in 50-knot winds and the feeling of being knocked down alone in the Southern Ocean was a sobering reminder of what was ahead of me. Dad was still struggling with the idea that this was really going to happen and so meeting Mike and seeing how another teenager was dealing with the adventure of a lifetime was (slightly) reassuring for him. I made sure he wasn't around for the more dramatic tales.

I know there are some who think that there is a fierce rivalry and competition between young sailors like Mike, Jesse Martin, Zac Sunderland and his sister Abby, but the truth is we support each other, email, share our knowledge and wish only the best outcome for all. I am very sorry that Mike had the problems he had with his autopilot but I am grateful that I got to spend time with him before I set out on my own adventure.

Meeting Mike made things suddenly seem so real and also served as a reminder for me to have fun with every part of the voyage and preparation. We renamed *Shanty* to *Youngestround* and Bruce and I sailed her from Mooloolaba to Rivergate Marina in Brisbane for a scheduled media launch. We cast off the mooring lines and set off into rain squalls and 20 knots of wind blowing straight on the nose for my first big sail in the boat. To begin with we made good progress, but then the wind dropped right off and the rain came down heavily. We ducked below to stay dry and soon discovered that the trusty autopilot had a few quirky personality traits – we christened him Mr Wonky.

After a few accidental tacks we slowly sailed south before discovering another problem – water in the bilge. I offered to take the wheel and Bruce gallantly set to work bailing the bilges. It was a great relief to realise the water was from washing the boat down the previous night and not some critical leak in the hull. I can't say we made great progress and at the top of Moreton Bay we were slowed even more by a strong outgoing tide. We got down to 3 knots with the assistance of the iron topsail (engine).

Things just kept going wrong. As we made our way down the passage, a shackle on the mainsail traveller snapped in a sudden 25-knot wind gust. We dealt with that and then discovered that the starboard lower stay (one of the wires that holds the mast up, so pretty critical!) had begun unravelling itself.

But the last leg across the bay was really special. As the sun was setting, the wind picked up and pushed us along perfectly and we sailed into the Brisbane River towards the glittering city lights. Magic. It didn't take long to find our designated berth at the marina but I was definitely ready for a warm shower and a hot meal by the time I stepped off the boat.

We learnt a lot about the boat that day and the list of things to do was a long one. The refit was going to be a major undertaking and I had my fingers crossed that the media launch and the upcoming Sanctuary Cove Boat Show would help me find enough supporters to keep my dream alive. We still needed a major naming sponsor and help with expenses and technical equipment. We'd set a tentative departure date for September so I had just four months to get everything ready.

On 13 May 2009, the morning of the launch event at Rivergate, none of us knew what to expect. We had no idea if anyone would be interested or if the response would be positive. It turned out to be beyond anything we could have hoped for. Media stories had been written about me before and I'd been interviewed by a few journalists, but nothing had prepared me for the media requests that came in that day. I spoke to journalists, suppliers and anyone else even remotely interested about what I was trying to do. I don't think I stopped talking until I went to sleep! One of the really important contacts I made on that first day was with Scott Young from 5 Oceans Media, a media, sport and entertainment company who manage people like Layne Beachley, Hazem El Masri and Lincoln Hall. Up to this point, I'd been coordinating the campaign with Mum and Dad and my family and friends, Bruce, Suzanne and Don, but it was such a huge undertaking we could see we needed help. Meeting Scott was great and he arranged for his partner, Andrew Fraser, to chat with us at the upcoming Sanctuary Cove Boat Show.

After such a huge day, and still running on adrenaline, I was riding high . . . but it didn't last long. After tossing and turning all night, I woke up really early to get ready for my first live television interview only to discover the clothes that I'd carefully picked out to wear had been put into a car heading in the wrong direction. This mightn't sound like a big deal, but I was nervous, sunburnt, and my voice was hoarse from too much talking the day before, so I'd been hoping to at least make a good impression with how I'd dressed. And, hey, I'm a teenage girl, we always worry about an outfit on a special occasion.

Things became a bit dreamlike when a limousine arrived to pick us up. I couldn't believe it. I was sleepy, feeling drab and riding around in a chauffeur-driven car with our driver, David, dressed in a suit. The best thing was the complimentary jelly beans.

After making it through the live interview without completely humiliating myself I thought it might calm down but the rest of the morning was a blur of radio interviews, filming for television news and more pictures. The response to my announcement and the launch of the boat was phenomenal. There was a flood of emails and phone calls coming in and I was completely taken aback by the offers of support and the encouragement I was getting. I was elated to find so many people were behind me. Every email and every 'good luck' message inspired me more.

But not everyone was encouraging. We'd also had a flood of criticism about me being too young and even more distressing was the way so many people were disparaging of Mum and Dad. I'd learnt to expect some criticism and it didn't really get under my skin anymore, but I was worried about how Mum and Dad would take it. It was my dream and I was ready to defend it, but I was annoyed that they were being judged so viciously and criticised because of it. I didn't have to worry. Mum did an amazing job of defending herself in front of the cameras and even Dad seemed to take it in his stride. But Emily, Hannah and Tom were equally affected. They hadn't chosen to have this harsh spotlight put on their parents and it was not good for any of us.

It was very weird reading headlines that said things like 'Schoolgirl's Solo Sail Irresponsible', seeing newspaper polls asking readers if I was too young and hearing that some group called the Australian Family Association was urging Mum and Dad to reconsider letting me go. Mum, Dad and I always listened to what people said and Mum would say 'people are entitled to their opinion'. I just wish their opinions had been better informed.

Not one of the people who were so vocal in their views knew me or my family or bothered to find out how I had prepared for my quest. I was really thankful that people like Jesse Martin and Don McIntyre stuck up for us. Don was quoted saying, 'She hasn't been pulled out of the bedroom, playing with dolls and plonked on a boat. Age isn't relevant here. It's who she is, what she is and what's driving her. Can she do it? I think she can. Will she do it? Only time can tell.'

Between the quest launch and the upcoming Sanctuary Cove Boat Show I passed another big milestone: my sixteenth birthday. No presents were needed when I had a boat, and after waiting outside the Queensland transport office for it to open I was the proud holder of a licence to skipper it!

With that important piece of paper in my hand, I celebrated by setting off with Tom, Dad and our cousin Ben, to sail down to the Gold Coast from Brisbane. It wasn't exactly the nice sail we'd hoped for. After clearing the river we were met with 25 knots of wind right on the nose and a short chop that reduced our speed to a frustrating 3 knots. I didn't care, this was the first time I was legally allowed to skipper a boat so I loved every minute of it.

Even better was the next day, when I finally got to sail the boat alone. The autopilot was still playing up and it stubbornly refused to steer the boat in a straight line. I had my hands full, especially when I reached a shallow part of the channel just as a rain squall came through and a local radio station called me on my mobile to do a phone interview. Talk about multi-tasking! Bruce would tell you this is exactly what it takes to be a solo sailor, you have to do everything yourself and often deal with a few things at the same time.

The next few days were a blur getting ready for the Sanctuary Cove Boat Show and then, before I knew it, we were dealing with 63-knot winds and sandbanks all around as we motored the boat around to Sanctuary Cove with Dad and Bruce to put her on display. I was stoked to have been invited to speak at the Rivergate Marina and Shipyards Annual Deck Party. I was still getting used to public speaking and I was pretty nervous, but I was introduced by world champion sailor and skipper of the four-time Sydney to Hobart winner *Wild Oats*, Mark Richards, and had the chance to talk about my proposed voyage and try and encourage more support. It was a great opportunity.

The show was another whirlwind of talking, meeting suppliers and gathering information, while still trying to generate sponsorship. I met David Campbell at his SatCom Global stand, arranged to talk to Duncan Curnow from Musto and lots of other suppliers. Meeting Scott again and being introduced to Andrew

Fraser was a huge turning point and we hit it off straight away, so we decided that Andrew and Scott would take on managing me and help attract sponsors and deal with the media. At first it was so strange to think I had a management company, but they soon became a critical part of the team, acting as support crew and so much more.

Another highlight of that show was when a man came down to the boat all fired up and intending to have words with my parents for letting me even think about sailing around the world at my age. After talking to me and Mum he walked away brushing tears from his eyes, completely converted and vowing to support me all the way. After all the negative publicity it was reassuring to find that even the most determined critic could change their mind if they took the time to talk to me and heard how extensively and thoughtfully the trip had been planned out and how we were keeping risks to a minimum.

There was no time to get cocky or rest after the show, as the boat went straight from Sanctuary Cove to Manly, on Brisbane's Moreton Bay – with plenty more drama on the way – where the mast was taken out and given to David Lambourne Yacht Rigging for a new rig to be made. David is one of the best and most reliable mast builders and riggers in Australia and we weren't settling for second-best with anything. From there, the boat was trucked to a huge shed at Rosemount, near Buderim on the Sunshine Coast, for the enormous refit. I wasn't too thrilled about having the boat welded firmly into the cradle that would be its home for the next eight weeks, but despite the fact it must have looked like we were rapidly going backwards it was all so exciting. Things were really happening.

The first week of the refit was spent stripping the boat right back to something very close to a bare hull and deck. Everything, from the near-new engine to the positively radioactive dunny, came off as we settled into the shed, set up scaffolding and got together all the tools and equipment. A lot of time went into planning exactly what we were going to do. I was used as a size guide as plans for the targa, dodger and various other pieces of equipment were sketched out on pieces of cardboard or measurements were scribbled in notepads.

At times I must have come across as pretty stubborn and pushy, but I was determined to get all the jobs done in time for the slightly ambitious deadline we'd set ourselves. Also, I had spent so long researching and preparing for the trip that I knew exactly what I wanted to have onboard. I am not stupid (believe it or not!) so of course I listened to advice, but I had been gathering opinions and recommendations from experienced sailors for years and had sorted through the things I had been told, weighed up all the pros and cons and made my own decisions. Don wanted me to use Air-X Breezewind wind generators because he has used them with great success. Jesse Martin also used them but I preferred the Rutland 913 because it was quieter and had a reputation for being more reliable. We built a drop mount so any broken blades could be replaced easily.

Another talking point was the targa, the frame on the stern that holds the solar panels and aerials. David Dicks used one with tilting panels and Jesse Martin did the same. I thought it was all a bit too high, which made it vulnerable, so went for a lower one. Then, as the rig was being built, there was a great debate over whether or not the storm jib should be on its own furler. I had to decide what was right for me and stick with it.

Don had given me that advice early on. He said, 'If you make the decision yourself after careful consideration and it goes wrong, you at least have no regrets.' Wise words from a wise man. I am responsible for every decision we made, good or bad.

We knew it was going to take a lot of work to get the refit job done and I didn't have the money to pay wages. Don placed an ad in *Trade-a-Boat* asking for volunteers to help and I was blown away by the responses we got. All these people arrived from all over the country to help and at times we had a dozen people hard at it – sanding, grinding and painting. Bruce had completely thrown in his support and he and Suzanne dedicated themselves to getting me on my way. Bruce had become the project manager, not just of the refit project but of the whole journey from start to finish. Mum and Dad did whatever was needed and then some, as well as feeding and housing many of the volunteers. You know the saying, well, all hands were definitely on deck!

They were an amazing bunch of people and it wasn't just their work that was priceless, being able to call on all their years of boating and sailing experience was invaluable when making decisions on equipment or at planning sessions around the dinner table. I am sure I will miss out someone if I try and mention everyone but there were some I have to single out. There was Ed, ex-US Navy, who worked away quietly; Richard, the carpenter who could turn his hand to just about anything; Jim Hawke, who came in a few days every week to install the new plumbing; Rod, with his strong and often entertaining opinions, whom I can thank for the dodger; Ricki, who always ended up with the worst jobs and kept coming back for more; and Pat, with his hilarious sarcastic humour who did a bit of everything and liked to work late when everyone had left and the shed was quiet.

Phil George the owner of Fleming Windvanes, not only provided and fitted the windvane but also built the targa frame with Dad; Damien worked hard but also kept us all entertained around the dinner table with his stories; Neil poured hours of work into completely rewiring the boat; and then there was Mick, Francois, Murray, Steve, John and Jim Williams.

With everyone working so hard towards the same thing, it became so much more than just my dream. By stopping in to help with an afternoon's sanding or running a quick errand for us, so many people played a huge part in getting me and the boat on our way and they were all a crucial part of the voyage.

It wasn't all serious though. One day I turned up at the shed early to write out the day's jobs on a huge bit of cardboard, then pinned it to the wall. Only a few minutes later I looked at it and saw my carefully planned list had been brutally vandalised! In between every item I'd noted down, someone had added 'smoko', then 'tea break', 'coffee break', 'union meeting', 'team-bonding session', 'sundowners', just to name a few. I still haven't been able to find out for sure who it was but I suspect everyone there was in on it. Jokes aside, even after days and days of hard work, everyone was in fine spirits and it was a privilege to have so many good people give up their time to help me fulfil my dream. I know I've said it before, and I am sure I will say it a few more times in the coming pages, but it was an amazing thing.

What was achieved in those eight weeks refitting the boat had to be seen to be believed. The list is impressive:

- Hull scraped bare, sanded, primed, epoxied
- Deck sanded, glassed and filled
- All hatches, windows, cleats, EVERYTHING, off and replaced with new parts
- Keel bolts ultrasounded and old rudder x-rayed by Pearl Street
- New rudder and tiller installed
- Four Johnson electric bilge pumps installed as well as two manual pumps
- All skin fittings, valves and hoses replaced
- New oversized cockpit drains designed and installed and extra chainplates for lower stays fitted
- New watertight bulkhead glassed in to hold new inner forestay chainplate
- Anchor locker filled and sealed to make a crash compartment
- All cockpit lockers made independently watertight
- A new galley and chart table designed and installed
- New engine box installed
- Brand-new Yanmar 3YM29-horsepower engine with Gori folding prop installed
- Diesel tank reconditioned, sealed and tested
- Water tanks removed, reconditioned, sealed and tested
- New Lavac dunny installed
- All new electricals rewired
- Beautiful new dodger put in place
- Everything painted in glorious shades of pink!

You may not believe me, but getting in some 'moping' is an important part of sailing around the world. With the frantic pace of refit, preparation and the building media attention it was essential to spend a couple of hours a week (at least) being completely unproductive. Vegging out by myself, not letting one single important thought cross my mind, was absolutely vital to recharge my batteries. Halfway through the refit I was wrecked and ready for a mope. I spent a wonderful Saturday evening watching mindless television and re-reading my favourite books while my amazing little sister, Hannah, made all the toasted sandwiches I could eat, forced second helpings of dessert on me and sent me off to bed early. It was just what I needed to ready myself for another week of fibreglassing, sanding and painting before heading down to Brisbane for a day to do a marine medical course. I was fitting all this extracurricular stuff around the physical work and the logistical planning for the trip.

With the time screaming by I still didn't have a major naming sponsor, but with Andrew and Scott now onboard (I know, but it was an unconscious pun so I'm leaving it there!) we could leave that to them and just concentrate on the preparation. It was a huge relief. It was important for me to take it one day at a time and focus on ticking off my 'to do' list, which was huge! No two days were the same and if I wasn't helping out at the shed I was in meetings, making more lists and adding to my skills.

I spent another weekend in Brisbane studying sea survival with Gerry Fitzgerald at the Offshore Training Centre. Gerry is a very experienced sailor who competed in the Olympics, raced in the Sydney to Hobart, made many long-distance sea journeys and skippered various general cargo, trading, military and federal-police vessels. This is a man who knows his stuff and I found the course really helpful. It covered just about every possible danger that could arise when alone at sea. We practised drills in the water with a life-raft, getting in and out – although I was used to this thanks to Don and Mike who had put me in a life-raft in the pool at night, turned the hose on me and made me get in and out over and over. We learnt about flares and how to use them effectively. Everything we did helped reassure me that it wasn't physical strength that was important in any crisis, it was technique and keeping your wits about you.

That time with Gerry in the classroom, going over real-life case studies of survival and disaster, putting together checklists and polishing up my knowledge on how to correctly use safety equipment, really hammered home that should something go wrong you had to be as calm and measured as possible in your reactions. I wanted to make sure I had as much survival awareness and information as I could get, just in case I ever needed it.

Being out of the shed for a few days was good for another reason. I'd developed a reaction to the fibreglass resin and what I'd thought was a heat rash soon became a little more serious when I got back from Brisbane and started back to work on the boat. When the rash spread to my face I was charmingly told that everyone at the shed found it too hard to look at me and was made to go to the doctor. On Mum's orders I was all but banned from working on the boat. As if that was going to happen!

With the boat well and truly on its way to an amazing makeover and booked to appear at the Sydney International Boat Show, it was important to continue to raise awareness for the trip. Andrew Fraser had organised a 'Name Jessica's Boat' competition through the *Sunshine Coast Daily* and it was wonderful to have the local community so involved. We wanted to thank all the people who had worked on the boat and all the suppliers and sponsors who were helping to make my dream a reality, so we decided to hold a bon voyage dinner on Saturday, 25 July 2009. The night was going to be part thank-you, part fundraiser and part media opportunity. We also planned to announce the new name of the freshly painted and absolutely gorgeous S&S 34 before she was trucked down to Sydney to star (yes, my opinion not necessarily that of the show's organisers) in the boat show. I would have loved to sail her down but there wasn't enough time.

Andrew, Scott, Mel and Liz and the 5 Oceans team organised the whole dinner and it was a frantic few days leading up to it. By this stage we were pretty much living in the shed. We'd arrive before the sun was up and leave long after night fell. I woke up on the Saturday knowing it was going to be a mega day.

The truck and crane arrived bright and early and the boat was carefully lifted onto the cradle that would stop it rocking around on the trip down to Sydney. She headed off down the highway with her shiny pink paint job and the gleaming stainless steel of the targa looking awesome. I was left standing there feeling a combination of nerves, relief and exhaustion. But there was no time for getting all misty-eyed. We had to clean up the shed and then hop in the car and pick up all the last-minute odds and ends for the dinner. I just had time to scrub off the last of the resin and paint in a hot shower before we were back on the road heading to the Novotel Twin Waters Resort for the evening.

What a night it was! Everyone looked fabulous all dressed up. I actually didn't recognise a few people without the layers of paint, resin and dust they usually wore. The night was extra special, because Andrew had arranged for me to meet Don McIntyre, James Castrission – who had recently completed the world's first Trans-Tasman kayak expedition from Australia to New Zealand with his mate Justin Jones – and Jesse Martin. After all these years of reading his book and being inspired by him it was overwhelming to meet Jesse, who was so generous with his knowledge and experience. Channel Ten journalist and newsreader Bill Woods was the emcee and between courses Don, James and Jesse spoke about their adventures. Then Bill asked me questions about my upcoming voyage. We announced the name *Pink Lady* (which had been suggested by local resident Bob Hughes) for the first time, and after the auction and the raffles it was well after midnight before it started to wind down. I was on such a high I didn't even feel tired . . . until I got home.

Thankfully, the next morning I was able to have a bit of a sleep-in before jumping in the car with Dad, Bruce and Suzanne for the drive to Sydney to meet up with the boat at Darling Harbour. All was well until we got a phone call from the truck driver telling us he'd had a problem. We arrived on Monday morning and found that the targa frame had been badly damaged by cables hanging down from a bridge on the Pacific Highway at Hornsby (so close to where she was heading!). Once we'd looked at it we could see it was basically a write-off. Seeing the targa in such a sorry state was hard for us all, but it was particularly tough for Phil George, who'd done most of the work building it. I could only look on the bright side; at least the hull and mounting points weren't damaged.

The day improved when *Pink Lady* was launched smoothly at Sydney City Marina and the Yanmar engine fired up straight away. David Lambourne arrived to put the mast in and, despite the mangled targa, she looked fabulous.

After a few hours sleep I woke at 11.30 pm to motor across the harbour and join the stream of boats lined up to get into position. We entered Darling Harbour so late at night because the Sydney monorail on the Pyrmont Bridge had to be dismantled to allow the masts to get in. It was the first time I had sailed the boat since the refit and the new tiller, prop and engine kept me on my toes while I manoeuvred into our berth. It all went smoothly and being back at the helm of this gorgeous boat was hugely exciting. *Pink Lady* and I were dwarfed by many of the other bigger vessels on display, but as far as I was concerned she was perfect.

Day one of the show was absolutely awesome. I think if I lined up all the 'good luck' and 'best wishes' we received I could just about bridge my way around the world! And everyone I met had an opinion on *Pink Lady*'s paint colour. They either loved the pink or hated it, there was no in-between. At one point I went for a walk and looked down on *Pink Lady* from the walkway above Darling Harbour. There was no missing her. In a tightly packed line of boats she may have been the smallest but she was also the brightest.

The whole atmosphere at the show was great and I was proud to have been included in the program to give daily talks with Don McIntyre; James Castrission and Justin Jones, who were promoting their book *Crossing the Ditch*, which told of their adventures kayaking across the Tasman; and Pete Goss, renowned British yachtsman and former Royal Marine, whose latest adventure was on the *Spirit of Mystery*, which was moored right next to us at the show. Pete is probably best known for saving the life of Frenchman Raphael Dinelli during the 1996 Vendée Globe solo around-the-world yacht race.

What Pete Goss did is an amazing story of courage and compassion. He was competing against Raphael in the race, but when he was told of Raphael's distress call he turned around to spend two days in the worst conditions the Southern Ocean could throw up searching for him. Pete found a near-frozen Raphael battling hypothermia and barely alive in a life-raft that had been airdropped by an RAAF plane just before his yacht sank. For his selflessness, Pete was awarded an MBE and the Légion d'Honneur by the French President.

Spending time with these men was remarkable. I listened to their talks and made sure I got to chat to them whenever I could. They all had a lot of great advice for me and kept reminding me to have fun and to enjoy every moment of my adventure, from the preparation to the end and each second in between.

They also kept emphasising the importance of complete preparation in any adventure. James and Justin say that over three-quarters of their record-breaking achievement took place before they set off. Pete says the same, believing that eighty per cent of any race is won before the start. I was very grateful for the great team I had helping me and knew that should I succeed it would be because of their efforts.

Listening to the guys speak and seeing pictures and video from all their adventures was incredibly inspiring and it was making me slightly impatient to get going myself.

I was still looking for a major sponsor. Andrew and Scott had put together a strategy and One HD (Network Ten's digital channel) had come onboard as the media partner for the trip. On the Thursday night I did a live weather cross with Tim Bailey for the Channel Ten *Live at Five* news broadcast and then headed off to the Network Ten studios for *Thursday Night Live* on One HD. Having my hair and make-up done was quite an experience. When I was all ready, I looked at myself in the mirror with my curly hair and made-up face and blurted out that I thought I looked totally ridiculous. I wasn't thinking, and felt so bad when I saw the hair and make-up ladies' horrified expressions. Oops!

The last few days of the boat show were a blur and I started to lose my voice from so much talking. Once it was over I was glad to have a bit of time to myself. I headed off to the National Maritime Museum to check out Kay Cottee's yacht, *First Lady*, which is one of the exhibits at the museum. I really enjoyed having a good look around the boat and I picked up some great ideas. Even though *First Lady* – a Cavalier 37 fin keel yacht – and my *Pink Lady* are completely different boats it was interesting to see the similar ways they'd been set up for strength and solo sailing. It was also great imagining Kay in the boat, alone at sea. After reading her book so many times I could almost close my eyes and picture her there, sitting in her bunk knitting while learning Spanish and monitoring for any unwanted noises from the deck.

By the Tuesday morning it was back to it. The once beautiful targa frame was dismantled, cut up and sent off to be used as a template for the new frame. It was horrible seeing all that work lying on the ground in a tangle of bent stainless steel. We pulled the rig out to get ready for the boat to be trucked home but . . . well, nothing ever goes quite to plan, and this time it was the truck that proved the problem. It was delayed by a day, so we spent the extra time in Sydney making still more lists and working out how we could iron out a few tricky problems. The 'to do' list was tallied up and we worked out we had twenty-one major jobs to do and twenty-four man (and woman) days to do them in.

We finally left Sydney on the Thursday afternoon after seeing *Pink Lady* safely hauled out of the water and onto the truck. Driving over the Sydney Harbour Bridge on the way out of town, I couldn't help thinking that the next time I'd be seeing it would be from a different angle, as I sailed towards it! We headed north up the Pacific Highway, with *Pink Lady* following, as my head spun with the stories I'd heard at the show, the faces of the people I'd met and the excitement I was feeling as my departure date inched closer.

After much discussion with many people, talking about weather patterns and different routes, the details of the journey I would take had been plotted out. There were a few basic requirements for anyone wanting to sail solo, unassisted and non-stop around the world. I know some purists believe that, with the technology available today, and the fact that I could call for advice on the satellite phone, I was not unassisted. In some respects they are right. I was going to be able to communicate with the people I loved and the all-important support crew I had around me. But I was not setting out to re-create the conditions of Joshua Slocum's journey and I was definitely not going to ignore all the safety and communication advances that are available to modern sailors (and let's face it, I am a teenager so too long without email, phone and Facebook can be harmful!). I *was* going to sail my boat myself, non-stop, carrying all the food and water I would need and I'd have to fix anything that broke without any assistance. I couldn't stop anywhere: couldn't take anything onboard that I didn't have before I left. I would have to deal with the weather conditions alone no matter what they were like and sail accordingly. If a sail ripped, I would have to sew it up. If something stopped working, I would have to make it right. The bottom line was: *physically* it was just me and *Pink Lady* for as long as it took to cover approximately 23,000 nautical miles.

After Jesse Martin completed his circumnavigation on 31 October 1999 and entered the record books as the youngest person to sail solo, unassisted and non-stop around the world, the World Sailing Speed Record Council (WSSRC) discontinued age records. There is now no official recognition of either the youngest or the oldest sailor to achieve this amazing feat, so Jesse Martin will always hold his place in the WSSRC official record book.

Just to be sure, in June 2009 I sent an email to John Reed, Secretary to the WSSRC to clarify the situation. I told him I was planning to sail from Sydney, northeast across the equator to the Line Islands then down to Cape Horn, under the Cape of Good Hope, across to Cape Leeuwin and home to Sydney. I asked if I changed that and instead went from Sydney below New Zealand and Cape Horn, up to the Azores Islands and home via the Cape of Good Hope and Cape Leeuwin – basically Jesse Martin's route – whether that would satisfy the WSSRC distance requirements and if they would then accept my journey as a WSSRC-ratified record attempt.

John Reed replied two days later to let me know that the WSSRC had a policy of 'not ratifying "youngest" claims or attempts' and so their rules did not include a category for me. That didn't worry me at all. If I succeeded I knew I would be the youngest person to have circumnavigated the world at the time but any age record is eventually broken. If all you are after is your name in a record book, then one day you'll be disappointed when someone else comes along to claim the prize. Ultimately, this wasn't about a record, I was looking for a challenge – though, it would have been very cool. So, if I wasn't able to officially break an existing record that was okay by me. I would set my own. David Dicks was eighteen years and forty-two days when he got home and Jesse Martin was eighteen years and sixty-six days. I wanted to try and achieve my dream of circumnavigating the world before my seventeenth birthday. If I could do that, I would be the youngest person ever to achieve this.

From the information we had from Jean-Louis Fabry, Vice-Chairman of the WSSRC, I was not required to pass through an antipodal point (if a hole was drilled through the centre of the earth, the place it broke through would be the antipodal point) to successfully claim a circumnavigation.

With all that information, I had chosen a route that is traditionally recognised for around-the-world sailors. It was similar to the one Kay Cottee sailed, except that I was intending to cross the equator before rounding Cape Horn to give myself time to settle into the boat before one of the most demanding stages of the trip. According to the WSSRC rules for solo circumnavigation, I had to depart from and arrive at the same port, cross all lines of longitude, cross the equator entering into the Northern Hemisphere at least once and round the southern landmarks of South America and South Africa.

I would also have to deal with some of the most demanding and relentless oceans a sailor can face.

Don had told me to think of the journey in stages and to consider the total voyage as one one-day sail after another. It sounded so easy when you put it like that! I broke the trip down into six stages and made notes on what I could expect during each stage.

Stage One – Sydney and North to the Line Islands

I was leaving from The Spit, at Mosman in Sydney, and the plan was to cross the starting line at Sydney Heads and sail towards northern New Zealand. Depending on the weather, I would choose a point where I turned left and headed towards Fiji. I wasn't sure if I'd go left or right of the Fijian Islands and would decide that when I got there, again depending on the wind. Once past Fiji and Samoa, I'd head northeast to the Line Islands. The equator lies just south of Kiritimati (Christmas) Island, the largest island of the Line Group, so I would round one of the islands in the Line Group that is north of the equator before heading back south.

Stage Two – South to Chile and Cape Horn

To make South America, *Pink Lady* and I needed to head a long way down before we could turn east. This area is known as the Roaring Forties because of its characteristically strong westerly winds; it is a notoriously difficult area for sailors. I planned to make my way south of the fiftieth parallel to make the passage between South America and Antarctica but was nervous about confronting the Everest of ocean sailing: rounding Cape Horn. Cape Horn is the southernmost headland of the Tierra del Fuego archipelago of southern Chile, a place Peter Nichols, in *A Voyage for Madmen*, calls 'the scorpion-tail tip of South America'. It divides the South Pacific from the South Atlantic and it's a particularly hazardous place because of the unpredictable weather patterns, strong currents, fierce winds and the huge seas that can subsequently be whipped up. Many, many sailors have come to grief there and I was determined to be as prepared as possible so I didn't become one of them.

Stage Three – North after Cape Horn

Once around the base of South America I was going to head due north to seek out some calmer weather and recharge the batteries (mine and *Pink Lady*'s). Because I was attempting a non-stop voyage I couldn't pull into a port, so time spent on calmer seas and refuge behind land would be essential to make sure I avoided exhaustion. I was going to head close to the Falkland Islands and most probably sail towards the east.

Stage Four – The South Atlantic Ocean to the African Continent

Once I was rested I'd move on to the next stage of the journey that would take me to the southern point of South Africa. As the crow flies it is about 3500 nautical miles from the southernmost point of South America to South Africa, but my route would be determined by the weather and was bound to be many more miles than that.

Stage Five – Rounding South Africa

The Cape of Good Hope is not the southernmost point of Africa, but sailors use it as the point where they start heading east. Cape Agulhas is the most southern landmark and divides the Atlantic and Indian Oceans. The Cape of Good Hope is another significant milestone in the journey, though I was not planning to be close enough to land to see anything. This area is notorious for very steep waves that can smash a boat in two if you aren't careful. I wasn't going to risk getting into shallower water and planned to stay well away from the landmass and associated undersea shelf.

Stage Six – The Southern Ocean to Home

From South Africa, the vastness of the Southern Ocean would be ahead of me. To get back into Australian waters would mean navigating over 4000 nautical miles of open and often unforgiving seas. I had read so many stories about sailing the Southern Ocean and was looking forward to the challenge. It is a very volatile sailing area with the threat of violent storms or days adrift with no wind, so I tried hard to stop myself from assuming too much in advance. I would just have to deal with the conditions as they developed. I knew I would have to keep my focus at this point because despite being so close to home there was still a long way to go. I had to travel across the Great Australian Bight and down around the South East Cape of Tasmania. From there I would head north to the mainland and then up the east coast of Australia back to Sydney Harbour.

By making this trip I was following in the wake of so many great sailors and I felt a little strange if I thought about my name being linked to theirs. I wasn't sailing around the world to become famous, to chase celebrity – that isn't what I'm about at all. I also wasn't thinking it was a great way to make money. That didn't even cross my mind. I was just hoping that when I got home I wouldn't have a huge debt dragging behind me and my family. I was setting off on this epic trip to challenge myself, to see if I could do it, and to show others that it is possible to make a dream a reality. My family and I knew the risks involved and we knew it was going to be a hugely demanding journey both physically and mentally. I had faith in the boat, my sailing abilities and the support I had. The thing that niggled me slightly was the question of my mental toughness. The only way to test that was to challenge myself, but up to this point that hadn't happened. All I could do was keep moving forward. I'd know soon enough if I had what it takes.

Once we got back to Mooloolaba from Sydney it was a very busy week finishing off *Pink Lady*. In the rush to get to the Sydney Boat Show a lot of jobs had been left undone and there was still quite a bit of equipment to be installed. This time transporting the boat went off without a hitch. On the way, the mast was dropped off at David Lambourne's workshop in Brisbane for some more work and finally *Pink Lady* was put back in the water and moved to a berth at the Mooloolaba Marina.

The weather was beautiful, and it was lovely to work on the boat under clear blue skies and the warm Queensland sun. I was involved in everything but sometimes being the smallest person around isn't a good thing. Whenever there was a spanner needed in a tricky little corner I started getting meaningful looks . . . then hinting comments. I'd end up crawling out of a locker half an hour later covered from head to toe in Sikaflex, a marine sealant.

Rod Cran tackled the job of installing foam for insulation and padding on the walls and roof, and Neil Cawthorne, the electrician, often worked late into the night, when everyone else had left, to finish the electrical systems. Power is very important on the boat because it runs the sat-phones, high frequency (HF) radio, computer, navigation equipment and, possibly most importantly for me, the stereo! Thanks to Neil, we were doing everything we could to make sure it was perfect, but I was also able to survive without it all if there was ever a problem. When it comes down to it, all *Pink Lady* and I really need to keep us going is some wind – preferably 15 knots behind us with sunshine. I was hoping it never came to that, but I had the sextant onboard just in case.

The boat was equipped with four 80 a/hr gel batteries and another for starting the engine. Then for charging the batteries there were two 80-watt solar panels, a 60-watt solar panel and a Rutland wind generator. The solar panels would give me plenty of power when the sun was shining and the wind generator would be constantly on the go, trickling in power little by little. For the days when the sun wasn't shining, the wind was down and I'd been playing the stereo too loud, I could run the Yanmar engine (out of gear) to give the batteries a little extra boost. I would be completely self-sufficient the whole time I was away.

I was going to be able to keep in touch with the rest of the world thanks to the awesome communications equipment I was lucky enough to have onboard. SatCom Global had provided me with all my satellite gear. The plan was to have two hand-held satellite phones – one for everyday use and one for the emergency grab bag ready for me to take if I ever had to abandon ship. I would also have internet connection through a small satellite dome on the stern called the Sailor 250. This would enable me to send video clips, pictures, blogs and emails. The boat was also equipped with an HF radio, which I would use for skeds (short for 'scheduled', meaning a prearranged radio link up) and listening in to see what other shipping was around me. I'd also have a TracPlus tracker fitted to the boat, which would send back a constant signal to the appropriate people to reassure them I was afloat and moving, and last, but not least, I would have all my different EPIRBs, which would hopefully make *Pink Lady* one of the safest and best-equipped yachts ever to sail around the world.

Dad installed the heater and finished a million odd jobs while Bruce and I fitted winches and other deck gear. Jason Mineff from Linemaster Marine Electronics installed and connected the sailing instruments, AIS, HF radio and other electronics and Richard Taylor made up storm boards. Various other people came and went and took on numerous small jobs and I am so grateful to them all.

Bruce, Dad and I often worked late into the evenings and during the day there was often barely an inch of spare room in the cabin as everyone worked away at their different projects. The job list seemed never-ending; there was so much to be done, from installing the wind generator to fitting a lee cloth on my bunk.

Meanwhile, the guys from Ullman Sails set to work finishing *Pink Lady*'s new set of sails, using cloth from Bainbridge, which was twice as strong as most. When David and his boys had finished the mast it was stepped back in late one evening and Phil George flew up from Melbourne again to fit the re-built targa frame, which had been trucked up. Iain from Panasonic arrived from Sydney to install the software on the four Toughbook computers that I'd be taking, and Rod from SatCom Global gave me the run-down on how to use my Sailor 250 satellite dome. To begin with all the flashing lights and switches had me a bit worried but it turns out the Sailor 250 is just like using a normal phone, and I sure know how to use one of them!

I was really excited about the new stereo I had onboard because Dad had always said that when I got my own boat I'll be able to listen to the radio stations I like rather than the ones he prefers. I suspect that Neil deliberately left this job till last so he wouldn't have to listen to my music either. And just to rub salt in the wound, I knew that when I finally got out there on the water by myself, chances were that the only station I'd be able to pick up would be Dad's favourite: the BBC. I guess that's what iPods are for!

There was not a moment to spare, when I wasn't working on the boat I was trying to practise my maintenance skills. I spent time with Jim Williams, the mechanic, going over potential engine problems and talked through the electricals with Neil. I was starting to feel I knew the boat inside out.

Mum was busy testing out all kinds of long-life food options on me to see what I liked and, more importantly, what I didn't. I don't want to sound fussy or ungrateful, but some of it was just a little too creative. Tom kept telling me to hurry up and get going because he wanted to get back to eating 'normal' food.

Finally on Thursday, 20 August we were able to set off for a sail. It was a beautiful Queensland winter day with a 15-knot wind, blue water and clear skies, perfect for gently testing everything out on a sea trial. All went well, but it made me anxious because I wanted to get out and do some serious solo sailing and it was all taking too long.

In the middle of the first sea trials a film crew from the American sports channel ESPN joined us. They filmed me on the water and then back on land, documented my check-up trip to the dentist and then tagged along as we did the big shopping trip to pick up the bulk of the food for the trip. With a lot of help and advice from other sailors and from Dr Gary Slater – a senior lecturer in nutrition and dietetics at the University of the Sunshine Coast – I ended up with a planned diet that I thought was amazingly close to normal food.

My main meals were going to be a choice of about ten different meals from a range called Easyfood, which lasts on the shelf for eighteen months. Breakfasts were easy, just normal stuff like cereal and porridge. I was planning to bake my own bread and things like scones in the pressure cooker. Mum had chased up all kinds of long-life food with the help of Nick Duggan, the owner of our local IGA supermarket. I'd worked on the list with Mum but it was still a shock to see the huge mound of boxes and packets we ended up with. I made sure I was in charge of the visit to the lolly aisle and, with Tom's help, we piled packet after packet into our trolley. Just to give you some idea of what I was taking, I had twenty-four tins of Spam, two hundred litres of milk powder, sixty-four tins of potatoes, thirty-two tins of pineapple, thirty-six tins of tuna and 250 popper juice drinks. An egg company had produced a special batch of powdered eggs for me and I also had heaps of the pre-packaged meals from Easyfood. And, of course, five crates of lollies for my sweet tooth!

After a couple of days filming, David, the producer from ESPN, asked if they could get some footage of me just hanging out in my bedroom or with friends. I had to tell him I didn't actually do things like that, all my time and effort went into preparing the boat and getting ready for the voyage. Except for the odd veg-out session, I didn't do anything but work towards getting *Pink Lady* to the start line. I was still going to the gym, jogging and often biking down to the marina in an effort to build up some extra muscle, and the evenings were for emailing, updating my blog and packing. I was obviously not fitting in with ESPN's idea of what a typical teenager does with their time!

After a few short day sails I headed offshore with Bruce for three days, which proved to be more challenging than fun as I was pretty seasick. I might have been struggling but *Pink Lady* sailed beautifully and with each trip we were working through any minor problems.

While I was on the water, Mum had completely taken over the downstairs living room at home for the enormous task of packaging and organising the food I was going to carry with me. She managed to do all this while still working part-time and giving the other kids their share of attention. Mum and Dad had both thrown themselves behind me, making sure I was as safe, well provisioned and well equipped as I could possibly be.

As always, most of the time working towards my goal was great fun, but the closer we got the more impatient I felt. The drawn-out nature of the preparations was really starting to do my head in. I just desperately wanted to leave. Sure, there was some pressure to sail by a certain date before the best weather window closed, but most of the pressure was coming from me. I was anxious to get out on the water solo. I didn't tell anyone at this point, but I had some niggling doubts and wanted to prove to myself that I could do it. With so much time and money committed to the voyage, I was extremely conscious that I hadn't actually spent any time alone at sea. I became quite moody and my attitude was all wrong. I was not in a good head space and was willing to cut corners in my rush to get out on the ocean. Luckily for me, my ever-pedantic Dad, along with Bruce and Neil, were there to stop me from making any foolish choices. They were determined to make sure nothing was overlooked or rushed. I didn't appreciate what they were doing at the time so in that last week or so there was a bit of friction between me and Dad.

Despite my grouchiness, I eventually saw good sense and pulled myself together, and when I set out on my first real solo sail on *Pink Lady* we were both ready for the test.

I left the dock late on a Saturday afternoon. The wind was blowing 25 to 30 knots and because of this, the local sailing club had cancelled its usual race. Although that meant the water was much less crowded, it also meant that the yachties who would normally have been out there were gathered around the BBQ having a few drinks and watching as we loaded up the boat. It was pretty clear that they thought it was a bit strange that I was heading offshore by myself when everyone else had chosen not to leave the harbour.

I motored out of the river and started pulling up the sails in a pretty steep sea just outside the entrance. Mum, who had been watching from the breakwater with everyone else, told me later how dramatic it all looked with *Pink Lady* flying out of the water as some of the steeper waves rolled past.

By the time I had everything in order and set the windvane to work, the sun was setting and I was just beginning to lose sight of land through the sea spray. I knew I was facing a long, sleepless night dodging the local fishing fleet but my confidence was growing by the minute. Despite the bouncy conditions, *Pink Lady* wasn't at all a struggle to handle.

The time and thought we'd put into laying out the cockpit had really paid off and it was a great feeling sitting there knowing that everything was right at my fingertips and perfectly under my control. As it got dark and the land dropped away behind us completely, all my doubts slowly dropped away, too. I knew I could handle this boat.

It was a busy night gybing in 30 knots of wind to avoid the constant stream of shipping, but all went well and in the early hours of the morning I brought *Pink Lady* around to the south. As the sky started to lighten in the east, the wind eased right off, so I managed to catch just enough sleep in short catnaps to keep me going. After the sun came up, I cooked breakfast on my stove, enjoyed a cup of coffee in the sunshine, and spent the morning playing around with different sail combinations. I spent an enjoyable day sailing up the coast with a steady breeze and I arrived back at Mooloolaba in the mid afternoon. I was in no rush to head home straight away, so I spent some time tacking back and forth in the bay, each tack was slightly faster and an improvement on the last. When I did finally pull down the sails and head back up the river I was worn out but happy that *Pink Lady* and I had proved ourselves perfectly compatible. I took a leaf out of Jesse Martin's book and brushed my hair with a fork (I forgot a hairbrush!) before I came ashore. Everything was coming together. I was feeling confident in the boat and in my own abilities. It was all good!

And then, to top off a great week, we got some wonderful news from Andrew Fraser. Ella Baché, the oldest family-owned skincare company in the world, had offered to become my major naming sponsor for the trip. Introduced into Australia in 1963 by Edith Hallas, a Hungarian-born beauty therapist, whose husband, George, was Madame Ella Baché's cousin, the company had stayed in the family and was now run by Edith's son, John Hallas, and his daughter Pippa. The company has a long history of supporting sailing and were heavily involved in the 18-foot skiffs in the nineties; that was all before my time but it was apparently a pretty big thing back then. When I heard Ella Baché's mission is to inspire you to be the best you can be, something that I also strongly believe in, I could see it was going to be a great partnership. So *Pink Lady* was proudly re-named again. She became *Ella's Pink Lady*.

Having this major support was just what we needed and really calmed Dad. He'd been getting worried about how we were going to fund the whole trip as fully as we had hoped. We would have struggled to get to this point without a management team like Andrew and Scott. For us, securing and looking after commercial deals was a whole new terrifying world, so I was glad these guys were there to work it all out. Thanks to them I had the broadcast partnership with One HD, who were going to follow the voyage; SatCom Global had provided me with all the equipment I was already getting attached to and most importantly phone contact with family and friends; and Panasonic were keeping me online and wired up. I had never imagined that so many people would give me so much wonderful support and I was touched and enormously grateful for their backing and belief in me. Let's face it; I couldn't have done it without them.

Despite my focus on making my own trip happen I wasn't completely ignoring the rest of the world. I had been following Mike Perham's voyage closely and we had kept in touch since he'd left Hobart. When I heard he'd crossed the finish line in Portsmouth on 27 August 2009 and become the youngest person, at 17 years 164 days, to sail solo around the world I was so happy for him. It was such a major achievement and totally amazing. Mike's trip definitely wasn't all smooth sailing, he'd had to pick himself up from setbacks and disappointments but he kept going. I have to say handling his Open 50 yacht alone isn't something I'd want to do. I'll stick with my gorgeous S&S 34, even if we can't quite match the speed he can get to!

Ever since I met Mike I've been grateful to be able to talk to him about all the different aspects of sailing around the world. To hear about his experiences and swap notes has been really cool. At fourteen, Mike became the youngest person ever to sail across the Atlantic single-handed and although I was working towards taking his claim of being the youngest person to sail around the world away from him, he has never been anything but generous with his knowledge. One of Mike's favourite catchphrases is 'You are only as big as the dreams you dare to live'. I love that and might have to borrow it next time I have someone tell me I am too young and too scrawny to do what I want to do.

Hearing about Mike's success made me all the more determined. I just wanted to get out there and start sailing. Thankfully, I was edging closer to a departure date and on Thursday, 3 September, my New Zealand-based Granny Billie Watson, organised for *Ella's Pink Lady* to be blessed by Stella Maris Father Geoff Baron. I'd take all the help I could get!

The next couple of days were spent fitting the mounds of food onto the boat along with everything else I needed. It all had to be carefully tied in place and anything that might get damaged or wet had to be wrapped up and stored in a dry bag. Luckily, packing my personal things was really easy because there wasn't room to take much at all, though I made sure I had all the good luck charms and cards I'd been given.

Finally I was ready and on Tuesday, 8 September 2009, I was on my way. I planned on taking around ten days to sail down to Sydney so that I could get plenty of time on the water to test all the systems and give *Ella's Pink Lady* a good run in. It meant when I got to Sydney there'd be time for any last-minute adjustments before heading out into the Tasman Sea for the start of my circumnavigation.

It was so nice to set off knowing that *Ella's Pink Lady* was completely ready with everything neatly packed, and the send-off I got was amazing. I wasn't at all prepared for all the people lining the river to wave to me or the small fleet of boats that saw me out of the harbour, not to mention the two helicopters buzzing around overhead. I was so proud to have my local community show their support like that and despite being tired I felt wonderful sailing out into the wide ocean, though we weren't travelling fast because of the wind conditions.

Even when the last boats had left me to head back into the river, I still wasn't going anywhere too fast, but eventually the wind picked up and I tried to enjoy the sunshine and hold off my seasickness. I cracked open my first can of potatoes to fry up into chips for afternoon tea.

By late afternoon I was sailing along at six knots off Cape Moreton. I was keeping my eyes open for the few fishing boats around and I'd spotted a few whales. It wasn't too bumpy but I was still being a bit careful to ensure my food stayed down as I hadn't got my sea legs yet.

By about 1.30 am *Ella's Pink Lady* and I were about 15 nautical miles east of North Stradbroke Island. I'd have liked to have been further offshore, away from the local fishing fleets and possible shipping, however the current and earlier light winds meant I hadn't sailed very far since leaving. After scanning the horizon, checking the radar and AIS and setting my alarms, I climbed into my bunk, still wearing my life jacket and harness.

A horrible bone-shuddering explosion of noise woke me as *Ella's Pink Lady* was suddenly stopped in her tracks and violently spun around. Jumping up as the awful grinding noise continued, a quick glance up through the companionway told me that we'd collided with something huge, a ship. The sky was a wall of black steel, obscuring the stars and towering over me. The roar of engines filled my head and my whole world.

Leaning out into the cockpit, I grabbed at the tiller, flicked off the autopilot and tried to steer us. It was hopeless. There was nowhere to go, nothing I could do. Shuddering and screeching, we were being swept down the ship's hull. Another glance told me that the ship's stern, with its bridges protruding, was fast approaching. The noises were getting louder and, knowing that the mast and rigging were about to come down, I rushed back below hoping for some protection.

With my hands over my head I sat on my bunk as a whole new and far more terrible set of noises began. A few short seconds passed but to me they felt like hours. The cupboard next to me ripped apart as the chainplate behind the bulkhead splintered it into a million pieces. The boat heeled to one side then suddenly sprung upright with the loudest explosion yet as the entangled rigging suddenly freed itself and crashed to the deck.

When the boat steadied and the roar of the engines started to fade I went back on deck. It was a mess. There was rigging, lines and huge rusty flakes of black paint and slivers of metal from the ship's hull everywhere. Beyond *Ella's Pink Lady* I could see the dark outline of the huge ship's stern slipping away unaffected, leaving us at a stop in the foaming white slipstream.

Shocked and disbelieving, my head still reeling, I desperately tried to come to grips with what had happened while checking the bilges for water and the hull for damage. All I could think was 'my poor boat', and while flicking switches to see what equipment still worked it became a sort of chant – 'my poor boat, my poor, poor boat'. I was numb and still shaking off the last remnants of sleep; being scared hadn't crossed my mind. My only thoughts were for *Ella's Pink Lady*.

Taking deep breaths to calm my shaking hands, I picked up the radio to call the ship and then grabbed the phone to tell Dad what had happened. 'I'm okay,' I told him. 'I'm fine, perfectly okay, but we've been hit by a ship, we've been dismasted,' I finished in a rush.

Back on deck, alone and miles from land, it took me over two hours to slowly clear the deck, lash the broken rigging in place and cut the tangled headsail away. I had to pause frequently to lean over the side and throw up as my earlier queasiness had turned into full-on seasickness. Finally, I turned on the engine to motor the six hours to the Gold Coast.

What can I say? I have so many questions about that night. I have no idea how I didn't see the ship. Once I was back on land I was running on adrenaline so it took a while to completely hit home how scary the whole collision was and how dangerous it could have been.

After I called Dad and then let everyone know I was all right and going to get myself back to port on my own, I spent the hours slowly motoring in going over everything that had happened. I had to try very hard to look at the positives and I had a bit of a cry to get it out of my system as best I could. The disappointment was overwhelming but I was so proud of the way the onshore team handled the situation. The Australian Rescue Coordination Centre (in Canberra) was brilliant and from my first call back to base everything was under control. All the years we had spent planning for an emergency meant everyone knew what to do, who to call and not to panic.

Many people might think it strange, but from the moment I started cutting the rigging and tying down the mast I knew that I could handle anything an around-the-world trip might bring. I never panicked and I instinctively knew what I had to do, and did it. Don't get me wrong, I am not playing down what happened at all, it was terrifying. But after living through it, I had no doubt that I was going to set off on the trip. I was more determined and more focused than ever. I knew that this one horrifying incident had given fuel to anyone who had criticised me and my parents for what I was trying to do. In their eyes I had proven exactly why I shouldn't ever be permitted to sail alone. However, in that same incident, I had proved to myself that I had the ability to achieve my dream. Up until that point the only thing that had niggled at me in my rare quiet moments was the question of whether I could deal with this mentally. I knew I had the skills, the boat and the support to successfully complete the trip. The only thing that had not been tested was my state of mind. After the collision I knew I had the mental strength to match whatever came along. I wasn't underestimating the isolation, the exhaustion, the fear or the danger, I just knew I could do it.

What I didn't know was how I was going to afford to repair the boat and deal with the aftermath of the collision. I wasn't so sure that Mum and Dad, especially Dad, would be as keen as I was to keep my dream alive. I knew that phone call at two in the morning would have freaked them out completely.

Just before I'd left Mooloolaba the negative comments about the trip and my age had been building but I had no idea what was about to happen. The helicopters that turned up to film me were a clue and I gave a few sombre waves to the camera-person. By the time I got to Southport there was a fleet of boats there to greet me and a number of helicopters circling overhead. Hundreds of people stood lining the breakwater and I could only hope that the majority were there to support me, not to witness what many assumed was the end of a very short-lived adventure.

I wasn't feeling good at all. Everything was quite surreal and the frantic media attention and hovering helicopters didn't help. The Queensland Water Police had met me at around 7.30 am and escorted me and *Ella's Pink Lady* to the Gold Coast Water Police base opposite Sea World. Mum and Dad were waiting there for me.

Andrew Fraser had flown up from Sydney and I was so relieved he did. There seemed to be cameras and journalists everywhere we turned and I wasn't sure what I should do. We were being inundated with requests for interviews and all I wanted was to go somewhere quiet so I could talk things through with Mum, Dad and Bruce and work out my next step. After discussions with the police, Andrew organised for a brief press conference to be held at 1.30 pm to give the media access to me in the hope that they would leave me alone afterwards. We were wrong. I obviously couldn't say a lot because there was going to be an in-depth investigation by both Maritime Safety Queensland and the federal government's Australian Transport Safety Bureau (ATSB) but I answered what I could. Once that was done we motored the boat to Pamela's parents' place at Runaway Bay. It was wonderful to get there and I was hanging out for a bath and a sleep. None of us were prepared for what happened next.

News crews, camera crews and journalists were everywhere. The Fredrics' backyard was on a canal with a jetty so we could keep *Ella's Pink Lady* close and unload. Any time anyone went out the back door several dozen people would jump up from the yards across the canal. I heard later that journalists were doorknocking and offering money to the neighbours for access to any yard or jetty that had a view of where my family and I were staying. Tom and Angus (Pamela's younger brother) had fun going outside every so often just to give the news crews some exercise but after a while they were bored by this and just found it annoying. I felt so bad that yet again I was the cause of such a kerfuffle that was impacting on people close to me. I couldn't understand what the journalists were waiting for. I am sure no one wanted to see pictures of me in my pyjamas or moping around with my hair sticking up.

The next day it wasn't any better and, if anything, the frenzy got worse. More and more people were calling on me to abandon my trip and the criticism of Mum and Dad really got bad. Queensland Premier Anna Bligh had initially said I should keep going but then changed her mind and urged me to reconsider. There was even a report that the Queensland government was going to investigate ways to stop me. I was very pleased when I later read that this wasn't true. I'm sure the government and child services have much more serious issues to worry about and many cases of abuse and neglect that deserve their attention. I know my friends and family were trying to hide the worst of the stories and comments from me but they didn't have much success. I found it all very upsetting but what made it bearable were the equally strong messages of support that we were receiving. So many people were sending their best wishes and urging me to keep going. Men like America's Cup legend John Bertrand and five-time MotoGP champion Mick Doohan weren't afraid to stand up for me in the media, which was lovely. Not surprisingly, Jesse Martin was asked his opinion on ABC radio. I was touched when he said, 'Everyone's got something in their mind they want to be doing and she's out there doing it like I did, and I think that's a great thing. I'm certain she'll probably get out there again . . . I still think she should.'

And the bloggers and newspaper readers from all over the world who added their comments and support online and on my website were remarkable. I had messages from people in Tasmania, Sweden, the United Kingdom, America, from everywhere. For every negative comment it felt like there were two positive ones to offset it. The local Gold Coast community were awesome and would give an encouraging nod or wave to me and my family whenever we stepped out.

I couldn't believe it when Dean Leigh-Smith from the Gold Coast Marina and Graham Eaton and Joe Akacich from Australian Marine Enterprises (AME) offered to repair the damage for free and make sure that *Ella's Pink Lady* and I were back on the water as soon as possible. The seventy businesses based at the marina were donating everything. Dean said that they'd stop at nothing to get the repairs done in record speed even if it meant working through the night. It was an offer too good to refuse. After motoring from Runaway Bay round to Coomera we hauled the boat out of the water and she was in a shed by Thursday with a team of people who had volunteered their time and expertise working on her. It was pretty hard for me to see the damage, but the shavings of metal and rust on the deck that had been scraped off the side of *Silver Yang* during the collision told us all how strong *Ella's Pink Lady* had been to withstand the onslaught. Talk about a tough little boat!

I was really grateful to have so many enthusiastic volunteers as I could very easily have wallowed in my misery and not fired up straight away. With blokes like Bruce, Chris, Black Joe, Scooter and Ryan around I was back into it instantly . . . whether they wanted me there or not. We had to remove the damaged rigging, lifelines and bow fitting and then it was straight to it, putting on the first layers of fibreglass over the damaged areas. There was a lot to do and we kept finding little things, like small holes where the mast came down. It was amazing how many things survived the crash. The Hella navigation lights were still working perfectly despite a direct hit and the Yanmar engine fired up immediately and brought me safely home.

Once everything had been assessed it was estimated that it'd take ten days to get *Ella's Pink Lady* looking her best again and the rigging wasn't going to take much longer. Luckily we still had some leftover pink paint!

The people at the marina didn't just work hard on the boat, they fed us every day and made sure anyone they didn't know was checked out properly before they were allowed near me or the boat. There were still journalists trying to get close but I wasn't as bothered once they had stopped impacting on Pamela's family and neighbours. Once we were in the shed it was easier to control and I tried to ignore the ongoing negativity surrounding the trip. There was one newspaper article that claimed it had a copy of a letter from the Queensland Department of Transport and Main Roads that was being sent to the federal government. I was so naive, up until then I thought a confidential investigation was just that. It was claimed that I had doodled on my safety checklist and drawn 'childish' pictures around it. I did have a notebook that I had written and doodled on and jotted key things down. I always have a notebook with me to write lists and things I have to do. It wasn't a log.

If it was just me I could have dealt with all the inaccuracies and misinformation but I was worried that the people who supported me would think everything they were reading was fact and be disappointed. Ever since the collision I'd been nervous that some of the sponsors might change their minds about me and pull out. Not one did. And then to have the local boaties and marine tradesmen pitch in was so amazing. It made me stop any time I felt slightly sorry for myself and get on with the task at hand.

Watching *Ella's Pink Lady* slowly come back together was great and after working so hard I was persuaded to go home for a weekend. I spent the time catching up with friends and hanging out with my family but I was looking forward to getting back to the Gold Coast and getting *Ella's Pink Lady* back in the water.

Just before I headed off to Mooloolaba we had a lunch to say thank you to all the people who had helped me out. I was blown away by the kindness and generosity of so many people and it was great to be able to tell them how much I appreciated them.

By Wednesday, 23 September, all the work to the hull was finished and the rig was due to arrive any day. I would have loved to give the boat a wash down to make her really sparkle but there was no point. A huge dust storm which had already smothered New South Wales had arrived on the coast with the strong south-westerly winds and everything was covered in a fine red dust. The sky was an orange haze and it made the world seem like a very strange place. As the dust got thicker I heard that construction sites were closed down, flights were redirected, roadwork stopped and workers sent home. You couldn't even see the sun. I was quite content to stay in the shed doing last-minute jobs to *Ella's Pink Lady* rather than venture outside.

Everyone in the shed was in good spirits despite the dust, working away at various bits and pieces that would make my life much more comfortable at sea. Over the previous few days Dad had built me a set of steps to make getting in and out of the companionway just a little easier and Chris, from AME, had tackled what had to be the world's most uncomfortable job: fitting one-way valves to the cockpit drains while lying upside down in a very tight spot. Because we had the time we were able to set up a system of pumps for transferring fuel and water from jerry cans into the tanks. As usual I kept writing up check lists (and doodling around them) and in any spare moment I studied charts and weather outlooks for the Pacific Ocean.

Finally, on Monday, 28 September, *Ella's Pink Lady* was ready to go back into the water. It was a remarkable achievement to have her repaired only nineteen days after the collision. It was a big moment for all of us but I think the pride on the faces of everyone at the marina who'd helped put her back together was priceless. Bruce and I spent that day out on the water testing everything thoroughly, and it all did exactly what it was supposed to do. We sailed back and then motored around to Runaway Bay to spend the last night with my family at Pamela's parents' place again. Her mum and dad, Gavin and Nadine, are good friends of my parents, and their place has always been a home away from home for us. But the way they helped us and put up with all the intrusions was truly remarkable. I am so lucky with the support I have had while building my dream.

The weather looked good with northerly winds predicted to hang around for a while so, all going well, the plan was to head

ABOVE: (LEFT TO RIGHT) Emily, me, Tom and Hannah at holiday sailing camp, where I first learnt to sail.

RIGHT: Swimming was never my thing when I was young. Here I am aged five with Emily (LEFT) and Hannah (RIGHT).

Hannah and I smiling for the camera when we were cruising up the east coast of Australia.

TOP: *Home Abroad*, the 52-foot motor (stink) boat that was our home for more than five years. Living on the boat meant all of us kids became really close.

MIDDLE: Mum, Emily, me, Tom, Hannah and Dad at Lizard Island after a big day of beachcombing. This is one of my favourite beaches ... so far!

RIGHT: Me, Hannah (trying to get in the photo) and Emily. This was taken in front of our bus on the last day of our trip exploring inland Australia. I was glad to be heading back to the water.

LEFT: Emily, Nick and I set off on all sorts of adventures. This time we'd paddled across a lake and instead of paddling the 8 kilometres back we made sails using our sarongs. Surprisingly effective!

BELOW: The infamous weekend sailing on Nick's little red yacht. This photo was taken as we left Mooloolaba when the weather was still perfect.

Don McIntyre, Mum, Emily, Tom, Dad and Hannah standing in front of my new boat. This is the picture they sent while I was away sailing in New Zealand, waiting impatiently to hear the results of the survey.

This was taken on my sixteenth birthday by my cousin Ben, the day I finally got my boat licence.

Don and Mike after a day sailing with me on *Shanty*.

With my family at the media launch at Rivergate Marina in Brisbane. We were calling the yacht *Youngest Round* at the time. It was our first really big experience with the media.

Ben Upton/Echo Imaging

ABOVE: Just some of the amazing refit team. (CLOCKWISE FROM TOP LEFT) Pat, Neil, Ed, Ricki, me, Dad, Mick, Richard, John, Bruce and Suzanne.
RIGHT: Another planning session around the dinner table – Terry, me, Suzanne and Bruce.

Ben Upton/Echo Imaging

Ben Upton/Echo Imaging

TOP LEFT: Dad spent most of his time on the phone juggling logistics during the refit.

TOP RIGHT: Ricki with the dodger slowly taking shape.

MIDDLE AND BELOW: It was frantic at the shed doing the refit on the boat.

Dad and I posing in front of the very impressive *Pink Lady*. It was a mammoth day as the boat came out of the shed and was trucked off to Sydney for the 2009 International Boat Show. She looked gorgeous! That night we held a combined 'Thank you' and fundraiser dinner at the Novotel Twin Waters Resort.

An OMG moment at the Novotel dinner...the first time I met Jesse Martin, with Don McIntyre looking on proudly. Both men have played a huge part in helping me achieve my dream.

off the next day and aim to be in Sydney early the following week. Just to be on the safe side, Bruce, Suzanne and Tom were going to leave at the same time as me and *Ella's Pink Lady* on *Big Wave Rider* and sail behind us for a while to keep me company and help navigate the busy shipping lanes. I knew I was going to have to do it by myself once I left Sydney, but I am not ashamed to say I had a few jitters about the demanding conditions out in those lanes for solo sailing. Apparently, since 1990 there have been thirty-eight collisions or near collisions between small vessels and larger ships and in more than fifty per cent of cases the ship did not stop to help. After becoming one of the statistics, having Bruce around for a little while was just the nerve-settler I needed to get my confidence back up.

I spent that night packing and finishing a few jobs and woke up ready to go. I wanted to make an early start and hopefully slip away before a media circus could develop. We didn't have any luck, though, because somehow word got out and we ended up with three news helicopters buzzing overhead. I'm sure Pamela's neighbours were glad that I was going! The wind was strong and we made great time away from the coast and then turned south.

It felt so good to be back on the ocean. I was by myself on the yacht and took my time settling back into it. The 15-knot winds and blue skies chased any remaining nerves away though, sadly, not the slight 'green around the gills' feeling I always have in the first few days at sea.

I had many thoughts running through my mind, but one stayed with me: the most amazing thing had happened the day before. Phenomenally successful British billionaire and renowned adventurer Sir Richard Branson sent me his best wishes. He had this to say to anyone who thought I should be stopped from setting sail:

> She's sixteen; she's not a baby anymore. I left school at fifteen and started my own business. At sixteen you are pretty grown up; she should go for it. It's risky, but it could be risky walking over the road, it's risky in cars, it's risky on bicycles. She'll have the adventure of a lifetime . . . you only live once and live life to the full.

Moments like this made me pinch myself to check I wasn't dreaming. I never imagined I would get the media attention I did or have people as famous as Richard Branson talking about me. I know the collision made it easier to attack what I was attempting to do but the support just kept coming. I am not special. I am an ordinary person, an ordinary teenager, who has been lucky enough (some may say stubborn enough) to keep following her dream. The day I set out from the Gold Coast I felt I had more people with me than against me. It was a good feeling to leave with.

I took five days to sail down to Sydney and the sea trial was just what *Ella's Pink Lady* and I needed to discover any potential troubles. It didn't take long to realise there were problems with the cockpit drains. There was a lot of water coming into the boat and at one point I was pumping out the bilges every twenty minutes or so. The lovely northerlies disappeared and a southerly change blew in so I was bumping around quite a bit with 23-knot winds and three-metre steep seas. It was pretty full-on sailing and combined with my seasickness, hypervigilance around shipping lanes and getting used to catnapping, I felt like I was finally doing what I had always wanted . . . challenging myself to an adventure.

On the last day at sea the ocean flattened out and I had to work hard to keep *Ella's Pink Lady* moving with very little wind and light rain squalls. Bruce, Suzanne and Tom had kept their distance the previous few days but we met up again to sail through Sydney Heads together. A few boats and a couple of media helicopters followed us in and Tom jumped off *Big Wave Rider* onto *Ella's Pink Lady* to help me dock at The Spit. I was still getting used to a tiller rather than a wheel and I didn't want to do a Tony Bullimore and stack in front of news cameras. It wouldn't be a good look, especially after the *Silver Yang* drama. The hilarious thing was that I was asked later by a few journalists who the handsome young man on the boat with me was (LOL!).

Once I stepped off the boat, my head started spinning and I stumbled about for a while there. Just like it takes a few days to find my sea legs, finding my land legs also takes some time. Goodness knows what I was going to be like after six or seven months at sea. Kay Cottee had absolutely no problems at all when she stepped off her boat after her circumnavigation but I saw what James and Justin were like after their kayak crossing of the Tasman: they struggled to walk after sixty-two days. I know they had less space to stretch out in and were almost constantly rowing, so it is a bit different, but I had a feeling I might be more like them than Kay.

I was so lucky that when we were planning where I'd be based in Sydney someone suggested talking to Andrew Short. Veteran Sydney to Hobart sailor Andrew Short had built up his business from a garage in Caringbah to a multi-million dollar boat dealership with interests at Taren Point, Yowie Bay and The Spit. When he was asked if he could fit us in at The Spit he was amazing. Not only did he give up a berth for *Ella's Pink Lady*, he also made space for *Big Wave Rider* and gave us access to any of the facilities we needed at his marina. I'd only met him for the first time that week, but Andrew was someone who understood what I wanted to do – he got it – and he, his wife Kylie and his children, Nick, Ryan, Sam, Mitch and Maddison, made us feel incredibly welcome. His eldest sons, Nick and Ryan, were wonderful and when I came through the Heads they brought Mum, Dad and Hannah to meet me on their family boat. Poor Hannah got seasick!

I had a bit of a sleep-in the first day after I arrived and then it was time to deal with a whole new job list that I'd put together during the sail down. In between maintenance, like examining the cockpit drains, more fibreglassing, trips to the local marine shops to stock up on armfuls of last-minute odds and ends and a few media interviews here and there, time sped by. Officers from the ATSB turned up on 9 October to discuss the draft report into the collision and they were absolutely wonderful. They were professional, friendly and solely interested in getting to the bottom of what had happened that night off Stradbroke Island so that it didn't happen again and I could learn from what had gone wrong. The last thing I wanted to do was to relive it, but it was important, and so we had a discussion around the table of *Big Wave Rider*, going through it all again. When we finished, they took me and Bruce to visit a shipping tanker. They had arranged a tour of the ship so I could get an understanding of how things might have been from the perspective of the *Silver Yang*'s crew.

After feedback from the ATSB, *Ella's Pink Lady* was fitted with a passive radar reflector to add to the active radar reflector she already had, and with my Aunty Vivienne's help I put together a more comprehensive fatigue-management plan. Reading through the report and talking through the findings showed me that there were a number of things that led to the collision that night and there were contributing factors from both me and *Silver Yang*. Learning about how it happened was invaluable to me to make sure it never happened again.

I was still completely focused on my trip but I did take the opportunity to have a bit of a break as well. We were staying at a pretty fancy hotel on the beachfront at Manly on Sydney's northern beaches (not our usual budget choice but they were helping out with discounted rates so we got to go a bit posh). Every morning I'd have double and triple helpings of fruit, pancakes and fresh cream knowing that I'd probably be losing a bit of weight in the first few days at sea. Down at the marina there was a constant stream of well-wishers stopping by to look at *Ella's Pink Lady* and to wish me luck. Phil, Ed, Pat, Judy, Aunty Cathy and Uncle Campbell all arrived to do what they could to help and to be there for the big day. One night, all the family and Bruce and Suzanne trooped off to have a big dinner with James, Justin and their families. It was a fun night and good to have a laugh and talk about someone else's adventure rather than mine for a change.

When I had first decided I wanted to become the youngest person to sail around the world, I never in my wildest dreams expected it would lead to meeting some of the amazing people I have. One of these people is seven-times surfing world champion Layne Beachley. Layne acted as the emcee at the huge media launch we had with Ella Baché opposite the Opera House. Beforehand I had been really nervous, but it turned out to be a whole lot of fun. Layne asked me questions about the trip and Jesse Martin was there to give me a hard time. It was all a bit of a blur of photos and questions but the fun part came when Jesse and I jumped onboard *Ella's Pink Lady* with a film crew from *The 7pm Project* to sail back to The Spit. I have to admit that I got a kick out of having Jesse there. Here was the guy who had been my hero for years, handling lines and crewing for me. To top it off we had an on-camera arm wrestle and Jesse only just managed to beat me. In his book, Jesse tells of how he sent off letters trying to raise sponsorship for his trip and how he'd waited at the letterbox every day for replies. Three of the knockbacks he got began 'Dear Ms Martin'. Jesse says it 'was a kick in the guts' that they didn't just think he couldn't make it, they also thought he was a girl. I would have loved to have won the arm wrestle just to pay him back for that line!

Outside my bubble of support there was still a steady stream of criticism that, for the most part, I could ignore. Probably the most distressing for all of us was when well-respected yachtsman Andrew Cape, who had completed five around-the-world races and had rounded Cape Horn seven times, sent an email on 8 October to journalist and author Rob Mundle asking him to pass it on to me but somehow it also found its way into the hands of the media and numerous articles were written quoting from it. Rob handed it to Andrew Short, who delivered the letter to me and my family. It began by saying Andrew Cape believed it was his duty to contact me to let me know that a voyage like mine took more experience than I had. He obviously had not attempted to find out what experience I *did* have and he used Dame Ellen MacArthur and Samantha 'Sam' Davies as examples of women who had accumulated several thousands of miles at sea before they set off.

If he had asked, I could have told him I had clocked up 10,000 nautical miles on open water and had already sailed around the south of New Zealand, among other places, as he advised. I had learnt about electrics, engine maintenance, meteorology, how to maintain my fitness and had the most wonderfully prepared boat I think anyone has ever had for this type of voyage. I had the most cutting-edge technology I needed but I also had the skills to sail unaided if that technology failed.

Without any informed knowledge of me, my skills, the boat or our preparation, Andrew Cape concluded that I had a thirty-three per cent chance of making it around the world, a thirty-three per cent chance of damage to boat and crew and a thirty-three per cent chance of total loss of boat or crew. *The Age* published his quote saying that what I was doing was 'like growing up on a farm and upon acquiring a .303 rifle you feel you are ready to take on the Taliban'.

It was a shame that Andrew Cape only sent this to me a few days before I left. Had his approach been made earlier I could have talked to him and perhaps benefited from his knowledge. Many other sailors with similar experience had generously shared their wisdom with me and I soaked it all up willingly. The fact that Andrew Cape had raced in his first Sydney to Hobart when he was sixteen meant he'd probably come up against the 'you are too young and inexperienced' comments himself.

It also would have been much better if his email hadn't simultaneously been used as a news story. The way it was all handled made me question the timing and the true intent of the email. I was angry that Andrew Cape's comments would be viewed as fact by many people but I couldn't waste my time or energy trying to defend myself. There was no point. I had to be as prepared and determined as I had always been and let my actions tell the story.

We were still finalising the boat and Paul from Aquatronics Marine was finetuning the electronics while at the same time Gavin Brennan was installing fixed cameras on deck and in the cabin so I could film while sailing, so there wasn't an inch of free space as we all worked away in different corners. I was also having to learn how to operate the cameras as we'd decided to make a documentary of the trip as a way of financing it. It was hectic and not everything was turning out. For some reason the cockpit drains refused to stop leaking. I felt so sorry for the guy who had to repeatedly wriggle back in over the engine to reapply fibreglass. I was glad that this time it wasn't me squeezing into a tight spot! Since I'd arrived in Sydney I'd stepped back a little and Bruce had taken over and was worrying over every detail. We did sea trials to practise deploying drogues (a parachute-like device that is thrown off the stern to act as a brake in rough, wild weather) and to test out the new light-wind sail and after that we thought, finally, the drains were fixed.

An inspector came to check that the boat and equipment was up to Category 0 racing regulations standard, which basically means I was fully equipped for offshore, cold-water, far-from-assistance sailing and survival below 5 degrees water temperature and 5 degrees air temperature. This category covers all boats sailing in trans-oceanic races and situations where yachts must be completely self-sufficient for lengthy periods of time, capable of withstanding heavy storms and prepared to meet serious emergencies without help from anywhere. The inspector looked at things like my medical kit, provisions, clothing, survival suits, EPIRBs and fittings, as well as every component of the boat itself. This wasn't a requirement for my trip, but it was something that we wanted to do to know we had done everything possible to give me the best chance of making it.

I was at the Manly hotel with my family on the Saturday morning, 10 October, when Andrew Fraser called with some devastating news. I knew that Andrew Short had left the night before to sail his 80-foot maxi yacht *Shockwave* in a race from Point Piper, in Sydney Harbour, to Flinders Islet, off Port Kembla, and back. Andrew was the skipper and his sons Ryan and Nick were part of the seventeen-person crew. There'd been a freak accident and the yacht had smashed into rocks as it rounded the Islet, throwing everyone overboard. Andrew and his incredibly experienced and respected navigator, Sally Gordon, had died. I couldn't believe it when I heard. It was like the air was sucked out of the room and we were all in shock. Andrew had been so wonderful to me and my family and so full of life only the day before. He was a man who made you feel safe and I wasn't surprised to hear later that one of the last things he did was throw a torch to Nick so he could signal where he was. Because he had that torch, a water-police boat found Nick and pulled him out of the water. His father saved his life.

We stayed away from the marina that day to give the family and the people who worked there – who were extended family to the Shorts – their space. We had a lot of calls from the media for my comments but it wasn't appropriate for me to say anything. I had only just met Andrew and his family and there were so many more friends of theirs and Sally Gordon's who had much more to share about them.

It was hard not to let the sadness wash over us all and want to stop for a while, but if Andrew Short showed me anything it was to live life to the fullest and to cherish the things that matter to you. For him it was sailing and his family. For me, it is the same.

There was definitely a change in everyone after Andrew died. In case we had forgotten, the accident reminded us that anything can occur at sea. It doesn't matter how experienced or how careful you are, bad things can happen. I didn't talk about it much with Mum and Dad, but I know it was a reminder to them as well. But we had all come to terms with the dangers involved in what I was planning so we didn't let this stop us.

In the last days before I left, everyone rushed around getting the final jobs done and then double-checking everything. I remained completely calm and composed as tempers frayed around me. I had a *60 Minutes* crew film me as all this was going on and journalist Charles Wooley interviewed me, Mum and Dad and Bruce. He is a good guy and I had fun taking him for a sail. He asked me if I could really know what I was in for and I told him, 'I don't. It's an adventure. I'm going out there to attempt to sail around the world, to see if I can.'

I surprised myself by being so matter-of-fact about it all and I actually started to find all the attention I was getting a little annoying. Looking back, I suspect it was part of me getting ready to say goodbye and to be alone.

I wasn't going to be there when the *60 Minutes* interview screened. They were planning to show it the night I left. I'm glad about that. I hate watching myself on television. After all his worry about me, Dad told Charles Wooley, 'It would be devastating if we lost her . . . but I think it would be worse to say, "No, you can't go" because of that risk, because of what she's put into it.' That's my mum and dad's attitude completely, they have always supported Emily, Tom, Hannah and me in our dreams, knowing that when you do push yourself, when you do step outside the everyday there will be risks. There is a quote someone sent to me from Irish poet and philosopher John O'Donohue that says:

> One of the most beautiful gifts in the world is the gift of encouragement. When someone encourages you, that person helps you over a threshold you might otherwise never have crossed on your own.

Thanks to Mum and Dad I was about to cross a threshold that in some ways was going to change me forever. No matter what happened, whether I succeeded or whether I failed, they had given me the greatest gift: the power and encouragement to follow my dream.

It was only as the leaving day kept getting pushed back that I began getting a little wound up. I'd get myself all psyched to go and then another small problem would be discovered, which would mean an extra day or two sorting it out. But things had to be right, and by this point I had kind of learnt to be patient. Finally, the afternoon before I left we stowed a few last things – like a box of books that made Bruce shake his head! – and then sat around eating pizza. We wondered if there was something obvious that we'd overlooked or had forgotten to pack, like when Jesse Martin packed the sextant but forgot the almanac of nautical tables you need to use with it. I was sure there'd be something.

That last night I slept onboard *Ella's Pink Lady*. I was about to be using that bunk for at least seven months and it seemed a good idea to give it another test run. But I also needed the time to settle myself as the last-minute nerves kicked in. That night, knowing that I had done all the preparation I could thanks to the wonderful team of people around me, I slept well. Moored at The Spit, the noise of one of Sydney's busiest roads didn't even register. I was calm and felt strong and completely at home on my pink yacht. I never expected to be as relaxed as I was so close to leaving. The last thing I said to Mum and Dad before they headed back to the hotel was, 'Tomorrow I am going to wake up and sail around the world.' I felt a shiver of excitement, anticipation and disbelief as I said it. After almost five years of dreaming about this voyage, it was actually about to become reality.

PART TWO

The Voyage

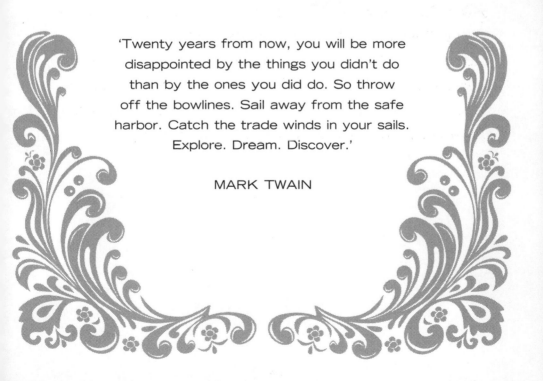

'Twenty years from now, you will be more disappointed by the things you didn't do than by the ones you did do. So throw off the bowlines. Sail away from the safe harbor. Catch the trade winds in your sails. Explore. Dream. Discover.'

MARK TWAIN

Do you remember when you were a young child feeling so excited about Christmas and Santa coming with presents that it was impossible to get to sleep and even harder to stay asleep? I was expecting that my last night before leaving would be a bit like that. But it wasn't. I spent some time fussing about organising things in the cabin but I didn't stay up late and I know I slept well because I didn't wake until my alarm went off. I lay there for a while, cosy on my bunk, listening to the light rain falling. I didn't get up until Bruce came looking for me. He knocked on the side of *Ella's Pink Lady* and told me Pat and Judy were cooking up breakfast for everyone on *Big Wave Rider*. Okay, so the thought of food helped get me moving.

After breakfast it was all a bit of a blur. The media throng were set up already and it made everything slightly strange. We had to restrict access to certain areas and everyone who worked at the marina or had their boat there was wonderful. They helped to keep the cameras at arm's length and give me and my family a little space. It was hilarious actually, because Bruce and Scott Young had to act as bodyguards to get me through the crowd of reporters and camera crews pointing cameras, thrusting microphones and shouting out questions. I'd had a grin on my face since I'd woken up because this was 'THE DAY' but I almost had the giggles as well because it was all so over the top. I only remember two questions being repeated by different reporters: 'How was I feeling?' Surely they could see the smile on my face? And 'What was the weather like?' Couldn't they see that for themselves?

I took special care to enjoy every second of my last hot shower. Dried off and dressed, I snuck out a different entrance and rushed back onto the marina before the cameras had time to swing around and refocus.

Back on *Ella's Pink Lady* we all fiddled around stowing the last few things and readying the sails, all of us keeping busy and trying not to think about the impending goodbye. People kept arriving to give me their good wishes and to wish me well, and I appreciated it but it also started to make me feel quite emotional. I had to hide down in the cabin after a while to say a private farewell to my family. I managed to hold back the tears for the first few goodbyes but after that I didn't have a hope. They weren't sad, frightened or even nervous tears, it was the thought of not seeing the people I love for so long. The laughing and joking had stopped. It was a very emotional scene and hard not to sob when everyone around me was weeping. I don't even remember who started first but it was a chain reaction as one by one we all set each other off. By the time everyone was waving me off and we were untying the lines, the whole dock seemed to be packed with crying people, their tears running down over proud smiles.

Saying goodbye to Dad was probably the toughest thing I had to do because he was taking my leaving pretty hard. He had supported me, once he knew how focused I was, but I also know he was always hoping I'd change my mind. At that moment I wanted him to know how perfect everything was for me and how happy I was to be chasing my dream but I couldn't stop my tears. I got a bit clingy and soppy with Hannah and Tom as well. I was holding Hannah's hand and hugging her and Tom over and over. I'd already said goodbye to Emily as she had to be somewhere else on leaving day. I hugged Mum so tight and I kept looking at her, trying to stamp every detail of her face into my mind. I don't think anyone really took any notice of the *60 Minutes* camera crew but they must have been getting some pretty full-on emotional footage. When I finally motored away, even tough old journalist Charles Wooley was crying with everyone else.

Turning the engine on and guiding *Ella's Pink Lady* out of her berth felt surreal but as soon as we were clear I took a last glance over my shoulder and saw my brave family, remarkable team and so many amazing people, like James Castrission, all standing there. It really hit home what we'd already achieved and I felt overwhelmed with pride.

But there was no time for reflection as I had to concentrate completely on pulling the sails up, getting *Ella's Pink Lady* out through the spectator boats to the Heads and across the start line. Things were pretty crazy with helicopters overhead and more than thirty vessels on the water to see me off. It was touching that people had taken the time to show such support but I had to pay attention as there was only a very light headwind and with all the wash from the boats and the swell rolling in, it was almost impossible to make any ground. I hardly noticed actually crossing the start line because it took so long, slowly tacking back and forth. We'd requested the Harbour Master, Steve Young, from the Sydney Ports Corporation act as the starter and witness for my departure. He was onboard *Big Wave Rider* to take down the time I crossed that imaginary line running between the north and south heads that marked the beginning of what I hoped would be a seven- or eight-month journey. There was no rule that said we needed anyone there because it is all recorded digitally, but for me and my team it was important to have this moment recognised by someone official.

As I got further away from The Spit the fleet of boats dropped away, and then the boat with Mum and Dad onboard turned back sooner than I'd expected. *Big Wave Rider* stayed with me the longest, but then all of a sudden they were gone, too. I was finally alone and I started to cry again. I was feeling wobbly and not quite right. All the emotion had shaken me up far more than I'd expected. But that didn't last long and neither did the solitude because the helicopters found me again!

I spent the rest of that day working to keep us moving in the light wind but, despite all my efforts, by evening I was still within sight of land. I'd shaken off my vague sadness and felt in high spirits, listening to a local Sydney radio station for as long as I could and making the most of patchy mobile phone coverage to use up the rest of my phone credit calling friends. No sense wasting it, right?

The rain had stopped and it had turned into a lovely clear day. By the time the sun set dramatically over the faint and fading outline of the lights glowing on the Sydney Harbour Bridge, I was feeling settled and ready for everything ahead of me.

Stage One

SYDNEY AND NORTH TO THE LINE ISLANDS

Monday, 19 October 2009
Across the start line

. . . I'll admit I was a little emotional for a while after all the goodbyes but on the plus side I already feel like I'm settling in, and with such calm conditions I haven't even been feeling any of my normal first-few-days-at-sea queasiness.

Not feeling even the slightest bit queasy or seasick in those first few days as I usually would have was a huge bonus. My normal approach to the beginning of any passage is to 'endure' till I get my sea legs. Not getting seasick meant that I felt cheerful right from the first day and was able to settle into a routine far quicker than I would have otherwise.

So after all the excitement of getting away, progress has been pretty slow. We're still only just over 65 nautical miles from the coast, currently doing a not very remarkable, but steady, 2.5 knots. It's a little frustrating but I'm not complaining. I'm just taking it one day at a time for now, giving myself a little time to settle in and waiting for a little more wind.

Later: Monday, 19 October 2009

Blues and pinks

Today's been a quiet one out here. For a while this afternoon we were completely becalmed again. I expected that it would frustrate me making so little progress but I really enjoyed the chance just to take it easy and start on a book between tweaking the sails. It's been so long since I've had any time just to relax for a while and the freedom is amazing. No deadlines, nothing to rush off to, I can eat whatever I like, whenever I like, no one to send me off to bed! It was pretty special this afternoon when the sea glassed right out, it was as if you could see right to the distant blue bottom, apart from huge schools of jelly fish floating past. We even had a couple of dolphins drop in to say 'hi'.

I've already discovered that a tidy cabin means a happy Jessica. I can only relax when everything on deck, in the cockpit and down below is in its place and ready for the unexpected. Right now the sun's setting and the sky's turned a shade of pink exactly the same colour as *Ella's Pink Lady* – very pretty! So I might get the camera out before finding something to eat (I'm thinking sweet and sour lamb and then pancakes), getting *Ella's Pink Lady* ready for the night, then calling in for evening skeds.

I actually had another unexpected visitor that day, and one that wasn't quite as welcome as the dolphins. A small plane gave me a fright when it turned up to circle around overhead. I had thought that out of sight was out of mind and didn't expect helicopters or media, let alone a light plane. Thinking I was finally by myself I'd stripped down to a bikini to enjoy the sunshine and I hadn't heard the roar of the aeroplane's engines approaching. It was a surprise when I saw how close the plane was and I quickly rushed back below to throw on a t-shirt and shorts!

And I have to admit, day two didn't go quite as smoothly as I led the world to believe in my blog. The conditions were still very calm but I'd discovered a problem with *Ella's Pink Lady* that could have potentially threatened the trip. I wasn't prepared to share this information with everyone (except my support team) and detract from all the good stuff. Even though there was quite a bit of shipping action around, I was starting to relax and get myself into a routine. I was feeling great until a screaming alarm went off and shattered the peace. The alarm meant there was water in the bilges. I can tell you it was not good when I pulled up the floorboards and saw water coming in. At least I knew straight away what the problem was. The cockpit drains (yes, those damn cockpit drains again!) were leaking terribly, despite the many layers of fibreglass patching that had been applied the week before my departure.

I didn't freak out because I knew there was no immediate threat. The water trickling in was simply pumped straight out again by *Ella's Pink Lady*'s seriously heavy-duty bilge-pump system, but considering the wild and deserted waters we'd soon be sailing into it was a problem that I couldn't afford. Keeping a close eye on the drains in case the leak got worse I called Bruce to talk through what I could do. We decided that I was going to have to get my hands dirty and have a go at re-fibreglassing the drains, something that I was not looking forward to after my recent experience working on the seriously hard-to-get-at drains while sailing down to Sydney from the Gold Coast. Not to mention the fact that I'd discovered, when we were in the shed at Rosemount, that working with epoxy (the stuff used with fibreglass to build boats) makes me break out in a terrible rash.

My dad's always told me that you should tackle a problem head-on and not put it off, but it turned out that the problem with the drains was an exception to his rule. I pumped the water out numerous times throughout that day and carefully monitored the situation to make sure it wasn't getting worse, but I decided to wait for a perfectly calm day to do the repair to give it the best chance of working. So every day I checked and pumped, and within a week the water trickling into the boat slowed and then stopped. The fibreglass repair we'd done before I left had kept curing and each day it hardened some more and finally set enough to stop the leak.

I was glad I didn't blog about it as I suspect the media and our critics would have had a field day and the bloggers, who were always so wonderful, would have worried too much. Although I had everything under control the words 'water coming into the boat' could have easily spiralled out of perspective and created all sorts of negative speculation. None of it would have really affected me but everyone back home would have felt the brunt and they had copped enough flak already because of me.

Tuesday, 20 October 2009

Moving!

Today was definitely a better day for progress with 13 knots of wind from the north-east pushing us along nicely. But, if anything, it's been a pretty quiet day out here again, just a lot of sparkling blue water and blue sky.

I was kept busy last night avoiding a bit of shipping and adjusting the Fleming windvane (which I've nicknamed Parker, can anyone guess why?*) when the wind dropped right out. It was so quiet and flat for a while that I brought my pillow out into the cockpit and grabbed a few catnaps of sleep under the stars.

It already feels like I'm settling right into a routine, grabbing a bit of sleep through the night and into the morning when I can, logging and plotting my position, digging through the food bags for meals and calling in for phone skeds twice a day. There's always something to do or check. I've been hard at work eating my way through all the last-minute presents and sweets that were shoved aboard just before we left. Every time I think I've eaten them all I seem to discover another packet stashed away somewhere!

Sleeping outside in the cockpit is magic, the blanket of stars overhead more than makes up for the discomfort of having no mattress. I find the quiet little jingling and squeaking of Parker working away next to me along with the gurgling and splashing of the water on the hull, and the tinkling of the rigging amazingly comforting. Some people buy wind chimes for the same reason. I remember reading in Kay Cottee's book that the noises really bothered her because she was worried about chafe and wear and when things were silent she knew everything was working smoothly.

---

* Parker is the name of a character from the television series *Thunderbirds*. He drives a transforming pink Rolls Royce for Lady Penelope!

I was equally as worried about the wear on the boat and the rigging, so I still kept an ear out for anything out of the ordinary, but for me those noises meant *Ella's Pink Lady* was on her way.

But apart from all that, more than anything I liked the idea of sleeping outside because it meant that I was right there ready to take control, change course or tweak a sail at a moment's notice. In those first few days, as I was getting used to everything and clearing the busier shipping areas, I was a little bit on edge. The sound of the 34-foot *Ella's Pink Lady* scraping along the side of the 63,000-tonne *Silver Yang* is hard to forget and being constantly ready for anything was the best way for me to feel more comfortable and in control and to make sure something like that never happened again.

Thursday, 22 October 2009
Out into the Tasman and sleeping

. . . Overall it's been pretty quiet out here, but after a great run of 155 nautical miles yesterday, the wind dropped off again and now we (*Ella's Pink Lady* and I) are back to plodding along slowly. So we're well and truly out into the Tasman now, near Lord Howe Island, with Australia well behind us. *Ella's Pink Lady* is under full mainsail and genoa at the moment and doing a slow but steady 3 knots. The sun's still shining and the water is an even more amazing shade of blue, but I've been finding that sunset is my favourite time of the day – the whole world turns pink! This morning I had a pod of dolphins pass by and the odd bird also dropped in to check us out.

I think keeping the cabin tidy is going to become one of those never-ending battles. Is it just me or does housework always take this long? And then washing up. There's no one else offering to take their turn, so I'm stuck with it after every meal!

Everyone's fascinated about what happens to *Ella's Pink Lady* when I'm sleeping and it's a subject that we've put years of thorough research into. I'd better start from the beginning so everyone understands, sorry if I'm boring you with the basics.

Firstly, I obviously can't be hand-steering the whole time, so *Ella's Pink Lady* has got three different self-steering systems: two electronic autopilots and Parker, the Fleming windvane mounted on the stern. The windvane is my favourite because, unlike the other two, which draw a lot of power, Parker steers us by responding to the wind over a blade and the water over a paddle trailing off the stern. I'll get to the power subject later.

Then I've got four different ship detection systems, which all sound loud alarms if there are any ships approaching. *Ella's* navigation lights and radar reflector also make us more visible to other ships at night. But even with all that, I never just put my head down and get a full night's sleep. If there's a bit going on I'll take a twenty-minute power nap, popping my head up to check on everything before going back to sleep. When things are quieter I'll sleep for forty minutes or longer at a time. It's amazing how used to the motion of *Ella's Pink Lady* I've already become. If the wind picks up a little the noise will wake me, or if we drift off course the sails luff (flap) and wake me. It takes a little getting used to, but I find that I can get all the sleep I need like this and wake refreshed every time.

Before I go to sleep I set up two different wake-up alarms so that there's no chance that I'll sleep through. You should hear how loud one of them is, it still makes me jump out of my skin every time.

All the equipment probably seems a little over the top but we're going to be out here for a while and the collision taught us that there's no such thing as being too careful!

Jessica Watson's Video Diary — Day 5
http://www.youtube.com/jessicawatsonvideo

I know they are totally essential and that they make my life easier in so many ways but you have no idea how much I came to hate those alarms. Yes, I know the alternative could be much worse and I should be grateful for the technological assistance in keeping me safe, but being woken from my precious sleep by the ear-splitting screech of the wake-up alarm is horrid. Worse still is the wailing of the AIS alarm, which tells me that there is a ship somewhere nearby. I constantly joked over the phone when talking to Mum or Dad or Bruce that I was going to come back with damaged eardrums. Believe me, those alarms are seriously loud!

Friday, 23 October 2009

Slowly

Still more slow progress out here, but past the 500-nautical-mile mark, which is a bit of a milestone. We spent last night completely becalmed next to Lord Howe Island, drifting along at less than a knot. But when we finally did get a light breeze as the sun was coming up, it made for a pretty amazing picture. The water was completely glassed out, reflecting the rising sun, so as we started picking up a little wind it was as if we were gliding along on a sheet of glass.

Today was more of the usual stuff for me, playing with cameras, catching up on a little sleep, keeping us moving, carefully monitoring my power ins and outs, feeding myself, the usual tidying up, listening to music (there's no one to complain about my taste or the volume I like to play it at!) and sending a few emails. It probably doesn't sound all that exciting but it's keeping me happy and I still can't see myself ever getting bored, there's always something to do. Sailing around the world sure isn't all high action and excitement but quiet days reading are part of what I signed up for.

Not much wildlife around today, just *Ella's Pink Lady*, myself and lots and lots of blue, what more could anyone ask for? We are not moving too badly again now, doing 6 knots under full main, headsail and staysail.

Sorry, I'll have to keep this short today because I'd better go and turn the HF on for a radio sked.

These days, with all the new satellite technology, less and less people are bothering with HF radios but in a critical situation they can be the only thing that works. We had installed one on *Ella's Pink Lady* and I enjoyed the chance to have a play with it. I did find it pretty amusing on the nights when the signal wasn't so good. After we'd struggled with the static to try to have a conversation, the radio operator at Tas Coast (the station I was skeding with) would often just give up and say they'd 'just check the blog' to see how I was doing. Gotta love the internet, right?!

Most of the time I was quite surprised at how comfortable, cheerful and at home I was. Having things like the sat-phone, HF radio and the internet was definitely a help because there was always someone at the end of the line or on email I could connect with. Since I first started dreaming about the voyage, I'd always expected that the first weeks out would be some of the toughest. Every solo sailor I'd talked to had told me over and over to just stick it out for the first week and that it would get easier after that when I'd adjusted to everything. I kept waiting for the crunch to come but it didn't . . . at least not then.

The quiet and easy sailing helped me keep that 'on top of the world' feeling, and I was as cheerful as ever. There certainly wasn't any need to 'stick it out'. I am not exaggerating when I say I was having the time of my life and my mood was boosted even more because I felt it was a personal triumph to somehow avoid this notorious 'down' period.

Mind you, I missed everyone. From the moment I sailed out of Sydney Heads I felt like I'd left something I needed behind. It was as if there was something physically missing, like a part of me was gone. All right, I know that sounds like something out of a soppy romance novel but it's the best way for me to describe it. Actually that feeling never went away but after a while I got used to it.

Saturday, 24 October 2009
Perfect conditions and food

Well, 'perfect' is about the only word for it out here today, we're doing 6.5 knots on a broad reach, heading for a waypoint below Norfolk Island. The wind was just getting up above 15 knots so I pulled the first reef into the main this morning to keep the motion comfortable and to make the steering easier on Parker.

It's such a nice day that I've just spent the morning sitting up on deck enjoying it all, watching *Ella's Pink Lady* sail along and listening to music. Today there's little speckles of white streaked across the water, as if they're there just to break up all that blue! Just think how great it would be if it were like this every day. On second thoughts, maybe it would get a little boring.

It's taken a while but I think the enormity of the voyage and everything that's happened over the last few months finally caught up with me today. Surprisingly it didn't make me feel at all daunted, just proud of all the people who got us here and a little overwhelmed – like, wow, this is it! And it's so much better than I ever dreamed. Still, there's a lot to get through yet but I know we can do it, one leg at a time. I'm about halfway between Lord Howe and Norfolk Islands now.

. . . Tonight I'm planning to have Easyfood lamb shanks (they are so nice!) with Deb (mashed potato) and asparagus.

. . . I'm off to enjoy the rest of the day and maybe have a bucket bath in the cockpit.

That last long, hot shower was a forgotten memory by day seven but I had my bucket baths down to a fine art. I'd unpack all I needed and carefully arrange the bottles and soaps in various places around the cockpit. Then I'd fill a bucket with salt water, scrub myself down, shampoo my hair twice so that it would foam up in the salt water, then rinse off with a precious cup of fresh water. Once clean I would sit and brush my hair in the wind (the all-natural hair dryer!). Depending on what sort of day it was, and how warm the air temperature, I'd either enjoy the dunking or squeal and wince my way through it. Either way, it was quite an event in my daily routine. All the little things (like baths or warm showers) that we take for granted on land become a big deal at sea. I hope that I keep this appreciation for the luxuries I am so lucky to have now I'm home.

With all the pressure of preparing the boat, dealing with media requests, ticking off checklists and everything else that was happening in the week before departure, my way of coping was to put the enormity of what I was about to do out of my mind. I didn't ever think about the big picture, I just focused on the small steps I had to take to get on my way. I knew that it had to catch up with me at some point, but I figured that it would be better to let that happen once I was safely offshore away from everyone. I was still expecting the downer that I'd been told would hit me but that wasn't exactly what happened.

It was a totally perfect day and I was sitting out on the cabin, soaking up the sun when a wave of emotion overtook me. I wasn't depressed but what was ahead finally hit me. I was overwhelmed but not scared and daunted like I expected to be. It was like a rush of adrenaline went through me and I was left in a state of dazed excitement for the rest of the day. It was like I had finally realised my dream was really happening.

Sunday, 25 October 2009
One week down and the shore crew

Well, we've been out here a full week now and into day eight today! I've just been doing the maths and we covered

740 nautical miles in week one, which is as much as I'd ever hoped for, and pretty good considering some of the windless days we've had. If anything, the first week's run puts us very slightly ahead of schedule, but I hate to say that so early on!

We're near Norfolk Island which sounds like a pretty interesting place so I'll have to add it to the list of places to stop off at next time. Not long now till the Tasman is ticked off and then it's on to the equator.

Something I maybe should have done long ago is to introduce you to my shore team. If you ask me, they're amazing, handling all the tricky stuff back home while I have all the fun out here! These are just a few of the people I rely on and talk to every day, the complete support network is made up of even more amazing people with all sorts of different skills. And that's not to mention all the people who worked on *Ella's Pink Lady* and all our sponsors, it's more like a huge extended family than anything. So along with all you guys thinking of me and *Ella's Pink Lady* I'm not really alone out here.

Firstly, there's Bruce the Project Manager [who I have already told you about]. Bruce and his wife Suzanne have worked on the voyage full-time for most of the year, were hugely supportive before then and a big inspiration to me. I love Bruce's calm 'can do' approach. I talk through boat performance, conditions, any potential shipping, etc. with Bruce.

I talk to Dad (Roger) on the sat-phone twice a day for the official skeds. Dad's great for talking through any little problems with me and is kept busy chasing up all sorts of bits and pieces. It's nice to talk to Dad and hear all the ins and outs of what's going on at home.

Then there's Scott and Andrew, who handle a lot more than just my management and media. Scott's always there to patiently help me work through the camera systems and some of the sat communication gear. Andrew looks after the blog, sponsors and other news updates.

Bob McDavitt (the ambassador for New Zealand's meteorological service) is providing all the weather forecasting and routing us around the worst of the bad weather. It gives me a lot of confidence to have such a good idea of what's coming.

And lastly, Mum (Julie) keeps me up to date with the outside world, forwarding on emails, sending me any news that I might find interesting. She's also the one who packed all the food so when I can't find something she's the one I call!

I can't stress enough how important it is to have such a great team of people behind me. I couldn't have made it as far as I have without them. To have this back-up and to know that any advice or reassurance I needed was only a satellite phone call away was an enormous comfort. All the advice I had about preparation being the most important part of the voyage was absolutely right and all the help and encouragement I received made a huge difference. But it isn't just the people I mentioned who have helped me and kept me steady. Just before I set out, there was a wave of positive media coverage, and then the flood of emails and comments on the blog when I left made me feel as if the whole of Australia was behind me. That is a pretty amazing feeling. For a while there it was heavy going, with so many loud voices saying I *couldn't* or *shouldn't* attempt the trip. Once I left Sydney that all changed. Though I'm sure there are still plenty of sceptics out there, they don't seem to be the majority anymore. Or maybe I just stopped paying attention.

Nearly the whole time I was at sea I didn't feel like I was alone. Sure, there were scary times and physically it was all up to me, but on the blog I always wrote 'we' and I didn't just mean *Ella's Pink Lady* and myself. As well as the immediate support team, I consider everyone who'd worked to get *Ella's Pink Lady* ready (and then re-ready) and all the people from around the world who were virtually sailing with me through the website as part of the team. I guess it might seem strange when you consider how far away I was but all that goodwill made a difference. I might have been by myself on the yacht but I never felt unaccompanied.

Though I have to be truthful, there were times I would have liked to completely disconnect and settle into the rhythm of the sea, like Joshua Slocum had to do, and test my resilience more – but that wasn't often. In those early weeks I was talking to both Mum or Dad and Bruce morning and evening for skeds. Sometimes it would just be a short call and I'd quickly run through conditions and how I was going but at other times we'd have a long chat. It was Dad who insisted I call in so often, and after all he and Mum had done for me I wasn't about to refuse. But I hoped that once we'd all settled in I'd be able to cut down on the calls. It sounds heartless, but right at the beginning I'd often dread these conversations as they felt a little like an interrogation. I hadn't been away long enough to miss everyone desperately, and the sailing I was doing was not unlike some of my previous voyages so I wasn't feeling out of my comfort zone. I can't blame Mum or Dad or anyone else for wanting to know exactly how things were going, but I was fine and I didn't think it was necessary to go over and over it all. Sometimes I just didn't feel like chatting (I know, very unlike the stereotypical teenage girl) and then other times I'd chatter away for ages, keen to hear every little detail of life back home. If my inconsistency bothered Mum and Dad, they never said.

Monday, 26 October 2009
Squid on the deck

When it got light this morning I did my usual check around *Ella's Pink Lady* only to find a whole lot of little squid lying on the deck where they'd clearly got stuck after jumping onboard during the night. One of them was a good 25 centimetres long and as I worked on the deck during the day I kept finding more little ones tucked into all sorts of unusual places. Hopefully I found them all or I'm going to know about it when they start smelling in a few days!

Conditions are still pretty quiet, we've had about 14 knots of wind right behind us all day so we're rolling along at a steady 5 knots.

After all the usual chores, I spent the morning catching up on a few emails and reading. I've been re-reading Kay Cottee's book about her non-stop trip around the world and of course Jesse Martin's book, *Lionheart*. I love comparing my trip so far with their voyages. After reading how organised Kay was with the housework side of things I've made a new resolve to do better myself!

Over the years I'd read and re-read these two books constantly and as my own voyage slowly came together I began to understand many of the things that Jesse and Kay wrote about in a whole new way. Every time I read their books I would react differently or learn something new. It was almost like I was reading them for the first time. Now I have not just followed Kay and Jesse on the ocean, I have also put my own book together and it is a very strange thing. I would love to whisper in the ear of the young girl I'd been and tell her, *anything is possible*. But actually, deep down, she must have known that already, otherwise you wouldn't be reading this.

This afternoon I kept busy on deck working out the easiest way to pole the headsail (using the spinnaker pole to hold the headsail right out) to make sailing downwind (with the wind right behind us) more comfortable.

The water was still a little chilly when I had another saltwater scrub down today and a quick rain squall came through so even *Ella's Pink Lady* had a nice wash down. So now we're both as fresh as roses! It's nice to have non-salty decks for a while and the rain was a bit of a novelty because it's the first I've had so far.

I've finally started getting a little more imaginative with cooking. Last night was cheese scones and very creamy soup (thanks to me adding maybe a little too much cream!). This morning was porridge with some of the last of my fresh fruit. Lunch was pasta again and I'm thinking Easyfood chilli beans and chips (fried tinned potatoes) for dinner tonight.

Tuesday, 27 October 2009
Cleared Norfolk Island

The comfortable routine I had been getting very used to fell apart today with the wind picking up to 25 knots. A short building sea has been making life, I wouldn't say uncomfortable, but certainly different to some of the quiet days we've had. It's nice to be guaranteed some good progress and even with two reefs in the mainsail, *Ella's Pink Lady* has almost been surfing along in the swell at up to 8.5 knots.

This morning we finally cleared Norfolk Island, which was a relief because I didn't get much sleep last night with land and a few boats around and have now settled onto a north-easterly course that should take us straight to the equator!

Jessica Watson's Video Diary – Day 10
http://www.youtube.com/jessicawatsonvideo

While rounding Norfolk Island I spotted another yacht and I talked to them briefly on the VHF radio. They were heading into Norfolk Island and then onto Opua, New Zealand. I told them I was doing a solo navigation but at the time I didn't get the impression they fully understood I meant around the world. Later, Richard, one of the people who regularly posted comments on my blog, came across another sailing blog written by Michael and Jackie Chapman. They were the people I'd spoken to and they described how small and determined *Ella's Pink Lady* had looked flying along out into the Pacific while all the other yachts in the area were headed to the anchorage to shelter from the uncomfortable conditions and rising wind. I love that they acknowledged the determination that *Ella's Pink Lady* and I share.

> This afternoon I was feeling a little down, so to cheer myself up I made a few phone calls, turned the music up, gave my hair and teeth a good brush, all the things that would normally make me feel on top of the world, before realising that I'd forgotten to feed myself! A good helping of tinned potatoes, fried into chips, later and I'm back to my normal cheerful self.
>
> No colourful sunset tonight with the overcast skies but it's a little too wet to be sitting around on deck enjoying it anyway.

During that first leg I didn't often feel anything other than cheerful and energetic, but I had my moments of sadness and depression. I tried to treat my mental health like I did the maintenance of *Ella's Pink Lady*. I worked at it and did everything I could to keep myself and the yacht in good shape.

The few times my mood turned dark and I felt slightly upset or mopey I really had only myself to blame because I had become lazy and hadn't made an effort. Maintaining good mental health had been something we'd put strategies in place for before I left. I'd talked to people like Mike Perham, Jesse Martin and Don McIntyre and I understood that the success of the trip was just as dependent on my state of mind as it was on the state of the rigging or the hull. There was rarely a time when I couldn't put myself in a good mood just by turning on some music, standing outside in the wind or doing any of the other things that I enjoyed, though there were definitely times when I had to really work at it. It was much more difficult when the weather turned bad and all I could do was strap myself in and ride out the worst. When that happened I tried to stay in the moment and not let my imagination run away from me. And if all else failed . . . chocolate helped!

Thursday, 29 October 2009

Night-time, little habits and on to the equator

I'm full of energy today after getting some good sleep during the night and a good breakfast with plenty of cream this morning!

There's still a good-sized swell but it's much longer and more gentle and the sun's even out at the moment, so I've been standing outside enjoying it. When we're in a trough between two waves *Ella's Pink Lady* feels small and a little lost, then up we go again to the top of the next swell, and with a good view out to the horizon. It's as if we're on top of the world. Then off rolls another wave giving us a little push along as it goes.

The wind eased off a bit overnight after blowing 25 knots yesterday, and this morning we've got a perfect 15 knots still pushing us along on a broad reach. We're making the most of the wind and loving the good progress while it lasts. Now that the Tasman is behind us I'm really starting to look forward to reaching the equator, it'll be my first time crossing the line so it should be pretty exciting!

I've been thinking about some of the little habits I've fallen into, like brushing my teeth every morning sitting out on the cabin top, keeping a packet of lollies or nuts beside me while working at the computer, and sleeping in my harness, life jacket and overalls, with a knife in my pocket and a headlight about my neck. It might sound a little uncomfortable but I get my best sleep knowing that I can be in the cockpit clipped on in less than a few seconds.

On the blog a few people have been asking about what it's like at night out here so I'll have a crack at describing it. I think a lot of people get goosebumps when they think about being out here all by themselves because I think most people imagine it to be like a night in the suburbs, all quiet and eerie. But it's not like that at all. Firstly, because there's the constant noise and motion of the boat, and then there's the waves and wind for company! On a clear night the stars are pretty amazing but I love the dark overcast nights almost as much when I can stand behind the dodger for protection, feeling *Ella's Pink Lady* ploughing along and not really knowing what comes next!

At this point I couldn't believe that the Tasman was already behind us. After so many years of, at times, excruciatingly slow preparation the actual trip itself felt like it was flying by. I knew I still had a long way to go, and that it was only a small step in something much, much bigger, but for years the crossing of the Tasman had seemed like such a big achievement to me. Even though it was the smallest of the oceans that we'd be crossing, it was still an ocean, and *Ella's Pink Lady* practically skipped across it, taking it all in her stride. It was easy to be cheerful because things were going well and I hadn't hit anything really challenging by this point. Until that happened the biggest test was keeping my head right and, really, that wasn't proving a problem.

Saturday, 31 October 2009
Flying along and power

Still overcast with a pretty bouncy sea out here but we're loving it and making some really good progress. I'm missing the sunshine a little but all the different shades of grey make for a pretty picture too. Looks like we're going to be on this course for a few days yet, with a steady wind slowly coming around to the south-east. Plenty of empty ocean in front of us for now before we start getting in among a few of the islands and reefs off the bottom of Fiji and Samoa.

Life onboard is really pretty simple with all the little things filling up the day, but when the sea is up, even the simplest task becomes an adventure. But the little things are keeping me more than happy. Food, talking with everyone back home, plotting our position to see how far we've come each day, music and standing behind the dodger watching the sun go down have become the highlights. Sure I'm missing everyone back in Australia, but mostly I'm having the time of my life out here. Bring on the next challenge!

Standing behind the dodger with one foot on each side of the cockpit for balance was my favourite place onboard. With my body protected from all but the most determined waves and my face and hair lightly stung by the wind I loved to look out as *Ella's Pink Lady* sailed along a rising and falling sea. I'd sing along loudly to whatever music I had playing and I never had to worry about sounding completely ridiculous as there was no one to hear me other than the odd bird, deck-lodged squid or dolphin.

With Missy Higgins or Powderfinger blasting out, no land in sight and the horizon calling me on, I felt so alive and completely exhilarated. It is easy to become dulled down at home, too focused on the next step to enjoy the moment you are living. On *Ella's Pink Lady* there was only the moment, it was a great lesson and I hope it is one I can carry with me forever.

It really was my own world and time started to mean different things out there. As I headed east into a different time zone from back home, I had four different clocks all set to the different time zones, just to confuse myself. The only thing that mattered to me really was what I started to call *Ella's Pink Lady* time!

I was sleeping less and less at night and more in the mornings and I ate whenever I felt like it. There was a freedom that came from deciding everything – when I ate, when I showered, what I read, everything I did – that I had never experienced before. It was another part of being in my own little world . . . and I liked it.

The only thing that had the ultimate power in my new world was the weather. I was a slave to that and though it was something I would struggle with at times, ultimately it was why I was there. I wanted to be pushed to the limit and have to find the strength and the knowledge within myself to get through the bad times. If it was all smooth sailing I wouldn't be doing that.

Sunday, 1 November 2009

New food bag, new chart and last orange

Well, that's it, the last of my fresh fruit. I've just been savouring my last orange and I'm sure going to miss it! And on the subject of food, today I pulled out my first new food bag. A food bag lasts 14 days. It feels like a bit of a milestone and I'm looking forward to dinner tonight because I get first pick of meals. By the end of the week all the good stuff will be gone and I'll be back to eating all my second favourites.

Progress has been a little slower today with the wind dropping right out to pretty much nothing for a while last night, then coming round on to *Ella's Pink Lady*'s nose this morning. But we're still eating away at the miles and getting very close to the edge of the chart. So I pulled out a new chart and spent the afternoon looking over it, studying up on areas we're sailing into. It feels like we're really getting into unfamiliar waters now, I've never sailed this far east before so it's all new and exciting stuff from here.

I'm a bit annoyed with myself at the moment after thinking it was calm enough to open a hatch and being quickly shown otherwise by a wave breaking over the deck and pouring right into the cabin. There's some wet salty clothing hanging up, but it's all drying quickly now.

All right, I'm going to sign off because I'm off to do something brave, daring and possibly a little reckless. I'm going to open the bag labelled 'Schoolwork'. Okay, so maybe I'm being a bit of a drama queen, but wish me luck on this one!

Monday, 2 November 2009
All's well and a busy day

Been a bit of a busy day and time got away from me so I'll keep today's update short. Just wanted to let you know that all's well. More than well, really, as we've been getting along so nicely out here. Loving every moment!

The wind's been sitting on about 15 knots from the south-east so *Ella's Pink Lady* is on a close reach [sailing at about 80 degrees into the wind] plodding along at a steady 6 knots. After passing reasonably close to Minerva Reef (below Tonga and Fiji) this morning, I've been spotting and passing quite a few yachts, so that's kept me vigilant on deck. Other than that, I've been poring over charts and forecasts again, chatting to a few people on the sat-phone and keeping up with chores and a little maintenance.

Tuesday, 3 November 2009
Slow day, communication and website

It's been a quieter day today, a bit too quiet actually. For most of the day the wind has been a bit non-existent. Any progress we did make could probably be put down to drift more than anything! But there's a nice breeze again now so off we go again. Rolling about not going anywhere started to get a little frustrating today, so I kept busy doing some schoolwork and I finally put the fishing line out. No luck catching anything but there's always tomorrow. I also didn't have much luck with the schoolwork. After completing the first English assignment I sent it off to discover that I'd opened the wrong bag and have been working on next year's assignments. Oops!

I sent off an email to Mum with the subject line, 'See! I told you so!!!! Schoolwork!' with my unit of completed English attached. I'd been working away mostly to prove a point because pretty much everyone scoffed and declared that I wouldn't get anything done when I told them I was taking some schoolwork with me. I was feeling quite good about it all until I got this reply from Mum . . .

Hi Jess

Hate to say it but . . . this work is for next year!

But please do carry on as you probably won't feel like doing it next year!

I'll find the stuff for this year and get it to you.

Lots of love, Mum.

(Sorry) Poor Jess!

Typical! Here I was thinking that I'd been diligently working away and it turned out that I hadn't even been working on the right year! If I'd followed normal terms I'd have been in Year Eleven, my second-last year of school, but with the full-time preparations leading up to my departure I'd let school take a backseat so I was pretty behind and only just scraping passes before I left. I'd brought schoolwork with me not just because I hoped to do a little so I didn't slip even further behind, but because I thought there might be quiet times when I'd appreciate something to keep my mind busy. I finished close to a term of English during the voyage, not a lot really, but enough to say to the scoffers that I did do some!

To cheer myself up I had scrambled eggs for lunch, made with powdered eggs and cream, really yummy! So I'll have to have them more often. Powdered eggs aren't exactly an off-the-shelf item, but all the effort Mum put into tracking them down was well worth it. Last night I brought my sleeping bag out to the cockpit and managed to get a bit of sleep under the full moon. It was a pretty cool sight with the moonlight making the waves sparkle and lighting up the sails. I have to keep reminding myself to make the most of nights like this as things are certainly going to change when we head back south and into the Southern Ocean.

. . . The other day I was having a major cheese craving and couldn't find the cheese anywhere, so I called Mum to ask whether she knew where it might have been packed. It turned out Mum was in Melbourne having lunch with Jesse Martin and his mum, Louise, at the time. My quick casual call about something as unimportant as cheese really highlighted the difference between my voyage and Jesse's. Back when he sailed around the world, satellite phone calls were so costly that they were saved for pretty much only emergencies and Jesse certainly didn't have luxuries like cheese! Anyway, they all had a good laugh at my expense and it sounded like they were having a good time.

Here's my recipe for *Ella's Pink Lady* Scrambled Eggs. Yes, I know it is simple but for me it was the perfect comfort food and never failed to hit the right spot whenever I made it.

Serves 2 (or one hungry sailor)
4 eggs (I used powdered eggs)
¼ cup milk or cream (I used cream if I could)
15 grams butter

1. Combine the eggs and milk and whisk lightly.
2. Melt the butter then add the egg and cook over a low heat.
3. Finish with dried parsley.

Wednesday, 4 November 2009
Rest, relaxing and reading

After some pretty interrupted sleep lately, this morning my head felt a lot like it was full of cottonwool. So I've pretty much spent most of the day in my bunk reading and dozing, popping my head out the companionway to keep a look-out and to tweak the sails. All the R&R today has left me feeling a lot better, so I'm full of energy again this evening, playing music and sitting up on deck watching all the shades of grey turn to pink and orange.

No sunshine at all today so we're a bit down on power, but progress has been reasonable. We've had a pretty consistent south-easterly so *Ella's Pink Lady* has been slipping along nicely under full sail.

A few people have been commenting on the blog how it must be nice to have other yachts around every once in a while but I can't say I really feel like that. Sure it was nice to chat to them over the radio, to find out where they'd come from and where they are heading to, but I can only really be comfortable when *Ella's Pink Lady* and I have the ocean completely to ourselves. Every time a bit of land pops up on the chart it weighs on my mind and almost feels a little claustrophobic!

The forecast is for more of the same weather for the next few days. Then as we keep heading north we should start seeing some tropical squalls. I'm starting to see more and more flying fish jump out of the water and am really starting to tick off the miles till reaching the equator.

That's it for today because my tummy is telling me that it's time to go cook something up for dinner. I'm thinking tacos (or maybe I should call them nachos, as they are a bit crushed up!) with freeze-dried mince, tinned tomato and tinned capsicum.

Thursday, 5 November 2009
Wet, bouncy and cupcakes!

With a good bouncy sea and water going everywhere today, everything's starting to feel pretty salty. Every time I come in from being on deck I seem to bring a lot of water with me. Also, despite all the effort we put into tracking them down before leaving, a few small leaks have made themselves known. The leaks aren't at all dangerous, they just aren't much of a help in the war against salt and damp. So I've been playing around with a tube of sealer and (fingers crossed) it looks like I might have put a stop to some of them!

We passed close to another boat this morning but I couldn't see him through the rain.

I pulled some sail out and in as the wind dropped off, then came back and right now we're doing a nice 6 knots with 20 knots of wind. We passed 2000 nautical miles today and my best guess is around 16 days to the equator, but it could be anything as it is all weather dependent over the next few weeks.

This afternoon I decided it was time to have a bit of fun in the galley, so I've been making chocolate cupcakes! It's been quite an adventure really, with ingredients and mixture going everywhere as *Ella's Pink Lady* bounces along. Life would be so much easier with a third arm but I got there in the end with all the mixture, less the stuff all over my face! (Maybe I should consider a career as a juggler when I get home?)

They are all cooked now and smell very good. So now the fun part – icing and decorating!

On the Friday the wind was up a little but it was a normal sort of day until mid morning when Parker started refusing to steer a straight course. I put my jacket on, clipped on and headed out to the stern to see what the problem was. My first inspection left me a bit stumped as I couldn't see anything out of place, but a closer look told me that one of the little circlips (a type of fastener) that connected the main shaft of the vane to the blade had come off. A good rummage through my collection of windvane spare parts told me that the one thing I didn't have was a circlip to fit. To keep us going for the short term I strapped the whole thing together with a bit of twine (covered with a little trusty duct tape!) and then put in a phone call to Bruce to tell him what had happened. Bruce set to work doing a bit of brainstorming with Phil over the best way to go about a more permanent fix. It was only a small problem right at that moment but it had me worried because I relied on Parker so completely and I knew that it was autopilot problems that had stopped Mike and a similar small problem (a missing bolt) that had stopped David Dicks from achieving his dream of sailing unassisted around the world. The windvane was one of the only things onboard that I couldn't replace and without it I wouldn't have enough fuel to power the electric autopilots. I spent a few hours imagining the worst but then had to just let it go and hope the repair held up. All was well in the end. I never actually replaced the bit of twine so all through the Southern Ocean trusty Parker kept us going held together with just a bit of string and, of course, the duct tape . . . that stuff is multi-purpose magic!

Saturday, 7 November 2009
Trade-wind sailing

Really loving the way *Ella's* been chewing away the miles over the last few days. With the wind sitting on 20–25 knots from the south-east it's good trade-wind sailing, even if the sun hasn't been doing too much of that shining business lately.

We're also really starting to make some good progress north. The GPS read-out now puts our latitude well into the teens. The temperature is just starting to get a little warm in the cabin, but with so much water over the deck, having the hatches open is completely out of the question.

But I'm sure this is nothing compared to how warm it will get over the next few weeks!

With a bit of a headache, plenty of sea room and *Ella's Pink Lady* not needing much attention from me today, I pretty much just spent the day wedged into a comfy position working away at a book and staying dry. Apart from the odd bird and flying fish there's not really been a lot of wildlife around lately and still no luck catching any fish. Then again, we have just passed over the Tonga Trench, one of the deepest places on earth. I'm not much of a fisherman but maybe it hasn't exactly been the greatest place to catch fish? I'll just have to keep trying!

The overcast skies have been making for some dark nights out here. The sky and sea are completely black with no way of telling them apart. It's pot luck whether or not I get a face full of spray when I stick my head out above the dodger for a look around. But even if I do get unlucky and cop a wave, I can't say it really bothers me. Normally I'll just laugh or squeal, even if I'm half asleep! So it's all going well and, at this pace, we'll be passing Samoa in the next few days and from there it really is a clear run to the equator.

Sunday, 8 November 2009
Sunday blog a little late!

Sunday has been much the same out here. Just had a nice dunking of cool salt water and am running my little fans to try and chase away that sticky humid feeling but I think it's just something I'm going to have to learn to live with.

My sleeping bag has been safely stowed away and I think a singlet and sarong have become my uniform for the next while. Sailing in the tropics! My breakfasts now have become cereal rather than porridge (still with my extra large helping of cream, dried fruit and honey).

The wind peaked at 30 knots last night so life's still pretty bouncy out here as we're sailing upwind. It's a little frustrating every time something goes flying across the cabin or when I discover that something else has somehow become wet and salty, but it only takes a glance at the log, and the miles ticking away, to keep me smiling. Only a little over 1200 nautical miles till the equator!

I was talking to my brother, Tom, who's spent the weekend tramping with some friends and it made me realise how much I'd love to stretch my own legs with a long walk right now. I hadn't realised how much I miss being able to take a walk or jog up the beach. The stretches and few exercises I do most days just aren't the same. It's funny how I never even thought to appreciate something like being able to go for a walk until now when I can't. Made me think of all you lucky people back on land. Hope you're all making the most of your Sunday afternoons and taking nice long walks!

Monday, 9 November 2009
Busy day and water

I've just come back into the cabin after pulling the fishing line in for the day. No fish, but the lures are covered in huge teeth marks, so looks like I've been getting some nibbles! Well, maybe nibbles isn't the right word! I've decided not to think too hard about exactly what left the great big teeth marks, but I'm sure it wasn't anything nearly as dramatic as my imagination would have me believe.

Looks like it's going to be another dark night out here and warmer than ever, but I'm a happy girl after a busy and productive day. The sea and wind finally dropped off this morning and the sun came out. I was out of my bunk bright and early ready to launch into a few jobs on deck that I'd been putting off due to the bouncy conditions. I got through my little list of maintenance and gave *Ella's Pink Lady* a really good check over for chafe and wear. Then the wind dropped off even more, to the point where we were left to roll a bit uncomfortably, not making any progress. But before it started getting too frustrating, a great big rain cloud came along and gave us a soaking in fresh water. Rain might not sound like something to get too excited about but I was just about in heaven!

Using the mainsail and the little gutters we strategically built into the dodger, I was able to collect enough water to top the water tanks up, fill a few empty containers and give myself a lovely fresh-water scrub down. In fact, I ended up with more water than I knew what to do with – even after washing all my clothes. So I decided to get right into it and ended up giving every surface in the cabin a wipe down. With the music up and the air temperature down for a while with the rain, I was really enjoying myself and I never thought I'd hear myself saying that about doing housework! I've never exactly been one to enjoy cleaning and washing so maybe I am going a little crazy out here after all? It provided me with some great exercise as well.

Anyway, this brings us to one of the topics that I haven't even touched on yet – water.

What am I doing for fresh water? Believe it or not, along with all the food, *Ella's Pink Lady* is pretty much carrying all the fresh water I'll need. It might sound a bit hard to believe but I'm only using fresh water for drinking and cooking and there's only one of me. Also, I'm relying on being able to top up the tanks again in squalls a few times before leaving the tropics and heading south. As an emergency back-up *Ella's Pink Lady* is also carrying a little hand desalinator, but judging by the amount of water I was so easily able to collect today, I don't think that I'll ever need it.

Another squall came through this evening, dumping a whole lot more rain and keeping my life interesting with a few grumbles of thunder, a pretty strong gust of wind and some random changes of wind direction. *Ella's Pink Lady* took it all in her stride. Compared to some of the more severe tropical squalls I'm sure we'll soon be getting, this little puff will just look a lot like a fluffy white cloud.

There's not a heap of wind at the moment, just a gentle 13 knots. But thanks to the quiet conditions this morning, the sea has pretty much flattened right out leaving *Ella's Pink Lady* to fly along on a reach, unstopped by any of those wet, bouncy things – waves! Just glanced at the speedo and we're doing a very healthy 7 knots. I wouldn't say no to more of this, but the wind is predicted to drop off again soon, so I expect the next few days will be hard work trying to keep us moving along.

That's me for today. I'm now off to open a tin of mandarin pieces with a double dose of cream for dessert!

Tuesday, 10 November 2009

Slowly but surely getting to the equator!

Not much in the way of wind today, so I spent the morning hand-steering and tacking to make the most of the few little puffs of wind we did get. All covered up from the sun in a big dorky straw hat, sunscreen (Ella Baché of course!), sunnies and a sarong, sitting at the tiller was the nicest place to be with a light breeze keeping me cool.

The Fleming windvane, Parker, does an amazing job steering, much better than me most of the time, but when the wind drops out to under 5 knots, even poor old Parker calls it quits. This afternoon the wind dropped right off to the point where I've just aborted the tiller, as there isn't much point in steering a boat that isn't going anywhere!

It's overcast again now with rain squalls sweeping across the ocean and marching along the horizon. Calm interrupted by towering rain squalls, it's been a pretty typical day for the Inter-Tropical Convergence Zone (ITCZ or the 'doldrums'). Lucky for me, the ITCZ is pretty weak at the moment, so it shouldn't be too long until we pick up a bit more of a breeze to take us to the equator. I think I'd be finding the lack of progress pretty frustrating if it wasn't for all the moody greys and blues looking so amazing on the glassed out water.

Despite this afternoon's poor progress, we've still only got 950 nautical miles until the equator (that is, to the actual point where I'm hoping to cross the equator) and I can't wait for that!

For me to be sailing alone through the doldrums was pretty cool. This was one of the mythic places that mariners talk of, people write stories and poems about and sailors are tested. 'The Rime of The Ancient Mariner' by Samuel Taylor Coleridge is probably the best-known poem that I know of that captures the spirit of the doldrums (I didn't experience anything like this here . . . but later I went a little crazy becalmed in the Roaring Forties of all places. I got a glimpse of that mariner's frustrating madness!):

All in a hot and copper sky,
The bloody Sun, at noon,
Right up above the mast did stand,
No bigger than the Moon.

Day after day, day after day,
We stuck, nor breath nor motion;
As idle as a painted ship
Upon a painted ocean.

I love hearing stories about other people's adventures and the way they coped with places like the doldrums or the Southern Ocean. The doldrums are known by sailors as a tropical dead zone. It is located between five degrees north and five degrees south, though this can vary depending on the seasons, and it is notorious for its unpredictable and fierce weather shifts. A yacht can be completely at a stop and then . . . Bam! . . . suddenly 40-knot winds can whip up in minutes. It all happens because the sun's rays are stronger here and so they heat the ocean and this causes warm moist air to rise. This warm air is unstable and can cause low pressure systems, thunderstorms and gales. Then, when you get cool air meeting this warm air, you can get severe weather systems.

By this point in my voyage, I'd already realised that I felt fine when we were moving but when *Ella's Pink Lady* and I were going too slowly I could get impatient and moody. If anything, this trip was definitely going to teach me patience. From all I had read about the doldrums, this was the perfect place to practise, and when you expect something – like being becalmed because so many others have had this happen in the same place – it is a little easier to deal with. It is the unexpected surprises that can be hard to cope with and that push you to the limit. I keep saying it, I know, but that's the reason I was doing this.

Wednesday, 11 November 2009
Robbed of dinner!

Exciting news to report today. I pulled the fishing line in to discover that I'd finally caught a fish! I'd love to tell you what it was, how big it was and how yummy it tasted, only someone (with rather big teeth!) got to it before me. Apart from a few bits of flesh left hanging on the lure, my beautiful fish had been gobbled up by something bigger. I can only keep trying!

Not much sleep last night because I was keeping an eye on a few nasty-looking squalls, nothing much came of them though and we spent the first part of the night drifting backward a little, ouch! There were a few jokes about that when I called in this morning.

Steady progress today though, I've been catching up on a little sleep and enjoying the nice sailing. The Southern Ocean certainly isn't going to be like this.

For all those having a guess at when we cross the line, the latest weather forecast from Bob gives us an ETA (estimated time of arrival) at the equator of the eighteenth, in about seven days' time!

Friday, 13 November 2009
Squally sailing

Sorry it's been a little while without an update.

I was told that my blog has become the most watched blog in Australia and stage fright has left me a bit speechless! No, just kidding, it's all good. Well, actually, it's pretty amazing and more than a little hard for me to comprehend out here all alone. Well, physically alone. It really is amazing to be able to share the voyage with so many wonderful people. To me, it is just sharing my journey with you, in what is sometimes a not very exciting life. Plodding along out here, taking whatever is thrown at us, just feels completely normal. I know I'm going to get a million cries of disagreement. But think about it. How strange would it feel to you to be describing to the world all the ins and outs of your everyday life? It is all a bit surreal. That said, thank you all for your support!

And talking of those little ins and outs, *Ella's Pink Lady* and I have been making good progress for the last few days. The latitude read-out now puts us in the single digits – wow!

Conditions have mostly been lovely (steady breeze from the east or south-east, sunshine and very gentle sea) but have also been frequently interrupted by squalls. Still nothing too severe but just enough to keep me working hard pulling a sail in and out and constantly keeping a look out for any particularly nasty black clouds. Last night a squall with a lot of lightning passed pretty close. Sitting there waiting for it to pass with all the electrics turned off got a little boring, so I made chocolate cookies in the torch light to pass the time. I suppose I should have been a little scared about all the lightning, but after doing everything I could, I figured there wasn't much point in worrying.

I'm finding it hard to believe how the days are flying. In between getting enough sleep, keeping up with the day-to-day maintenance and chores, checking that fishing line, feeding myself and keeping in touch with everyone back home, time just flies and I'm constantly wondering what happened to the day.

Even though *Ella's Pink Lady* is built and set up for strength, endurance and easy handling when the weather is nice, I've really been enjoying playing around, tweaking the sails for a little extra speed. Of course, as soon as the weather is up it's all about being totally conservative!

. . . Six hundred nautical miles till the equator!

Saturday, 14 November 2009

Fish, first aid, 'Parker' and bread

My resolve to catch a fish was strengthened again yesterday when I called in to have a nice long chat to all the family as they were having Friday night fish and chips. I've got it all worked out now. First, there will be sashimi with soy sauce, then steaks lightly fried, maybe with a light batter and lemon juice (not fresh of course) and possibly some kind of fish curry. All depending on the size and type of fish. Sadly, it seems to take more than resolve to catch a fish — still nothing!

With all this talk of food I've noticed that a few people have been commenting on the blog about me having to watch my figure. Not to worry, I do! I'm actually proud to report that after years of struggling, in the last few weeks I've actually put on just a little weight. You must be thinking that really is the strangest thing for a sixteen-year-old girl to be saying, but I've spent years being told by all the old salts that I need to bulk up and have a little in reserve, as it could be helpful as *Ella's Pink Lady* heads south and around Cape Horn.

No squalls at all today so I've been able to get plenty of uninterrupted catnaps. It really has been lovely sailing, Parker the windvane has been doing his job amazingly and nothing much has needed attention. Last night was something special with so many stars that I could swear that the air felt thicker for them. Also, there's been a bit of phosphorescence in the water lately so the wash around *Ella's Pink Lady* is speckled with glowing lights.

I got my first minor injury for the trip today, nothing at all serious, just a little burn from the stove on my thumb. Treatment involved sitting out in the cockpit with my hand in a cup of water enjoying the sunset then a little cream and, of course, the all-helpful bandaid! Not exactly anything to write home about and believe me I'm about to regret it because as soon as this blog gets published, the phone's going to start ringing and I'm going to be subjected to several full medical interrogations. Talk about being wrapped in cottonwool! Well, actually, while today's little mishap really wasn't anything serious, the chance of me giving myself a real injury out here is.

Thanks to Mum, local pharmacist and sailor Suzy Rasmussen, Mark White and the St John Ambulance Cadets from Dromana Secondary College, and my doctor Margaret Williams (who sailed solo round Australia a few years back), *Ella's Pink Lady* has a first-aid kit to rival any hospital. I've also completed my marine medical course, know the kit inside out and, as I mentioned, have plenty of advice ready at hand.

I just baked some lovely fresh bread so I'm off to go nibble at the crusty bits before they cool down. Of course covered with jam and cream, then bread and soup for dinner.

Just one more thing, with all this talk on the blog of me being mature, I have to say I had a bit of a giggle as I looked down at my bright pink toenails!

Now just over 500 nautical miles till the equator!

Monday, 16 November 2009

Mixed progress and dolphins

Progress has been a little on and off over the last few days. When we have a little wind, *Ella's Pink Lady* flies along the flat water amazingly. But there's also been a few times with not any wind. This afternoon particularly was a little unexciting, just rolling around not going anywhere in the heat. I started on a bit of schoolwork this morning, thinking that if I couldn't be achieving forward progress, at least I could be achieving something. But I can't say I stuck with it for very long.

Instead, between dunkings of cool salt water and prodding the tiller to at least keep *Ella's Pink Lady* pointed in the right direction, I ended up giving the little Yanmar engine a full polish up and scrubbed out the bilges. As the sun set I was able to stand back, hot and greasy but happy that I'd at least achieved something for the day. I'm sure that after another few months at sea, poor old *Ella's Pink Lady* won't be looking quite as great as she did sailing out of Sydney, but I'm at least going to do everything possible to try to keep her looking good. And it's like I'm constantly being told: 'Look after the boat and she'll look after you.'

When people talk about all the things needed to sail around the world they never seem to mention patience, but I'm fast learning that it's as important as anything.

This afternoon was pretty cool, a pod of dolphins spent a couple of hours hanging around and I had a great time sitting in the shade of the sails on the bow, feet dangling over the side (and, yes, clipped on!) watching them play in clear water. I'm not sure what kind they were (small and completely grey) but they hung around for ages, so they can't have thought my music was too bad! I loved the way they would play around, riding and shooting along the swell, and can only imagine how much fun they must have in a big sea.

I'm really getting down to the dregs of the latest food bag so I've been eating a bit randomly lately (dinner tonight was mince, tinned fruit and noodles!). Funnily enough, I'm really looking forward to pulling out the new bag.

I've only just realised how late it is. So that's going to have to be it for the night.

P.S. Thanks to Dad and Bruce over the last few days for being so patient with me over the phone and for understanding that sometimes a girl just doesn't feel like chatting!

P.P.S. Even with all the slow progress, now only about 370 nautical miles until we cross the equator!

Tuesday, 17 November 2009
Thirty days at sea and company

Tonight I've got company out here, let me introduce you to Silly. He's a little brown sea bird who's landed on the Sailor 250 satellite dome on the stern of *Ella's Pink Lady*. Silly earnt his nickname because of his dangerous fascination with the wind generator and his amusing attempts to land on the bendy windvane blade. Even though the wind genny isn't spinning too fast at the moment, watching him fly so close to it again and again was a little nerve-racking!

Anyway, he's been sitting there for well over three hours now and seems to have made himself quite comfortable perched on the dome.

Other than Silly, I've been seeing a lot of birds out here today, mostly little jesus petrels and brown gannets, (at least that's what I think they are!) which is kind of surprising as the nearest island is about 200 nautical miles away. Apart from when some light rain came through this morning it's been pretty close to perfect sailing all day.

It's really hard to believe, but as of tomorrow we will have been at sea for thirty days, exactly a month since we left Sydney on 18 October. One down, seven more months to go! Leaving Sydney really does feel just like yesterday, but it's crazy to think that I haven't seen another person for thirty days. I have to say, I honestly don't feel any different for it. It's a lot like someone asking whether you feel any different after a birthday. But it's just the same old me!

I pulled out a new food bag today so it's back to all my favourite treats. I'm planning on having pasta for dinner. I wonder if Silly likes pasta . . .

It doesn't look like we'll make the equator tomorrow as I'd hoped, but with only about 240 nautical miles to go, it won't be long now. I'll keep you updated as we get closer. Getting pretty excited!

After crossing the line, I'll be sailing north another 200 nautical miles up around Kiritimati Island, my rounding point in the northern hemisphere, then south back across the line and on to Cape Horn.

That's it from *Ella's Pink Lady*, Silly and myself for tonight.

In her book, *First Lady*, Kay Cottee wrote 'how even the sanest person can go slightly potty after long periods alone' and how on one solo Trans-Tasman race she was totally exhausted after almost 48 hours without sleep so she decided to have a nap. As she settled into her bunk five people were sitting opposite her and they told her they were going to look after the boat while she napped. She told them to make themselves at home and when she woke two hours later they were gone but all was well. I have never really experienced anything like this. But I did have some pretty full-on conversations with my stuffed-animal crew members and my trusty friend, Parker.

Parker and I developed a very strange relationship. Have you ever seen the movie *Cast Away* with Tom Hanks? Well, I'm not saying Parker and I were as close as Tom Hanks' character and Wilson (or that I was as crazy as Tom Hanks' character) but you get the idea.

I would constantly talk to him, telling him to watch our course. I'd yell out 'up' or 'down, down' if he veered the wrong way. I have to admit they were rather one-sided conversations as he wasn't a great talker. But he was definitely a great listener and I shared with him important things like my dreams for the future and even more important things like what I was planning for dinner.

When I was feeling a bit nervous about one thing or another, like in the build-up to a gale or some particularly bumpy seas, I'd talk to *Ella's Pink Lady*. I would give her a pep talk after one of Bob's forecasts came through predicting some nasty conditions – give her some encouragement and let her know how great she was in a very positive voice. The truth is, I think I got more out of our chats than she did!

During storms I'd constantly call out to Parker and *Ella's Pink Lady* to hold steady as we fell off or surfed a particularly vicious wave. When I wrote about 'we' in the blogs it was because I had to include my 'friends' in the adventure.

Wednesday, 18 November 2009

Shooting star and crossing the line tomorrow!

I'm not much of an astronomer but with all this talk of meteor showers last night, I was keeping an extra good eye out and did see the most amazing shooting star. [Apparently every year around mid-November the earth passes through a trail of dust particles left behind by the Tempel-Tuttle comet. The media were reporting that this year's was going to be especially spectacular.] It was so bright and big that I was actually a bit spooked before realising what it was. But I can't tell you what I wished for!

Well, Silly left us this morning but it was nice to have someone to talk to and have company for a while. He really did have the most interesting opinions on the subjects of fashion and boys! He wasn't at all interested in any of the food I offered and didn't seem to mind the flash of the camera.

Not a real exciting day out here today, other than the usual chores – sail trimming, HF radio skeds, etc. – I actually slept through most of it. I'm becoming more nocturnal lately because it's so much easier to get things done when it cools down after the sunsets. It was good to get a few extra catnaps in while I've still got plenty of open water and nice conditions.

Dinner tonight was the yummiest omelette with powdered eggs, tinned butter, bacon bits and dried parsley.

I also attended (via a phone call!) my first equator-crossing party tonight. Some of my aunties, uncles and cousins, my Grandma and Granddad, and all their friends got together in Cromwell in the South Island of New Zealand to celebrate *Ella's Pink Lady* and I crossing the line – but they were a little early!

The winds have been nice and steady all day so we've made good progress and only 50 nautical miles to the equator! Anything could happen, but right now it looks like we'll be crossing in about ten hours, which is Thursday morning back home in Australia. So it's a big day tomorrow.

Thursday, 19 November 2009
A big day

Today I crossed the line! I celebrated with a lot of slightly melted chocolate and the traditional dunking of salt water necessary for any first-time equator crossing. I had to use a bucket and dunk myself but I can't say it was all that bad!

Crossing the equator was one of the major milestones of my trip. I was so excited to reach this point. The equator is basically an imaginary line that runs around the earth at zero degrees latitude an equal distance from the North and South Poles. It is 21,600 nautical miles long and it is here that the earth is divided into the northern and southern hemispheres.

Sailors have a tradition of celebrating anyone's first crossing of the equator and I was all for upholding the tradition, so I was going to make sure I marked the moment well. I've been told that at one time it wasn't the nicest of initiations and that in some navies the ritual could be very cruel and was seen as a test of a sailor's abilities to handle rough conditions. I don't know exactly what was done then, but I do know that cruise liners morphed the tradition into something much nicer and anything that could include chocolate was fine with me.

Friday, 20 November 2009
Northern hemisphere

No change that I can see. The water is still blue, the waves are still rolling and the wind is still blowing, but apparently the water now splashing across the deck and slipping away behind *Ella's Pink Lady* is northern hemisphere water!

I couldn't have asked for a better day to cross the equator: flat seas, 15 knots of wind and sunshine. We crossed the line at 2017 UTC doing 5.5 knots and celebrated with the usual toast to Neptune, the traditional dunking in salt water and plenty of excited phone calls. I also had a few presents stashed away, especially to open for the occasion. Neptune was toasted with fruit juice and plenty of chocolate. I'm not normally one to toss good chocolate into the sea, but I figured that this was my chance to get myself into Neptune's good books. I'd hoped that my generous offering might be rewarded with a fish on my line but no such luck!

I thought that crossing the line would be just like any other day out here, so I surprised myself a little by getting a bit emotional as I juggled three different cameras while counting down the latitude read-out on the GPS. It's not so much physically crossing into the northern hemisphere that had me so worked up (you can only get so excited about an invisible line in the water!), but the fact that it meant the end of the first leg. Sure, this has probably been one of the easier legs (call it the shakedown!) compared to some of the sailing to come down south, but the distance we've already covered is pretty amazing. Getting this far (and through everything that happened before the start line!) has given me the confidence to know that even though we've got some seriously tough times ahead, we're going to have fun tackling whatever comes our way.

Great sailing overnight again so we're well into the northern hemisphere and on our way to Kiritimati Island, which we might be rounding by late tomorrow. It's been a slightly eerie feeling with overcast conditions all day, but I think it was more my imagination than anything, and *Ella's Pink Lady* has made steady progress so I can't complain.

After all the celebrating and fun yesterday I got back into a few jobs today – not that jobs and maintenance aren't fun too! I'm sure keeping on top of even the slightest little potential problem will pay off in the end and staying busy keeps me happy.

We've finally got a bit of a moon out here this evening. I'm not sure about dinner yet but I'm thinking of attempting some kind of apple crumble with stewed fruit for dessert. A bit of ice-cream on top would go down pretty nicely too, but maybe it's better not to think about that!

Thanks to everyone for all the congratulations on my blog. Sounds like plenty of people had a great time celebrating on my behalf as well! But I still say the credit all goes to *Ella's Pink Lady* and the amazing team that got her to the start line. I'm just along for the ride.

Sunday, 22 November 2009
Around Kiritimati Island

Winds on the nose and a current against us for the last few days has made for pretty painful progress. We're only just getting close to Kiritimati (Christmas) Island now. All going to plan we should be around and clear by the morning. It'll be a relief to have a bit of sea room and to be making progress south again.

Kiritimati Island sounds pretty interesting so I've added it to the list of places to stop off at next time! Apparently it's the world's largest atoll and thanks to a few random changes in direction by the date line, it's also the world's easternmost country. From what I've read it sounds pretty picture perfect with white sandy beaches and coral lagoons . . . but don't worry, I'm not tempted to stop, in fact I'll be lucky if I can even see a distant glow of lights as I pass by tonight. Oh, and it's said to be a good spot for fishing!

We passed a boat (three actually!) for the first time in over a week yesterday – they were big fishing boats but the crew didn't appear to speak English. I also got a bit of a fright yesterday, I was sitting down below at the nav station and heard the horrible noise of something rubbing down the hull. I climbed outside in time to see a big brown buoy caught up in the windvane but luckily it freed itself before I could do anything and there wasn't any damage.

I spotted a few more buoys during the day but have no idea what exactly they are and what they're doing just bobbing about out here.

Many clear and starry nights lately and I've been seeing plenty of them because, even though it seems to have cooled down a little lately, it's still much easier to get things done after the sun sets. I was a little jealous to hear that everyone back home was heading out to the movies last night so I had my own movie night watching a DVD on my Toughbook and making some popcorn! Still plenty of tropical sailing to go yet, but I'm already thinking more and more about the south and Cape Horn.

That's going to have to be it from me because it's time to go tack over again, fingers crossed this should be the last one to get us round the island!

The day before I left Sydney I'd sent Tom off with a friend of his, Andrew (not Andrew Fraser), to buy some DVDs for me to take on the trip. I gave them strict instructions to get girly stuff but, of course, they couldn't help themselves and I ended up with heaps of *Top Gear* episodes and a learn-to-fish DVD on top of *Bridget Jones's Diary* and a few other chick flicks. Tom was obviously hoping that if he sent me off with lots of *Top Gear* I'd come back all clued up about cars. Sadly, it didn't quite work like that. I did watch all the episodes but I'd always fast-forward through the boring car review bits. Sorry, Tom!

I also had the DVD set of the television show *Bones* with me and I enjoyed watching the odd episode now and again. I quickly learnt not to watch one before going to sleep though, after more than once waking up to the most vivid and creepy dreams. One time I dreamt that the whole *Bones* investigation team was on *Ella's Pink Lady* with me. Even weirder was the fact I didn't talk about some complicated murder case with Booth and Bones, I ended up having a very serious discussion about the weather conditions.

It was always strange to wake up to the rattles and bangs of the boat after some very full-on dream and find I was all alone. During my time away I dreamed that all sorts of people were onboard with me. They weren't all American television stars. At different times I'd have friends or family members show up and when I was feeling homesick I'd replay those dreams over and over in my head to help me feel closer to the people I loved. I liked those dreams.

The ones I hated were the nightmares I'd have when conditions were tricky or during the tougher parts of the voyage when I was really tired. Half the time I wouldn't remember exactly what I'd been dreaming about but I'd wake up confused and my mind would be blurry. It was horrible because at those moments I'd flash back to being jarred awake as *Ella's Pink Lady* scraped down the side of *Silver Yang*'s hull. For a few seconds I wouldn't know where I was. I'd have a feeling of helplessness that reminded me of being swept along by a current. I'd want to fight it, swim against it, but I couldn't. I hate that feeling of weakness. In a way it was what my trip was all about. I wanted to strike out, be in control and not just get swept along by life.

Monday, 23 November 2009

Finally, a fish!

Yes, I'm more than a little pleased and very relieved to report that I finally got a fish! [See the photo in the picture sections.] That was starting to get a bit silly. My best guess is that it's a yellowfin tuna. It's not huge but I'm sure that there will be plenty for everyone! I can't say that there would be many fishermen who would be proud of the mess I made filleting it. I'm just glad there was no one here to witness the whole thing, but practice makes perfect, right?

(I never did it but before I got home I was quite tempted to delete the footage of me pulling that fish in . . . I am embarrassed for people to see the mess I made.)

Turns out that wasn't my last tack last night. The wind and current weren't going to make things easy for us, so it was a particularly sleepless night as we tacked and inched along ever so slowly. Every time I thought that we'd finally cleared the island, the wind would change slightly and we'd have to put another tack in. It's all a bit frustrating but as always it's hard not to feel cheerful when the stars are shining and the music's turned up.

I spent a lot of the day on deck enjoying the shade from the sails and trying (without much success!) to give the stainless steel a polish up. Also, I've been noticing quite a bit of chafe on the windvane lines (not to worry, I've got plenty of spares) so have been playing around trying to stop some of it. It's a good reminder of the way Parker is constantly working. There's always something to keep me busy, whether it's wiping the salt crystals off the solar panels, replying to an email or trying to keep up with the housework (boatwork?!) side of things.

There's been a lot of birds around again and I've really been enjoying listening to them call out to each other as they swoop low around *Ella's Pink Lady*. It made me think about all the other land noise that I haven't heard for so long and that made me a little homesick. But I know as soon as I do get back to land I'll miss the constant noise of the water along the hull and all the little creaks and groans as *Ella's Pink Lady* sails along.

When I checked my emails this morning I found a very serious email from my clearly worried Mum, telling me to watch out for all those 'boys' – I think they must have been able to see me rolling my eyes from here!

I'd love to write more but it's time for some fun in the galley and the long-awaited fish and chips!

Crossing the equator was my first big milestone and saying goodbye to a big chunk of the Pacific was amazing. I'd had near-perfect sailing conditions and things were going better than I'd ever expected. I was loving the sailing, had settled into my own comfortable routine and we'd had no major technical problems.

Looking back at my averages throughout the voyage, our speeds through the Pacific were some of the best. I found that really interesting because this is where I'd expected to be the slowest because of the flukey headwinds and the notorious doldrums.

There's a few things that explain why I was going so well. When I started out I had a lot to prove to myself and I was determined to get rid of any small doubts I still had early on so I pushed myself harder in that first leg. The weather was also a major factor. Spending time tweaking sails on deck in the warm sunshine isn't exactly unpleasant, whereas further south I would spend a lot more time cooped up in the cabin just trying to keep warm rather than making the small adjustments I might have if I'd still been in the tropics. I loved the south, with the amazing swells, albatross and moody grey skies but, let's face it, if I had to choose I wasn't going to say no to day after day of sunshine, moderate winds and sleeping under the stars!

Of course it wasn't all idyllic trade-wind sailing during that first stage. Getting enough sleep and trying to develop good sleeping habits was hardest during this first leg. I was still settling in and because the Pacific is full of islands, reefs, yachts and fishing boats I was on constant alert and wouldn't allow myself to sleep too long because I had to keep watch. It was the other small yachts that most worried me because, unlike the big ships, small cruising boats (or most of them) don't carry AIS and they are almost invisible on the radar. Obviously hitting a small yacht is going to pack a lot less of a punch than a tanker (and believe me I know all about that!) but it still weighed on my mind and meant I was not taking any chances. I was looking forward to sailing further south and, though it would bring its own challenges, I was hoping to have the ocean to myself.

Stage Two

SOUTH TO CHILE AND CAPE HORN

Tuesday, 24 November 2009

South again

We crossed back into the southern hemisphere this evening, it's nice to be back home! I said a quick 'hello' to Neptune and thanked him for the fish. Still no sign of the big red line though, I'm starting to think that all this water must have washed it away!

More of a quiet day out here, nothing too exciting, just keeping up with all the ins and outs, doing a little schoolwork, reading and napping. Mostly we've made great progress and have had some light squalls come through. The squalls didn't give us any more than gusts of 20 knots of wind but that was just enough to make conditions just a little too wet to have the hatches open, making life pretty hot and sticky. Did I mention I'm looking forward to some cooler weather?

Plenty of open water ahead for the next few days so it will be nice to have some more uninterrupted sleep and I'm itching to put some miles behind us. Bob's latest forecast predicts south-easterly winds, so looks like we'll be able to make some good progress south, but none east for a while.

Wednesday, 25 November 2009
Washing machine

It hasn't been the most amazing day out here today, overcast, squally and the sea has been a bit of a mess – it must be a lot like the inside of a washing machine! Bob predicted that the swell would become a little uncomfortable with an east-going current clashing with the south-easterly wind and, believe me, he was right! I have to admit my mood was reflecting the grey sky for a while this afternoon so I had to give myself a good talking to. It didn't take much and I'm right back to feeling one hundred per cent positive again. No point in wasting a single minute of my time out here feeling miserable! I really don't have anything to complain about because even though the sun hasn't been shining we've made great (and slightly bouncy!) progress south. Oh, and even when things were looking a little blue I still couldn't think of anything I'd rather be doing. I'm sure that there are not many people who can say that, so I'm a pretty lucky girl!

It's still such a long way off but I've already started counting down the miles to Cape Horn (5450 nautical miles to go!) – it gives me something to stay focused on. Can't wait to see albatross again and to see what those huge Southern Ocean swells are really like!

Sounds like there are already Christmas decorations going up on land so there's another thing to look forward to!

Should be plenty more fast sailing over the next few days and plenty of lovely sea room, apart from when we pass quite close to a little island called Starbuck Island. If I wasn't doing this unassisted, I'd put in a stop for coffee!

Time to go find something for dinner again, I'm thinking something along the lines of spaghetti bolognese and then maybe having a good dig in the goodies locker to see what I can find.

I wasn't hiding things from people reading the blog but I was reluctant to really go into depth about my blue days. More for my own protection than anything, but also because I didn't want to worry Mum and Dad. It was up to me to pull myself out of the bad times and writing about it didn't help. What I had to do was distract myself, or get busy on something else.

There hadn't been too many tough times but it wasn't all easy-going emotionally either. At first I tried to hide any little hitch from everyone back home but then I realised that it was all a part of learning about myself. A big factor in sailing around the world alone was seeing if I could do it and learning how strong I was and what I could do to deal with the bad times. I had a few rubbish times in that week and felt alone, headachy and lethargic but I tried to keep it all in perspective. I'd had much worse at home. It was weird because most of the time I was fine and loved being by myself and then, boom, out of nowhere I'd just want someone there to give me a hug and look after me. At one point in that week there were things I absolutely had to do and I had to force myself to keep going when all I wanted to do was get into my bunk and sleep for days. I was dreading talking to Mum and Dad and Bruce in the mood I was in but I managed to snap myself out of my funk. It really was the small things that helped, things like tidying up the cabin, talking to friends, reading, writing and eating well – something I didn't always do! I don't think I mentioned in the blog that I had popcorn for breakfast a few times. I tended to write about food when I was being good.

I was having the occasional chat to Mike Perham as well as Tom, Hannah and Emily and other family and friends. It was great to talk to Mike as he'd been home about three months and was settling into life back on land. It was good to share the highs and lows with someone who knew exactly what I was talking about. I was also getting news about Abby Sunderland's progress. Abby was planning to sail solo, unassisted and non-stop around the world and she had chosen an Open 40 yacht for her attempt. Mike had sailed an Open 50 and he'd had problems. I was really happy with the decision I'd made to go with an S&S 34 and I knew already that *Ella's Pink Lady* was one tough little yacht and the perfect choice for me.

Friday, 27 November 2009
Flying along and mangoes

Heeled over, under full sail and throwing water everywhere *Ella's Pink Lady* has been flying along today. It can't just be me that's busting to get south! The wind has come round to the east a little more, meaning that we've been able to ease off the wind, making life a little more comfortable, and reach along directly south.

While giving the galley a reorganise today I was pretty thrilled to come across a stash of tinned mangoes! I've been hearing all about how lovely the mangoes are back home at the moment, so finding I had my own supply onboard was a lot like Christmas! Sure, they are not quite the same as fresh but they're not bad either. I have a feeling that this just isn't something that I'm going to be able to ration! Oh, and I think I can safely say that tinned mangoes are every bit as messy to eat as the fresh ones . . . Or maybe that's just me.

Nothing much else to report out here today so I thought I'd explain a little more about the plan for the next leg to the cape. The distance (5450 nautical miles) that I gave yesterday as the distance to Cape Horn is the distance in a straight line, but weirdly we're actually going to be sailing a slightly shorter route, I know it sounds really strange but it's all to do with something called the great circle route and the curvature of the earth. I'm probably not the best person to explain it, but as an example, if I were to plot out our course directly to South America taking into account the earth's curvature the fastest way to get there would actually be to sail in an arc to the south. Our great circle route, or the fastest way to get to the cape, is to sail south and then gently arc over to the east (5130 nautical miles). So if we can keep up an average speed of 5 knots, ETA at Cape Horn should be around the first week of January. But who knows? There's every chance that we might pick up a little speed down south and get there a bit earlier.

That would all be easy enough but then there's all these annoying islands and reefs in the way! And to add to the fun, it's not like the wind ever just lets us go where we want to.

I'm going to finish up by apologising for my explanation as it may have made you all just completely confused!

That's me for the night, Parker's wandering off course a little as the wind is dropping off slightly, so I better go set us back on course. Then I'm faced with a bit of a tough decision, do I or do I not open another can of mangoes?

P.S. Thanks for all the Happy Thanksgivings from America!

Saturday, 28 November 2009
Another day

Mostly just the usual out here today, still flying along really nicely, any tips on avoiding speed cameras? A few squalls have kept me busy reefing in and out and I spent a lot of my down time today catching up on a little sleep after being kept awake last night by a passing boat and a few little squalls.

I'm not sure how best to put this, but a lot of people have been wondering and asking so here goes; yes, it's definitely me writing the blogs (and my book)! Having someone write under my name is a big 'no go' for me. Can you imagine letting your mum or anyone else describe your feelings to the world under your name? Ouch! Well, maybe it's just a teenage thing! But I do have to confess, my updates have to be spellchecked before being published. My spelling is, can we just say, a little notorious!

While I'm on a roll with these confessions, I've got another one for you too. Sorry everyone, but I don't just blog to satisfy your curiosity, but also because I love writing!

Oh, and yes, I did open that can of mangoes and quite a few cans after that. I've been justifying my total mango pig-out by telling myself that, as a tropical fruit, the mangoes need to be eaten while still in the tropics. There's plenty of other treats stashed away for the cooler legs.

Everyone back home is out having fun at the local Christmas lights parade tonight. I'm a little jealous, but right here on *Ella's Pink Lady* is still my first preference. So, not to be outdone, I think I'll have another movie night with plenty of popcorn and chocolate. Anyway the stars out here would easily get first prize in any lighting competition!

No, all those mangoes didn't make me ill. Apart from the occasional headache and odd sad day I was feeling great. And I think the headaches were partly from the heat and partly from my erratic sleeping patterns. It really was a case of *Pink Lady* time and if I didn't have to make skeds I would have had a completely topsy-turvy routine. Having to make those radio skeds at certain times and calling home meant I did have some deadlines to answer to. And if I missed one I knew it! I know everyone was worried about my safety but like I said earlier, sometimes I just wanted to be completely alone. That sounds weird . . . I was alone. But being asked about what I was eating, how I was sleeping, whether I'd checked some equipment or other could get on my nerves sometimes. Of course, Mum and

Dad would want to know all about what I was doing but all I wanted to talk about was what was going on at home and what Tom, Emily, Hannah and my friends were doing. It didn't happen that often, but just occasionally I'd get annoyed by it all and be grumpy and short with my answers when we spoke.

Monday, 30 November 2009
Wind getting up again

Today started off with a passing squall giving me a very wet wake-up while reefing down and trying to catch it on camera. I'd have thought it was pretty clear that I was wide awake after the first wave but apparently not. To think that some people start their day with a quiet coffee!

As usual the squall was far more bark than bite, looking very dramatic as it approached as a great big dark cloud, but not coming to much more than 30 knots of wind and some rain. Although I was a little surprised at how fast a messy chop built up on top of the swell. It's been overcast and drizzly ever since, but at least the wind settled into a steady 18 knots this afternoon. *Ella's Pink Lady* is hard on the wind again but it's life as normal, passing the time reading, doing a little schoolwork or, my all-time favourite, just standing behind the dodger, wind and spray in my face, watching us blast along. I can't see myself ever getting bored of that one!

I've had the charts for French Polynesia out, swotting up on what's coming our way in the next while and have been thinking about a few of the jobs that need to be done before we hit the south. I've been a bit lazy with my cooking lately, mostly just heating up an Easyfood meal or snacking on crackers. I probably shouldn't be admitting it (I'll ruin my reputation), but I've even resorted to eating two-minute noodles when I really don't feel like cooking.

Tuesday, 1 December 2009

Cooler weather, rubbish and new food bag

Still good progress south but the big news for today is that I actually turned off one of my little Hella cabin fans this morning for the first time in weeks! Two little fans probably don't sound like anything to write home about, but believe me they've been a total lifeline, running constantly and doing a great job of helping me keep cool. Maybe it's too soon to start hoping, but it finally feels like it's started getting cooler over the past few days. You can be sure that it will be no time at all before I'm complaining about the cold!

It's still been very squally out here, with the squalls leaving behind a messy chop on the swell and making a mockery of anything I'd like to call sleeping patterns. I've been catnapping all afternoon to try and make up for lost sleep. *Ella's Pink Lady* is still making good ground south at the moment. Sometime tomorrow morning we'll be tacking over to make some ground to the east to hopefully pick up a more easterly wind. We passed back over the date line today, putting the local time zone at GMT-12, not that that means all that much to me. If anything, I'm still running on Queensland time!

One of today's little jobs included my weekly attempt to compact and package up my rubbish for storage in the bow. Obviously anything that's degradable goes over the side and anything that's left, which is pretty much only plastic packaging, gets washed out if needed and carefully packaged up till I get home.

With nothing left in the last food bag but a tin of baked beans and a packet of banana chips (dinner wasn't looking very exciting!) today marked the start of a new food bag. Lots of exciting new treats, and there's even a present from Grandma in this one!

For me the sleep deprivation is one of the hardest things about solo sailing. Learning to snatch sleep when you can and survive on interrupted sleep is critical to staying safe. I can really appreciate what mothers with young babies go through and what my own mother went through with four young kids. And recent scientific studies have found it is official: teenagers love to sleep in! Something that we'd been criticised about by Maritime Queensland after the collision with *Silver Yang* was not having a 'fatigue-management plan'. We'd put a lot of thought and time into working out how I'd handle the irregular sleep that is part of a solo voyage but without anything recorded on paper to support the statements we made and the preparation we'd done the officials considered me underprepared. They encouraged us to put all the information into one document. Aunty Vivienne (Mum's sister) came over from New Zealand to stay with us in the final stages of our preparation and she offered to write up my fatigue-management plan for me. I'm very proud of the extensive, beautifully researched and beautifully presented document I have onboard. And I am the first solo sailor I know of to actually have the physical evidence on the yacht!

Wednesday, 2 December 2009

Just briefly

Just a quick update. It's been another squally overcast day and tonight's become a bit bouncy with the wind gusting to 30 knots and the seas standing up as we pass over a shallow patch. The wind has been very shifty, every time I put my head on the pillow to catch some sleep something always seems to happen and back on deck I go. It's a pity that Parker can't also trim the sails and navigate! No complaints though, and we're still making great time south.

The clouds have finally parted a little just now and the moonlight shining down on the messy sea makes it look like seriously scrunched up tinfoil, only far more shiny and of course moving!

Saturday, 5 December 2009

Doesn't get much better!

We've had that messy sea and squally conditions for the last few days, but the clouds and squalls have well and truly cleared out today, leaving *Ella's Pink Lady* to fly along in picture perfect trade-wind conditions. The trade winds are the name given to the band of steady south-easterly winds in this part of the world but what the books don't say is how lovely the sunshine is, how nice it is to have a steady breeze and how amazingly blue the water looks speckled with whitecaps. Maybe it's just that I'm in a particularly good mood and seeing everything through happy glasses, but I don't think it gets much better than this!

It was funny how some of my comments like this one about the happy glasses were picked up and quoted by lots of people reading the blog. It was amazing to me that other people were reading what I wrote and even more amazing that they were applying my positive thought strategies to their own lives. As silly as they sound, I really do believe in 'happy glasses'. One thing I learnt at sea was that there are very, very few situations that can't be turned around and made more positive and less threatening by just looking at things in a different way. Sure, I had my mopey, wallowing moments when I was scared or sad, but eventually I would realise it was up to me to change how I was feeling (no one else was there to do it for me) and I would manage to shift my headspace to a better place.

On the downside, the south-easterly trade winds are also a bit of a pain, because south-east is exactly where I'd like to be going! We've been able to make some great progress south but we're not getting anywhere when it comes to making ground to the east. Still nothing to worry about because as we go further south the wind will drop off and probably come from a bit of everywhere (this area's known as the variables or subtropics) before settling in from the west when we get down south to the Roaring Forties. Bob's latest forecast gives us around another week on this course with similar conditions before we're able to turn on to a more direct line to Cape Horn.

We're now well clear of French Polynesia. With the wind we ended up getting, it turned out that we avoided most of the islands and reefs anyway. Other than a few little islands that we are set to pass tomorrow it's just open water between us and Cape Horn, 4380 nautical miles of it!

Oh, and one thing that I'm sure everyone is quietly wondering – no, I'm not at all sick of the pink yet! *Ella's Pink Lady*'s slightly 'out there' colour scheme still gives me endless smiles and turned out to be a pretty good colour for the tropics, keeping the cabin cool and making a nice change to the blues and greys, which is just about all I see out here! Still, I've got quite a while out here yet, so I'll keep you posted on just how I feel about pink as time goes on!

Well, I'm off to heat up my current favourite Easyfood meal, beef stroganoff, for an early dinner, and after yesterday's success with some scones I think I might have a go at making some more, maybe with cheese this time.

Sunday, 6 December 2009
Quiet Sunday

It's been a nice and pretty uneventful day today. Being so far from land and home it must seem a bit of a strange thing to say, but it feels just like a Sunday out here!

Ella's Pink Lady is still flying south and it's definitely starting to get cooler. Sitting outside in the breeze, I actually had to put a jumper on this evening. It's not exactly cool yet, with the air temperature down to 28 degrees (I recorded a top of 38 degrees in the cabin above Kiritimati Island), but what did surprise me was the change in water temperature today. It dropped from 26 degrees earlier today to 24.5 degrees, and compared with the 30 degrees we've had for so long it felt just a little cool when I had a scrub down this afternoon – *brrrr*!

With the sea flattening out even more, I've been doing the typical Sunday thing: catching some extra sleep and generally not getting up to much. I spent most of the day buried in a book which turned out to be just what I needed, it was so nice to completely put my head in another place for the day and I feel like I'm all recharged and ready for another week.

Wednesday, 9 December 2009
Ready for some wind!

I've been having a busy few days doing jobs and double-checking everything before we get too far south, all the while flying along in great sailing conditions. Of course, possibly the most important job of all had to be the installation of a safety strap for the crew – my stuffed toys!

The cabin has copped a full re-arrange, with everything properly secured, light-wind sails shuffled to the bottom of the pile to be replaced with the storm sails, all my warm clothing has been dug out along with wet-weather gear ready for easy access. Sorting out the bow area had been something I'd been dreading as it had become a bit of a dumping ground, a lot like the way I've always shoved stuff under my bed at home! But it turned out to be good fun as I discovered all sorts of things that I'd forgotten were there, including all my Christmas presents! Don't worry, I managed to restrain myself and save them for Christmas.

Turns out to be good timing, as it looks like I'm going to be in for some pretty strong weather tomorrow. Although the wind has been nothing severe today, the clouds have slowly been rolling in and the wind is expected to start picking up any time soon. Chances are that things are going to get pretty bumpy for me tomorrow. Call me crazy but hearing that *Ella's Pink Lady* and I are finally going to get some rough stuff was in one way a big relief, as it's been keeping me in suspense waiting!

I'm a tad nervous but mostly just excited knowing that I've done everything that I can. Well that's it for me, I'm off to have something good to eat and to try and catch some sleep while the going is good.

Jessica Watson's Video Diary – Day 53
http://www.youtube.com/jessicawatsonvideo

Friday, 11 December 2009

Banana muffins and watching the world go by

For the last few days we've had a dark and slightly eerie sky and a building sea. The wind picked up for a while and was expected to hit about 40 knots and I have been waiting for some action. But it looks like we've missed out this time as we've just sailed clear of the squash zone (an area where two weather systems come together).

Oh well, there's always next time. I can't see there being any shortage of strong winds further south. Call this one a practice run!

My favourite pastime lately has become standing in the companionway, under the dodger, sheltered from the wind, watching the world go by. You could say that I'm entertained by small things but I still find watching each wave roll under *Ella's Pink Lady*, with the occasional one dumping over us, just fascinating.

The weather really hasn't been anything special with the heavy overcast skies and occasional rain giving us pretty poor visibility, but in its own way it is just as spectacular as some of the stunning cloudless days.

Climbing into my cosy sleeping bag is already becoming something I look forward to. Getting out again is more of a challenge though. I even pulled on a set of thermals today, probably over-reacting really, as the temperature is only down to 20 degrees, but for now the cooler weather is still a bit of a novelty.

As always I'm in good spirits, but couldn't help thinking this morning of how nice it would be to be able to take a few days off, to think of something other than sailing and to be able to let down my guard for a while — just wishful thinking really and after all, it's just part of the challenge.

I discovered something this morning that I can see becoming a favourite, hot custard for breakfast! And talking of food, in an effort to get rid of some of the banana chips that Mum must have packed for me (on the off-chance that I actually might start liking them!) I had a go at making banana muffins this afternoon. Everyone present voted that they turned out perfect! They must have been pretty good as I'm eating the last one now.

The thing about doing a non-stop voyage like this is that there is no chance for any time off and you can never stop paying attention to the weather and the boat. As much as I had chosen to do this, it was relentless and, though I enjoyed myself most of the time, I'd have killed to have been able to say 'time out', to let my hair down, have a good laugh with my friends and ignore the latest barometric pressure reading. I could never completely wind down while at sea, losing myself in a book as an escape was really difficult when I had to stop every few minutes to stick my head out the hatch to keep watch. You know that saying, 'It's a marathon not a sprint'? Well, that sums up long-distance solo sailing perfectly!

Sunday, 13 December 2009
Lucky not lonely!

For the first time in weeks I saw something man-made other than *Ella's Pink Lady* – drum roll please! It was a small white piece of plastic that floated by this morning while we were becalmed for a short while. Not all that exciting, but it made me think about just how completely in the middle of nowhere I really am and about how every mile is taking us further into a pretty much empty stretch of ocean. It's still strange to think that I'm probably hundreds of miles from the nearest person, in fact it's now almost two months since I've seen anyone. Sure, I've seen other boats but none of them have come close enough to actually make out the crew.

Maybe stranger still, I can honestly say that I've not once felt lonely out here. Homesick, sure, and I've missed everyone since the moment I sailed out of Sydney, but not lonely. Lonely is the word for a Friday night with nowhere to go, sitting at home feeling sorry for yourself. The difference is that I chose to be out here. For some crazy reason I chose to be on a little boat in the middle of the ocean. Maybe the dictionary puts it better than I do (yup, I'm actually quoting a dictionary!): 'Lonely: a depressed feeling of being alone'. I might be about as physically alone as you can get, but I'm not depressed about it at all. How can I feel lonely with people all over the world thinking of me, talking about me (my nose just doesn't stop itching!), some probably still hotly debating whether or not I should be out here. And with my family and friends waiting for me back home. Lonely isn't the word. Actually, I feel like the luckiest girl in the world!

Another first for today was a little blue sky, it's been four days since I've had any sunshine and I hadn't realised how much I'd missed it. Living on the Sunshine Coast with its often endless stretches of perfect weather, I used to love a rainy or overcast day just to break up the monotony, but out here nothing makes me smile faster than a little sunshine. I've even got a few stars tonight. How spoilt am I?

So, other than that patch of practically no wind this morning that left *Ella's Pink Lady* rolling uncomfortably in the swell, we've been able to make good ground to the east, just plodding along one day at a time!

This was taken at the 2009 Sydney International Boat Show. I was thrilled to have been included in the Adventurers' Lounge presentations with such inspiring people. (LEFT TO RIGHT) Pete Goss, *Spirit of Mystery* voyage; me; Don McIntyre, Bounty Boat Expedition; Justin Jones and James Castrission, Crossing the Ditch.

This was one of my first sails on *Pink Lady* after the refit. Not much wind but a magic sunset.

RIGHT: Not a great moment as I motored back to the Gold Coast after the collision with the 63,000-tonne *Silver Yang*. *Ella's Pink Lady* was badly damaged and the generosity of the Gold Coast community, especially the people at the Gold Coast Marina, when I returned was amazing.

MIDDLE: The day I left Sydney on my voyage we had a visit from customs to make sure everything was in order. Suzanne, Dad, me, Mum, Bruce and the customs officers.

BELOW: Mum, Dad and me with the Certificate of Registration for *Ella's Pink Lady*. I was only hours from leaving and I am sure I had a million thoughts going through my mind, but I wasn't feeling as worried as I looked.

The first week was magical for me as I spent time settling into the trip.
ABOVE: This was an amazing day in the Pacific, an endless blue on blue.
BELOW: I loved every minute – even when a squall blew up I was having fun.

After the first few weeks, *Ella's Pink Lady* was holding up beautifully but I can't say the same for my hands. They were constantly wet and I was glad no one was around to see how manky they looked!

Climbing the mast can be full-on so I picked a very calm day to go up and check for wear. I called Bruce before I went up and as soon as I got down. I loved seeing *Ella's Pink Lady* sailing along from this angle.

LEFT: This is Silly. He kept me company for a while and I had a great time chatting to him...or her?

MIDDLE: Most of my food while I was at sea wasn't bad (well, not too bad!). This is me getting ready to cook an omelette, one of my favourite meals.

BOTTOM: In the doldrums after a rain squall, in which I managed to collect enough water to wash some clothes.

I went a bit overboard (ha!) with my Christmas at sea celebrations and put up so many decorations. My family didn't forget about me, making sure I had lots of presents to open. The fog was a stark contrast to the summer Christmases I was used to.

Rounding Cape Horn was a huge milestone. The weather was a bit iffy – you could only just see the outline of the cape. With the albatross overhead the whole scene was almost mythical. I became even more excited because the next day Mum and Dad flew over.

This was one of my biggest tests. A storm blew up and we were knocked down four times. I took these pictures as the sea was building. Waiting for the storm to hit was the worst part; once I was in it I just had to ride it out.

Monday, 14 December 2009

Amazing Sunset

Mostly it's just been a normal day out here, not a lot of wind but just enough to keep us moving on a gentle sea at a steady 5 knots.

Tonight's sunset was far from normal though, it was amazing! I thought it was good to start with, but then the colours just kept getting better and better as the sun disappeared.

Well, it's just going to be a quick update for today as my tummy is telling me I'm way overdue for some food!

Watching an amazing sunset, or sunrise, was one of the things that could lift my spirits, especially after a few gloomy days. The different colours that move across the sky as the sun sets, the pinks, blues, inky indigos and purples could be absolutely breathtaking. But whenever I saw a red sky at night I couldn't help but recite to myself the old sailors' saying:

Red sky at night, sailor's delight;
Red sky in the morning, sailor's warning.

Even if Bob's forecast was totally different it always planted the thought in my mind that the colour of the sky could predict what was coming. Where does that saying even come from? I had a bit of a search on the internet and it was fascinating to see it goes right back to biblical times. They didn't have people like Bob giving them weather forecasts then, so sailors – and shepherds (which is the other version you hear of the rhyme) – had learnt by noting the changes around them, things like the colours of the sky or the direction of the wind, and memorising the weather that seemed to follow on. Makes sense to me. I liked to think of sailors long ago, people like Joshua Slocum, watching the sky just like I did as they sailed alone around the world. I might have been able to contact home effortlessly compared to him but when the wind is strong, the sea is building and all I can see in any direction is an endless ocean meeting an equally endless sky the feeling of being a small part of something much bigger surely would have been similar. Slocum said in *Sailing Alone Around the World*: 'I found myself once more sailing in a lonely sea and in a solitude supreme all around.' Some people find the thought of being alone for a long time frightening but it never really scared me, though I had a few times when I craved having someone there with me and really wanted a hug and some company. Mostly, though, that solitude that Slocum wrote about is one of the things I love about sailing. I said it earlier, but when I'm sailing the world slows down and what matters, if I let it, is only that moment. Everything is very easy.

Thursday, 17 December 2009

Up the mast and into the Roaring Forties

Yesterday was a nice calm day so I decided it was time to have a go at climbing the mast. Down came the mainsail, on went the main electric autopilot, on went my dorky helmet and up I went. *Ella's Pink Lady* hasn't got the tallest mast and there wasn't much of a sea, but I certainly felt every little roll up there!

It was good to have a look around up top after being at sea for so long and before we hit the bumpy stuff. I'm happy to report that everything looks to be in perfect condition. The view was definitely great and it was really cool to see *Ella's Pink Lady* sailing along from another angle. If I can say so myself, what a cute little boat! The trip back down was the most interesting part because I didn't manage to give myself a very smooth ride, ouch!

Typically, while I was swinging around at the top of the mast, the wind, which had been steady all morning, started knocking us about (changing direction to come from the direction we were headed). Luckily I had my remote commander (a gadget that controls the main autopilot and displays information like our heading, the wind strength, etc.) with me and was able to bring us around to a better course. It wasn't exactly a high-drama situation as there was only a light breeze. Worst-case scenario would have been an even more uncomfortable trip back down, but I got a thrill out of the fact that here I was swinging around at the top of the mast sailing *Ella's Pink Lady* like a remote-control car. Pretty amazing!

It wasn't till yesterday morning that I noticed that my adventure up the mast didn't leave me completely untouched. I'm just a little stiff all over and have a few extra bruises. But all good.

I was twelve the first time I went up a yacht's mast and I was pretty scared. It happened the same day as another big first for me, the first time I raced offshore. I learnt a very valuable lesson that day: don't let go of a halyard (a rope used to raise or lower a sail up the mast). Letting go of the end of a halyard when attaching it to a sail will result in the person (on this day, me) who let go having to climb the mast to fetch it!

That first time the trip up the mast was fairly easy as I was strapped into a bosun's chair (a seat-like harness) and then someone hauled me up. Being small and usually the lightest member of just about every crew I sailed with, whenever the need to climb the mast arose I was the one chosen.

Of course, when you are solo sailing there is no one around to haul you up, so things get a little more complicated. A lot of people have steps up the mast and simply clip on at different points on their way up or down. I didn't want to fit steps on *Ella's Pink Lady* because they can catch on halyards and sails and cause problems, something I was looking to avoid, so instead I used a rock climber's ascender/grigri system and a harness to pull myself up and then slide back down.

When I started sailing with Bruce he showed me this system and I was able to practise a lot on *Big Wave Rider*'s huge mast while in port. After I got the hang of it I started practising when we were at sea. I learnt that, if it was possible, attaching myself to a sail car on the back of the mast stopped me from being thrown around too much if the boat was rolling. And it just shows that if you don't let your fears stop you from doing something (like I almost did that first time) who knows what you are capable of?

We've made great progress lately with the wind a steady 14 knots. *Ella's Pink Lady* loves reaching in conditions like this and yesterday I hardly saw our speed drop below 6 knots. I love this sort of sailing too because the motion and heel is nice and comfortable. It's a treat being able to move around the cabin without doing the arms and legs everywhere thing (spider impersonation!) that it often takes to stop myself being thrown about.

Also, yesterday we sailed into the forties. The wind didn't suddenly start roaring or anything but I'm sure that part comes later. Today's been a pretty average day. Not average as in bad, as everyday's great, just nothing much new or out of the ordinary.

I dug out all my Christmas music today (my favourites would have to be *Snoopy at Christmas* and *Christmas with the Wiggles*) and have been singing along very loudly and very, very badly!

The Roaring Forties is another of those sailing names that instantly brings to my mind images of huge seas and wild gales. This is the name given to the area between 40 degrees south and 50 degrees south. It was an area I'd read about endlessly and couldn't believe I was experiencing. I was a bit nervous about this part of the trip because I knew about the storms that could whip up. As much as I told myself not to imagine what was going to happen and to stay in the moment and deal with everything as it came, I couldn't help thinking of Francis Chichester's words, 'Wild horses could not drag me down to Cape Horn and that sinister Southern Ocean again in a small boat. There is something nightmarish about deep breaking seas and screaming winds; I had a feeling of helplessness before the power of the waves came rolling down on top of me.'

I didn't have a feeling of helplessness at all but I was a little nervous. I was learning that my imagination was the worst thing and if I could let myself stay in the moment I was fine . . . or as fine as you can be in 12-metre waves!

Friday, 18 December 2009
Quick update

It's been an overcast day today and the wind has been pretty light, but we've been able to make reasonable progress with the big light-wind reaching sail up. That was the one sail that I didn't expect to be using at this latitude!

It's cooler again with the temperature down to 17 degrees and over the next few days I'm expecting to see a low of 12 degrees.

I spent the afternoon tackling a little electrical problem. The battery monitor (a gauge that tells me the condition of the batteries and all the ins and outs of my power) had stopped working. I thought it was well and truly a 'goner' and that I'd have to go without, but thanks to some really detailed and helpful instructions from Neil, our astute electrician, combined with an afternoon's hard work, I'm very happy to report that I had a win! With all the tricky little details involved, I can't say that I was that confident that it was going to function. So you should have seen how thrilled I was after replacing the last fuse to see it fire up again!

That's it from me, it's past midnight local time and I'm feeling a little overdue for some shut-eye.

Good night!

Monday, 21 December 2009
Grey and misty

I've just come inside from sitting out in the wind with a cup of hot chocolate and watching the light fade. No sunset as there's heavy cloud and poor visibility, but the light misty rain and big rolly grey swell is just as lovely as any sunset.

I've been seeing quite a few birds around and I love watching them fly low over the waves and around *Ella's Pink Lady*. I'm pretty annoyed with myself for not bringing a bird book, but I think I'm mostly seeing big petrels and I spotted my first albatross for the trip this morning.

It's been a pretty uneventful day, just giving the cabin a tidy up. I also put up a few more Christmas decorations in the cabin. We've been keeping up a nice speed but the motion has been a little rolly, as downwind sailing isn't *Ella's Pink Lady*'s strong point. I'm just going to have to get used to rolly though, as a pretty big percentage of the voyage from here on is likely to be downwind – fast downwind sailing!

My best guess is twenty days to Cape Horn and just four more sleeps to Christmas!

Tuesday, 22 December 2009

Foggy

We didn't exactly get anywhere today, with very little wind. This morning was misty and overcast again, but this afternoon has been pretty special with a really thick fog closing in. It feels like there's a great big grey moist blanket draped over the world and just before it got dark the fog got so thick that I could hardly see 50 metres ahead. It's really a pretty amazing sight, but along with the almost complete silence, it's not far off feeling downright eerie.

I've been working hard not to let my imagination run away with itself, but it just feels so surreal sitting almost motionless with a big rolly swell passing underneath and the white swirling fog surrounding us. Now that it is dark, *Ella's Pink Lady*'s navigation lights at the top of the mast are lighting up big rays of red and green fog. It feels like something out of a movie!

I think I've got the complete opposite to the sunshine, heat and the craziness of the last-minute Christmas shopping that everyone's experiencing back home. Out here in my own little world things couldn't be more different!

I have to say I've been feeling a bit homesick on and off today but I refuse to let it stop me from appreciating every moment out here. I've been carefully planning out my Christmas dinner and the light winds mean that I'm almost constantly on my toes adjusting Parker's course. It's not exactly the most difficult task. I can normally correct Parker without even leaving the cabin by reaching out and adjusting the windvane line on the tiller, but the constant adjustments get a bit tedious when trying to get some down time.

Less than 2300 nautical miles to Cape Horn now, so despite all this slow progress we are slowly getting there. If this fog keeps up I'll be having a white Christmas of sorts!

There was one point in that foggy weather where I spooked myself a bit. I had turned my music off so I could listen to *Ella's Pink Lady* and experience the fog that rolled around us so thickly. It was like a heavy blanket that wrapped around everything and it really was beautiful in a weird way. But after a while I started to get a bad feeling and I didn't like not being able to see what was going on around us. I knew there was no one else out there with me, but that didn't stop me from feeling freaked out and imagining there was someone or something very close by. It was silly and I shook it off but I can't say I was unhappy when the fog started to lift and I could see the swell around me. There was a proper Southern Ocean swell rolling in and patches of fog settled in the troughs of the 3-metre waves, they looked like clouds between mountains and made me feel much better for some strange reason.

Being so close to Christmas and being so far away from my family was hard. I was exactly where I'd chosen to be but I was still a bit emotional about it all. I'd been so caught up in myself and my own mood that I'd missed a few calls to Mum and so we hadn't spoken properly for a while. When we finally talked we both got a bit emotional. I know I am supposed to be a selfish teenager but I did realise what a huge gift my parents had given me by trusting me and my abilities, so knowing that she was struggling set me off as well. I started feeling even more homesick and all I wanted to do was give Mum a hug. I then had a chat to Hannah and that made me even worse. Hannah is very funny and I missed her. When I heard that Tom had got his first job I was really proud of him and started crying because I wasn't there to tell him. (Luckily they couldn't see my tears 'cause they would have been horrified!) The combination of the fog and Christmas was bound to make me a bit weepy so I kept putting up more and more Christmas decorations to ward off feeling bad.

Thursday, 24 December 2009

Christmas in the middle of nowhere!

It's still been pretty foggy and grey out here but we've been able to make good progress with 15 knots of wind from the west. Both the air and sea temperatures have dropped a few more degrees and this morning we pretty much sailed right over Point Nemo, which is known for being the point of ocean furthest from any land. You really could say that I'll be spending Christmas in the middle of nowhere!

With pretty steady conditions and a reasonable forecast for the next few days I took the Christmas decorations in the cabin to the next level, there's now tinsel and little bauble-balls everywhere swinging in time to *Ella's Pink Lady*'s motion.

Well, that's it from me as it's getting late and I'd better get going to bed or Santa might catch me awake. I really hope he can find me out here!

Till tomorrow!

Point Nemo is also known as the Pacific Pole of Inaccessibility (which is a bit of a mouthful so I can understand why it needed a nickname) and is the furthest away you can get from any land. It is one of the most remote places you can be and is found at 48°52.6'S, 123°23.6'W. I've been told that it is named after the character Captain Nemo from Jules Verne's *Twenty Thousand Leagues Under the Sea*. I haven't read it but I might have to soon.

Friday, 25 December 2009
Merry Christmas!

Merry Christmas everyone, from out here in the Southern Ocean! It's Christmas morning and I'm about to make a start on my big pile of Chrissie presents, and then I'm looking forward to a long call home to everyone on the sat-phone. After that, I've got quite a bit of food to munch my way through. I'm going to start with my favourite Easyfood lamb shanks with roast tinned veggies and move on to some cream and custard with plenty of Christmas pudding and chocolate mousse – so I'm really looking forward to that! I'm having a bit of a white Christmas out here today – it's really quite foggy again, all grey and misty. It's quite cool, a bit chilly, but we're also moving along nicely which is great.

I just also wanted to say a huge thanks to everyone for their support. It means a lot to know that everyone's thinking of me out here today, and I hope you all have a wonderful Christmas!

By Christmas Day I was back to feeling good and even though I'd crossed the date line and it wasn't technically Christmas where I was, I kept myself to the time zone back home so we could all celebrate together. I'd said I was going to bed so Santa didn't catch me awake and then I did something I hadn't done since I left Sydney: I slept for five hours straight! And of course the wind changed while I was out to it so we ended up sailing completely in the wrong direction for over an hour. I think we lost about 6 nautical miles (make that 12 nautical miles if you count the ground we could have made). I was really surprised that the change of direction didn't wake me as it normally always does.

I had a great day talking to family and friends, and I really enjoyed quizzing everyone about what exactly they were eating and how they were spending Christmas Day. I was pretty lazy and did the bare minimum to keep *Ella's Pink Lady* moving, but after all my conversations I felt like I'd been part of multiple Christmas celebrations. Anyway, doesn't everyone just kick back on Christmas afternoon? Besides it was so cold outside it was much nicer to stay in the cabin and keep warm. Despite people worrying and my own doubts about being alone on what is normally a special family time I was completely cheerful all day. I am kind of glad no one could see me babbling away to myself and giggling as I opened my presents as they would have thought I was mad. Mum gave me four fancy notebooks among other things. I always struggle to write in beautiful notebooks because I feel like I'm ruining them with my bad spelling and messy handwriting. I normally use plain old notebooks that don't matter. When I asked Mum later how I was going to fill them all she said she was challenging me to try. How can I not do that after I'm always saying nothing is impossible?!

Saturday, 26 December 2009
Fearsome Fifties

Christmas wasn't just an exciting day for all the obvious reasons (presents and food!), but also because we passed into the Fearsome Fifties and now have less than 2000 nautical miles to go till Cape Horn.

Also, as many people pointed out, yes I did celebrate Christmas a day early for the time zone I'm currently in, but I figured that it would be far nicer to celebrate with everyone back home rather than a day later and truly alone!

Christmas must have been my foggiest day yet and I have to admit I spent it being pretty lazy, just doing the bare minimum to keep us moving vaguely in the right direction and staying out of the cold. Phone calls, eating all my favourite foods and opening the presents that had been stashed on *Ella's Pink Lady*, kept me busy all day. Down to the smallest, silliest thing, I enjoyed and treasured every present far more than I ever would have back home and believe me there were some silly ones, including a blow-up Kiwi (the New Zealand national bird, not a person!) and a pink doll which expands in water (known as a 'grow your own best friend'!). Other than that, there was also the normal collection of warm socks, books and other odds and ends.

No watching the start of the Sydney to Hobart yacht race or Boxing Day sales for me today, but I'm pretty thrilled to have been treated to a couple of hours of sunshine and an albatross doing a few close circles of *Ella's Pink Lady*. The albatross really is an amazing bird. No matter how long I watch them for, I never seem to see them flap their wings. They make flying look so effortless and seem completely relaxed weaving in and out of the swell, thousands of miles from land.

Sunday, 27 December 2009
The not-so-fearsome fifties!

It's been a bit of a slow day with only a little wind and drizzly rain. You wouldn't guess that this is the Southern Ocean! Well, apart from the long swell and albatross, oh and of course the cold.

I've been finding the light winds and slow progress a little frustrating, but I shouldn't complain because life is so much more comfortable in the light conditions, and the wind chill is going to be quite something when it does eventually pick up. Thank goodness for all my warm Musto gear and the protection of the dodger!

One thing that's really cool (that wasn't meant to be a joke!) about being so far south is how few hours of dark there are.

Lately I've been keeping in touch with another solo sailor Dilip Donde who is from India and part way through his own circumnavigation. It's been great to talk to him and compare conditions as he's not far to the west of us and also heading for Cape Horn. At 47 feet, Dilip's boat, *Mhadei*, is quite a bit bigger than *Ella's Pink Lady*, so he's catching us up pretty fast!

That's all for today.

Dilip Donde is a forty-two-year-old trained clearance diver in the Indian navy. He left India on 19 August 2009 to attempt to become the first Indian national to sail around the world and he was doing it in the first fibreglass yacht built in India. I really enjoyed exchanging positions with Dilip. He is a lovely man to talk to and email and I hope one day I can meet him in person. It was amazing to know he was only a few hundred nautical miles away from me and was facing similar conditions. It is strange how close I felt to him. Talking to Mum and Dad or Bruce was good but as much as they tried to understand how it was for me out there, they didn't really know. Dilip did, and I think it was pretty amazing to share part of my voyage with him (well, as much as you can share when you are both on different boats a long way apart).

I didn't know he felt the same way until someone sent me this from his blog:

Midnight of New Year's Eve, just as I was getting out to change the windvane with the wind dropping, the phone rang. Finding it a bit odd to receive a phone call close to midnight, picked up the phone and what a pleasant surprise! Jessica calling to wish New Year's! So very thoughtful of her! Amongst all the New Year's wishes I have received in all these years and at various places I think I will cherish this, from this gutsy girl 350 nautical miles away and the nearest human being to me, as the most special! With wishes like these how can 2010 not be anything but great!

On 19 May 2010 Dilip sailed back into Mumbai Harbour after 276 days at sea. He had become the 175th solo circumnavigator and he had achieved his dream of becoming the first Indian national to achieve this feat.

Tuesday, 29 December 2009
Better wind

I'm pretty thrilled to have made good progress to the east over the last two days. We've finally had 15 to 20 knots of steady breeze and *Ella's Pink Lady* has been surfing along nicely. The wind is also expected to keep increasing, so you never know, it might start getting a bit more like the Southern Ocean down here after all!

The light drizzly rain has become a constant and the temperature seems to drop a little lower each day. At least the fog seems to have disappeared now. There's still plenty of birds around, but I'm not doing so well at getting pictures of them as they just won't sit still for me!

When I venture up on deck these days, I feel a bit like a clumsy elephant with all the gear that I have to wear. First there's all the thermals and various different layers, then boots and wet-weather gear, a hat, life jacket and what feels like half the hardware on the boat stashed in the pockets of my overalls. I'm always carrying my knife, PLB (personal EPIRB), shifter and more often than not a selection of various other tools. It's far easier to just take most of the spanner set with you, when picking the wrong size means an extra round of clipping and unclipping tethers and opening and replacing washboards.

I'm still having the time of my life, doing a lot of reading keeping up a constant stream of hot drinks, having fun with my cooking (my chocolate pudding was a great hit with the crew yesterday!) and today I've had a few little jobs to do when shackles on the vang (which holds the boom down) and windvane decided to give up the ghost. But a bit of improvising and we were all good again.

So just 1500 nautical miles to Cape Horn and 2009 almost over. I can't believe how fast this year has gone. It's nearly 2010 already!

Thursday, 31 December 2009
First gale with a dolphin at our side

Sorry I didn't update you all yesterday. I've been catching up on a bit of sleep. I've certainly had an interesting few days. The wind started picking up pretty much right after

I sent Tuesday's blog and topped at 44 knots mid morning yesterday, which makes for my first Southern Ocean gale.

Ella's Pink Lady and I came through beautifully and I learnt a lot about how she handles when the sea's up. There's a good chance that we'll see worse somewhere along the line, but apart from a bit of fast surfing (a bit too fast for comfort!), everything went really smoothly this time. After a while, some of the waves started to knock us around a bit which got just a little hard on the nerves. But one thing I'm really happy with is what a good job Parker did keeping us on course!

The sea was really quite something. My best guess would be, conservatively, 5 metres and far more amazing than any of the pictures or how I'd imagined it! The ocean in a state like that is downright spectacular and fascinating to watch, but I think it's really one of those things you have to experience first hand. I'm not sure I can really describe it and pictures don't do it any justice.

But the most amazing thing of all was the dolphin that swam along next to *Ella's Pink Lady* for over six hours while the wind was at its strongest, just as if he was keeping an eye out for us! Every time I'd glance out the porthole I'd get another little flash of fin or tail, as if he was reassuring me that he was still there. I haven't seen a dolphin for weeks, so to have one see us through the gale like that was something special and very comforting!

I was just starting to think the wind was dying down and I was sitting at the nav table feeling calm and smug that we'd ridden it out so beautifully when out of nowhere we copped a really big wave. Water poured in from the vent right above me (which was closed) and I was covered in ice-cold water. The nav table isn't a great place to dump a whole lot of water but after a few shrieks I checked it all out and everything was okay. The wind picked up and was sitting between 36 and 44 knots as the waves started to build again. Once I'd dried off I spent a lot of time with my face up against the porthole watching the amazing greens, greys and streaks of white. Finally the wind calmed right down to more like 20 to 25 knots and after what felt like a few very long days I was pretty stuffed. I managed about three hours sleep over twenty-four hours and knew I had to watch myself. I made a list of things to do.

- Pull out new chart and charts for the cape
- Clean up the galley (a never-ending job)
- Re-stow and organise the cabin (after the water came in)
- Proper check over deck for wear
- Wash hair and strip-down wash
- Lots of good hot food!
- Rest up

> The wind and sea kept dying off today, so we're making good ground with a nice 15 to 20 knots of wind and 3 metres of sea. It's currently the middle of the night for me but it hardly seems dark as for the first time in weeks I got a sky full of stars and a brilliant full moon! It's such a novelty than I've spent the last few hours bundled up in more layers than I would have thought possible, braving the cold and sitting out in the cockpit taking it all in.

With my mind on other things for the last few days, New Year's Eve has crept up on me a lot faster than I'd realised, so I think I'll save my New Year's party for tomorrow in my own time zone. But I would like to wish Happy New Year to everyone out there celebrating tonight. Looks like I'm going to miss the fireworks so make the most of them for me!

Friday, 1 January 2010

Happy New Year!

I've had a very different day again. We've spent the day almost completely becalmed. But the novelty of having a clear sky, sunshine, a slightly warmer temperature and the company of two albatross has kept me from getting too frustrated.

There was so little wind that even the albatross were flapping their wings today. I had the chance to get some great close-ups as they kept landing on the water right next to *Ella's Pink Lady*. An albatross taking off without any wind is very clumsy, as they have to flap hard to lift themselves off the water which is very out of character for such graceful birds.

So it's New Year's Eve for me and now just five minutes away from midnight. There's quite the wild party planned out here, all the big names from miles around are attending. Entertainment will include party poppers, and a range of my favourite treats will be served – believe me, the treats are one part that you really don't want to miss!

This makes it the second New Year in a row that I've spent at sea. Last year I was out in the Tasman sailing another 34-footer to New Zealand. As it was only the third day out and quite bouncy, we were still all feeling a bit queasy. So the treats that Mum had packed for us were completely ignored. But not this year.

Deciding on my New Year's resolution wasn't exactly hard. I think that getting back to Sydney safely will be quite enough of a challenge and my main wish for 2010.

Happy New Year everyone and thanks so much again for all your support!

It was that time when people reflect on the year that's been and what they want for the year ahead. I'd always wondered whether I'd change much while on my voyage. Doing something like this has to impact on the person you are in some way but for the first month I didn't feel any different at all. It sounds strange but over the days heading towards the cape something had changed and I felt different. I don't know how to explain it really, maybe calmer, more centred, older? (Hah!) I'm not sure. All I can say is I felt different. I didn't blog about it because I didn't want to sound stupid and I almost didn't put it in the book because it is nothing I can pinpoint exactly. Something in me changed, that's all.

Saturday, 2 January 2010
Calm before the storm

It's been calm and sunny again today. I spent the morning doing jobs on deck and soaking up the lovely sunshine. Talk about a treat to have such lovely conditions!

I end-for-ended the headsail sheets, runners and windvane lines (as they were all showing signs of chafe), re-lashed the spinnaker poles, scrubbed at a few rust stains and re-stowed all my rubbish in the aft locker.

It doesn't look like the calm is going to last though, with the wind forecast to really start coming up again tomorrow. It sounds like this one is going to be pretty nasty, so this is probably the last time you'll hear from me for a few days, but please don't worry as *Ella's Pink Lady* and I are completely ready for it. The wind is not expected to be too much stronger than last time, but it is blowing straight up from Antarctica, so it is expected to be very cold – the little diesel heater will probably cop a bit of a workout. My action plan for this one is really very simple: stay calm and confident. And if I can't manage that, then Plan B is to fake it!

I'm off to get some sleep while I can.

This was the only point during the voyage that we were worried about icebergs and rime ice (icing of the deck and rigging). We'd timed my departure so I'd be rounding Cape Horn in the height of summer so the chance of me coming across any icebergs was very low, but this gale was blowing in straight from the Antarctic and so there was a possibility it could drive in small bits of ice along with some very cold wind. There wasn't much I could do because there was no way I could keep watch 24/7. Really, I was more worried about staying warm than hitting ice at this time of year.

Just before I made it home, on 7 May, an English family of four were sailing their 55-foot yacht *Hollinsclough* in the South

Atlantic after leaving South Georgia when they hit a growler at 2 am. A growler is an iceberg that sits just below the surface of the water. They are really hard to detect at the best of times but at 2 am they'd be pretty much impossible to avoid. Luckily, this family were rescued from their sinking yacht by a British warship, the HMS *Clyde*, which sailed 200 nautical miles to rescue them.

Tuesday, 5 January 2010
Cold!

The good news is that so far the wind hasn't been nearly as strong as expected. But on the downside, it sure has been, and still is, very cold!

The cabin temperature has been sitting on 4 degrees Celsius and the wind chill outside is really quite something. Mostly I'm staying toasty warm in all my layers, but handling wet lines on deck is just downright painful. Unfortunately, the heater is no help – it picked a great time to blast cold air rather than hot! I think the problem is fixable, but that's going to have to wait till things are a little quieter.

Actually, the heater hadn't been working for a few days but I didn't tell anyone because, after looking at the forecasts, Dad and Bruce were pretty worried about how I would cope with the low temperatures during this gale. I figured they were already concerned enough so didn't want to add to their pressures talking about the heater until after the worst had passed.

I've also got a little problem with a block on the mainsheet (the line that controls the mainsail). Again it's not a biggie, but for now I've got the mainsail down and seeing as there's still plenty of wind, *Ella's Pink Lady* is making good ground with just the headsail up.

So, as I'm writing this, the wind is sitting at about 30 knots and it's just become daylight again to reveal an angry, grey ocean. Nothing too serious, but I'm still a little on edge as there's more wind expected again today and the odd big wave is knocking us around a bit.

With everything in order, there's not really much for me to do for now, so in between frequent glances at the instruments and out the companionway, I've been reading, watching the occasional DVD and working my way through all the messages and comments on my blog.

I hope I don't sound like a broken record, but once again thanks so much for all the messages of support. Whenever I sit down to read them, I normally laugh and smile the whole way through!

Ella's Pink Lady handled all this nicely under the storm jib but after a while I was really feeling how tired I was. The waves were knocking us around and it sounds like no big deal when I write it but even though it wasn't too dangerous I was feeling the pressure and my nerves were a bit jangled. Sometimes I could hear a big wave coming and I'd brace myself but other times I'd be concentrating on something and wouldn't notice until we were slammed. I was getting a few bumps and bruises and it wasn't fun at all. I was talking to Bruce for a sked when probably the biggest wave of the gale hit us hard. It wasn't the best phone call because I wasn't in a great mood and neither was Bruce so we kept it short. After I hung up I lost it for a minute and let loose a few tears. It is funny how whenever I was feeling a little too close to losing it, talking to someone could really set me off. I was much better if I just kept it all to myself. You'd think talking would comfort me and make me feel better but most of the time it would make things worse. Finally the wind died down and I slept on and off. The next day I felt much better despite the cold and a broken heater. Bob sent through a weather forecast and I was pleased that it didn't look like I'd get anymore bad weather until after I rounded the cape. After catching up on my sleep I started to crave a proper cup of coffee but that would definitely have to wait until I got home – coffee just didn't work with my rubbish-tasting water and powdered milk.

Thursday, 7 January 2010
Closing in on the cape

The wind hit 40 knots again on Tuesday which kept life interesting and a little bouncy. Since then it's steadily dropped off to the current 8 knots, which is really only just enough to keep us moving.

In typical Southern Ocean style, the visibility hasn't been great, with almost constant light, misty drizzle and not the slightest hint of a clear sky. But no complaints from me. Like I've said before, in its own way it's just as pretty as sunshine and blue water. Looking at it another way, you could always say that at least the low visibility means that you can see very little of the bad weather!

The good news is that I was able to fix the little problem with the mainsheet block easily. But the bad news is that despite spending yesterday morning trying to fix the heater, it still won't play nice! Oh well, on the scale of things, the heater not working really isn't much of a problem, just one of those optional extras.

I'm really starting to get pretty excited about Cape Horn as we're getting so close now, with just over 500 nautical miles to go.

That's going to have to be it from me today as my fingers are pretty keen to slip back into some nice warm gloves!

Friday, 8 January 2010
Becalmed

Just a quick update. Becalmed today, but the albatross have joined us again. Only 450 nautical miles to Cape Horn, and I'm even more excited now as Mum and Dad flew out of Australia today to watch *Ella's Pink Lady* rounding the cape!

That *Becalmed* blog was really short, and there was a reason. I was having to fight sliding into a real slump and I could feel a sadness and frustration just at the edge of my thoughts. This was the first time in the voyage where I kind of lost it in a big way. Keeping my head in order and having the mental toughness to make this voyage is what I pride myself on so to lose that, even for a little while, is hard to admit. The excitement about getting close to Cape Horn wasn't enough to keep me up and I crashed. It was because we weren't moving, it almost felt like we were going backwards. I was okay that Friday and the Saturday was bearable, I *almost* enjoyed looking out at the huge swell all glassed out and the moody sky, but when Sunday was the same and we were becalmed again, going nowhere and just flopping about, I couldn't stop crying.

We were so close to the cape and it was just so frustrating, especially because Mum and Dad had been flown over to Chile by News Limited and were going to fly out of Punta Arenas to see me round the cape. I'd been told a few days before that a plane was going to come out and take a photo of me rounding the cape and I was really excited about it and then I was told that Mum and Dad were going to be on that plane. It was almost too much for me to handle. I didn't want to keep them waiting and cost people money but I couldn't do anything about it. I probably would have coped better with the slow progress if I was in the tropics and could laze about in the sun hand-steering but it was so cold and so I was spending as little time as possible on deck. I was stuck in the cabin listening to the constant slap of the mainsheet against the boom. Normally the noises of *Ella's Pink Lady* were comforting but we were making no headway and the monotonous thwacking, rattles and thumps were enough to send me a bit crazy. I didn't have any energy to even put on some music and so I just sat there crying and feeling sorry for myself.

I think being out of my routine and knowing Mum and Dad were off somewhere different was part of it. I was really glad for them and I felt like it was a bit of payback after all they had done for me but normally whenever I felt a bit sad or homesick I could just picture them at home and work through it, but hearing about them flying over the Andes and all the amazing things they were seeing made me a bit envious. I was going nowhere! I couldn't wait to get to Chile myself so I was jealous.

This was one of those days where I just couldn't find the energy or motivation to pull myself out of a slump. I couldn't do much more than feel sorry for myself and I didn't want to hear about everyone diving, swimming and surfing back home in the sun when I was cold and miserable, so phoning and emailing weren't going to help. Everything just built up and the cold seeped under my skin and made doing anything really hard. There wasn't much I could do except ignore the rolling and banging and try not to think about us drifting in the wrong direction but I couldn't pull myself out of the hole. After a good cry I finally had to give myself a talking to. I pulled out a book to try to get my head somewhere else. I can't tell you how relieved I was when the wind finally picked up and we started moving forward again!

Monday, 11 January 2010
Closing on the cape. Slowly!

I'm really not having the most exciting time down here at the moment. We've still got very, very little wind meaning very, very little progress towards the cape. All this slow progress and light wind really wasn't something I expected in these latitudes, so I've sure had to adjust my expectations.

Yesterday the wind dropped out again to the point that *Ella's Pink Lady* sat completely stationary, rolling on a glassy swell for quite a few hours. Making any ground at all in conditions like this means a lot of sitting out in the cold, either hand-steering or constantly adjusting Parker to keep us on the right heading. I have to say I'm a lot more prone to giving up and just letting us drift and going back into the warmer cabin, than I was when we were becalmed in the warmer areas in the doldrums!

To try to take my mind off the tedious speeds and uncomfortable rolling, I've been working away at a few books, totally throwing myself into the stories. Mum keeps asking me what books I'm reading and I think she's a bit surprised at my replies. I've hardly picked up an adventure or sailing story since leaving. Instead I've been reading and re-reading the most mindless, trashy stories that I have. When part of your mind (and often all of it) is constantly thinking of nothing but sailing and all the different aspects of looking after *Ella's Pink Lady*, the last thing I feel like doing is reading about more sailing!

So things out here couldn't be more different to all the stories of swimming, sunshine, diving and surfing from back home. But as always, I wouldn't be anywhere else. Having no wind can completely drive you up the wall, but at the same time seeing the surface of the big, gentle swell become so glassy that it reflects the moody, grey sky is just incredible. So good things still do come with the bad.

Anyway, down to business. The wind has finally picked up to a steady 12 knots in the last few hours, so *Ella's Pink Lady* is pushing along nicely again now. You have no idea how good it feels to be moving again! We've still got about 270 nautical miles till Cape Horn and if the wind behaves as expected, we are aiming for the rounding sometime on the thirteenth.

I've got all my fingers, toes, limbs and everything else crossed hoping that the weather works out okay for the flyover with Mum and Dad. Rounding the cape is sure going to be a huge milestone.

The weirdest thing happened once the wind picked up. As I was sailing about 213 nautical miles away from the cape the sun came out and I had the strongest déjà vu sensation. There we were at 56 degrees south and for a while it felt like I was somewhere near Mooloolaba sailing towards Mudjimba Island, a place also known as Old Woman Island, with Emily and Nick. I couldn't believe I was nearly halfway around the world and I felt like I was back home. As the wind got stronger and the sun disappeared the feeling vanished, but it was lovely while it lasted.

Wednesday, 13 January 2010
A stone's throw from the cape

With the wind gusting to 35 knots, *Ella's Pink Lady* is really surfing away the last 80 nautical miles to Cape Horn. It's looking like we'll be rounding the cape first thing tomorrow morning – super exciting! Fingers crossed that the cloud lifts a little and I get a half-decent view as we sail past.

Up in Punta Arenas, Chile, Mum and Dad are getting ready to take off later today and will be circling around overhead in a plane. We'll be able to chat over the VHF radio, so I'm looking forward to that.

Also, boats from both the Chilean Navy and the Argentinean Navy are expected to swing by to give us a wave. It's been over a month since I've seen another boat and almost three months since I've seen another person, so I feel totally thrilled and spoilt to have so many guests all at once! I was extra careful brushing my hair this morning, (which is of course completely pointless in this wind!).

The other exciting news is that I heard from Dilip that he and *Mhadei* rounded the cape ahead of us and are now on course to the Falklands to sort out his steering problems.

Anyway, there's plenty happening and things that need my attention out here, so I'm going to sign off for now.

That day, and especially that afternoon approaching Cape Horn, I was absolutely bouncing with excitement because I was only hours away from rounding the cape and was expecting Mum and Dad to fly over any minute. The building sea and moody sky only added to the atmosphere and being so wound up in the small space of the cabin probably made it even more extreme. When I suddenly spotted the Diego Ramirez Islands south-west of the cape, I shrieked. Land! After so long at sea it was a huge buzz. As time crept on and I didn't hear from Mum and Dad I started to suspect something had gone wrong and got a bit worried. I thought maybe they hadn't been able to spot us from the plane. Finally, Dad called on the sat-phone and told me the pilot had to turn back because the weather was so bad, so they never made it close to me at all. I spoke to Mum and Dad and they both sounded pretty flat. It had been a rough flight with a lot of turbulence and Dad got quite airsick. They were disappointed but not even that could get me down as I sailed closer and closer to such a huge milestone. They told me that they were still determined to find me so they began planning another attempt for the next day as soon as they got off the phone. The photographer they were with, Gary, was equally as focused so I crossed my fingers that it would happen.

Saturday, 16 January 2010

Highlights from an incredible few days!

I'm going to apologise in advance for the overuse of exclamation marks (!), but it's certainly been an amazing few days! Sorry not to have updated you all earlier, but after running on not much more than adrenaline for a good four days, I've only had one thing on my mind – sleep!

So much has happened lately. So many highs. But I'm going to start at the beginning with Wednesday and 80 nautical miles between us and the cape. Passing squalls, the waves standing up a little as we passed in to shallower water, the wind settling into a consistent 40 knots by nightfall, all made life pretty interesting.

But the fast disappearing miles till the cape and sighting land on that afternoon had me completely pumped up and totally bouncing with excitement! Seeing land after so long was incredible. I can hardly remember feeling so thrilled, which when I think about it, seems like a bit of an over-reaction considering I couldn't actually see anything more than the outline of a grey bit of rock disappearing frequently, as we dropped into the troughs between waves. Through my eyes at the time, that distant bit of rock was the most beautiful and incredible thing I'd seen. It's amazing how deprivation can make something look a million times more special. I imagine that my first long hot shower when I get back home will be much the same!

That night was a busy and sleepless one as we approached the cape. To ensure that we didn't just go surfing by in the dark, I put a bit of effort into slowing us down and just as it was getting light, there it was – the distinctive outline of Cape Horn!

Against the grey sky and with albatross flying in the foreground, it was just as I'd imagined for so long. Mythical and striking pretty much sums it up! The poor visibility didn't exactly make it the best sightseeing weather, but if we'd drifted comfortably by on a nice sunny day, it wouldn't have been half as special. In-between taking pictures and phone calls, it was an extremely proud moment!

Then the flyover with Mum and Dad sure turned out to be quite an adventure in itself. With pretty poor weather conditions it was only on the third attempt that the plane managed to find *Ella's Pink Lady*. I'm sure you can imagine what an emotional roller-coaster it was for me, not to mention Mum and Dad. First I'd hear that they'd just taken off and would be overhead within a few hours. Then would come the bad news that they had to turn back! When the plane finally did find us, the forty-five minutes that they spent overhead passed in an extremely fast blur. I got myself very dizzy and totally tangled up in my tethers watching them fly around in circles! In the end I think it was a good thing that I couldn't really make out Mum and Dad through the windows, because if I had been able to I don't think that I would have managed to keep my composure. I owe a really big thanks to everyone who made the flyover happen.

This is what Mum wrote back to a friend about it all:

WE FOUND JESS! . . . and no wonder we had trouble the previous attempts, she looks so very small out there in the ocean . . . There was so much excitement in the cabin of the plane, we quickly steamed up the windows and sent Gary, the photographer, into heart attack mode (but he handled it with his usual cool and calm dignity!). Not only did he have a difficult task, now we had steamed up his windows. Anyway we sorted that out and spent the next forty-five minutes circling her. Sometimes high, sometimes low, sometimes banked over with lots of 'Gs' and sometimes straight past. We did it every way possible! It was just fantastic to see her, the boat and sails just look as if she was sailing out of Sydney, looked perfect!

We made VHF contact before we saw her and had a chat and then I think we were unable to speak for a fair while, so after we had all composed ourselves we radioed her up again. She wanted to know how they looked from up there! And how was Dad (and he was getting fairly green). I asked if she had done her housework and she replied that maybe it was better that I was up there! She was making complaints about getting all tangled up with the tethers as she was following us circling the boat! (So that means she was in fine form.) It was so great to see her waving and up front of the mast. It made me feel really proud of her that she was just sailing on, through wave after wave. She's out there doing it! The thing she has been planning and dreaming about for so very long.

Mostly the wind has been nice to us over the last two days and we're already very close to the Falklands. But with quite a bit of shipping around and with the side effects of all that adrenaline, I hardly managed any sleep at all till yesterday. Today I was treated to full clear skies and tonight I've got stars like I haven't had in a very long time!

But I haven't been the only one not getting a lot of sleep lately. Mum, Dad, Bruce and Andrew have all been keeping very strange hours and they're only a few of a very long list of people who played a huge part in seeing *Ella's Pink Lady* and I safely around the cape. Thanks a million!

Some people might think, 'What's so special about sailing around a lump of rock in a windswept ocean?' The weather conditions meant I didn't get to see a whole lot really. It isn't an amazing natural wonder like Uluru or the Twelve Apostles. But when I finally saw the outline of the cape through the squalls I just stood there staring for ages. I wanted to soak every little bit of the moment in. I called Mum and Dad in Chile, then Bruce and then the rest of my family, who were having a get-together with some of the team back home.

It was great to share the moment with them all because they had helped me get to this point. It was Bruce's birthday that day and he told me that rounding the cape was the best present I could have given him.

After I hung up the phone from my last call it was like someone had flicked a switch in my brain. While I'd been talking I'd been full of energy but as soon as I stopped I could hardly hold my head up. The conditions were still not good but I had to shut my eyes for a while. I didn't even get out of my dry suit and I basically passed out strapped into the wet seat.

For me, the power of sailing around Cape Horn was the combination of the area's fierce and demanding reputation, the years I spent dreaming about doing it and the weeks of build-up as we edged closer and closer to this achievement. After a physically and emotionally challenging week before we got there, rounding Cape Horn was better than I'd ever expected. Forgive the cliché but it really was a dream come true.

The absolute high of rounding Cape Horn was just brilliant but there was a long way to go and I had to keep myself on my toes and ready for anything. As well as talking to Bruce, Mum, Dad and my brother and sisters, I called Don. I wanted to share my excitement with someone who really understood what it felt like. Don was on the ship *Orion* just coming back from leading an expedition to the Antarctic with about a hundred passengers. It was great talking to him and he patched me into the PA system so the guests onboard could listen in. We couldn't chat too long but I couldn't believe it when I heard that Kay Cottee was onboard with Don. Small world, hey!

Stage Three

NORTH AFTER
CAPE HORN

Tuesday, 19 January 2010
Typhoon Jet Fighter and north again

After a few days of light winds, we're only just properly clearing the Falkland Islands now. The birds, kelp and shipping that I've been seeing a lot of lately are steadily becoming less common as we head out into the South Atlantic. I'm sure that it can be just as nasty as any ocean, but after looking over all the latest charts, I can't help being a bit surprised at how small the South Atlantic seems after the never-ending Pacific!

The other day while slowly drifting off the coast of the Falklands, I was treated to a flyover from an RAF Typhoon Jet Fighter. Even though I was expecting him, I still got quite a fright when he turned up making a pretty amazing noise as I was finishing my breakfast. He did a couple of passes, put a big smile on my face and then headed off again. Very cool!

After seeing the pictures taken from the two fly-overs, I'm totally thrilled at how great *Ella's Pink Lady* is looking, cute as ever! It's sure a credit to the many coats of anti-foul from International Paints that the hull is completely free of growth, and also to Ullman Sails that the sails are holding up so well and still looking almost new! It's great to have come this far with so few signs of wear and tear.

With Cape Horn being the subject of all my attention for so long, it's strange now to refocus and start thinking ahead to the rest of the voyage and the other milestones along the way. Even though it's all been very exciting and a total novelty, I'm also glad to again be clear of land and the shipping that comes with it. It's nice to be able to settle back into some sort of vague attempt at a routine and to be able to sleep better knowing that it's just *Ella's Pink Lady* and me again. Actually I don't really think that you could describe my random sleeping and eating habits as routine!

Even out here I've been hearing all about the terrible earthquake in Haiti, I can't imagine what it must be like for the survivors and for everyone working with aid organisations in what sounds like horrific conditions. My thoughts and good wishes are with them. It's great to hear about all the support pouring in for them from all around the world.

This stage of the voyage was always planned as a bit of a rest and recovery following Cape Horn. After all my reading I thought I knew what to expect at every stage but by this point I realised that anything could happen . . . at any time. All the emotional highs and lows leading up to Cape Horn meant I needed to recharge my batteries for a few days. I didn't realise how soon *Ella's Pink Lady* and I would be tested.

Stage Four

THE SOUTH ATLANTIC TO THE AFRICAN CONTINENT

Thursday, 21 January 2010

What I miss the most

Ella's Pink Lady has been steadily plodding along north and east out into the Atlantic and yesterday I was treated to a day of incredible sunshine. It was so lovely that I actually drifted off to sleep, sprawled out across the cabin top (of course, with my Ella Baché sunscreen on!). The warm sun and the sound of the water against the hull had me nodding off within minutes.

Better still, I was woken up by a pod of beautiful black and white dolphins swimming along next to us. As always they were a treat to watch, playing in the greeny, blue swell. Then there was the pretty pink sunset that I could actually enjoy while sitting outside without feeling like my fingers and toes were about to fall off. Sorry, I feel like I'm bragging!

Seeing as I've been out here for over three months and almost one hundred days, I thought I'd put together a list of what I miss the most:

Family and friends pretty obviously come first. Particularly my brother and sisters. Second is being able to relax without the constant feeling of needing to be ready for anything. Third would be sleep – long, uninterrupted sleep with no alarms and nothing to wake me. (That's how I intend on spending my first few weeks back home, so please don't make any plans for me!)

Then there's walking. I really miss being able to stretch my legs on the beach or anywhere actually. And food. Even though I'm still not at all bored with what's onboard, I'm often having cravings for various types of fresh food – a crunchy salad, any type of fruit, even vegetables. I'd give a lot for a good cup of coffee, as you can't do much with slightly gross tank-water and powdered milk! A long hot bath goes without saying and I can't even express how much I'd appreciate someone else taking a turn at washing the dishes for a change! Oh, and chocolate that hasn't been melted and re-set, I certainly miss that. It just doesn't taste the same!

It's another nice day in this part of the Atlantic. *Ella's Pink Lady* is reaching at 5 knots with 13 knots of wind. I'm off to put the fishing line out again. Something that I've neglected since it got cold. I'm not sure what there is to catch down this way, but no harm in trying right?

Turns out there was harm in trying! Only a few minutes after putting the line out a bird that had been circling high above *Ella's Pink Lady* swooped down and got himself caught up in the lure I'd just put out. As soon as I realised the poor bird was dragging behind us I pulled the line in but he was not in the best shape by then. I felt so bad about it that it was a very long time before I put the line out again. Besides Parker, and my stuffed-animal crew, the birds were my only regular company. I'd spend hours watching them swoop around *Ella's Pink Lady* so catching one like that was absolutely horrid. I didn't have too long to dwell on it though because pretty soon my mind was full of other things.

Over the previous week I'd had a few fronts pass through which had been forecast to bring some gales but had turned out not to pack much punch. I wouldn't say it made me complacent but when Bob sent through another forecast predicting a mild gale I didn't really expect it to come to anything. I was very wrong!

Sunday, 24 January 2010
Wind, waves, action and drama!

My quite sunny conditions ended with a bit of a bang. *Ella's Pink Lady* and I have been having a very interesting time out here. The wind had been expected to rise to a near gale, but none of the computers or forecasts picked that it would reach the 65 knots that I recorded before losing the wind instruments in a knockdown!

That much wind means some very big, very nasty waves. To give you an idea of the conditions, they were similar to and possibly worse than those of the terrible 1998 Sydney to Hobart Yacht Race. We experienced a total of four knockdowns, the third was the most severe with the mast being pushed 180 degrees in to the water. Actually pushed isn't the right word, it would be more accurate to say that *Ella's Pink Lady* was picked up, thrown down a wave, then forced under a mountain of breaking water and violently turned upside down.

With everything battened down and conditions far too dangerous to be on deck, there wasn't anything I could do but belt myself in and hold on. Under just the tiny storm jib, the big electric autopilot did an amazing job of holding us on course downwind, possibly or possibly not helped by my yells of encouragement! It was only the big rogue waves that hit at us at an angle (side-on) that proved dangerous and caused the knockdowns.

The solid frame of the targa (the frame that supports the solar panels) is bent out of shape and warped, which gives a pretty good idea of the force of the waves. A solid inch-thick stainless steel tube doesn't exactly just bend in the breeze, so I think you could say that *Ella's Pink Lady* has proven herself to be a very tough little boat!

With my whole body clenched up and holding on, various objects flying around the cabin and *Ella's Pink Lady* complaining loudly under the strain, it was impossible to know what damage there was on deck. It was a little hard at times to maintain my positive and rational thoughts policy, but overall I think I can say that the skipper held up as well as *Ella's Pink Lady*. It was certainly one of those times when you start questioning exactly why you're doing this, but at no point could I not answer my own question with a long list of reasons why the tough times like that are totally worth it!

So in the middle of all the drama, back at home Mum received just about the worst phone call possible from the Australian Rescue Coordination Centre (RCC), telling her that one of my EPIRBs (emergency signalling devices) had been activated. One of the knockdowns had caused the automatic EPIRB mounted under the dodger to turn on without me knowing. Luckily I called in only a few minutes later before anyone could really start to panic. I was pretty annoyed at the stupid thing for going off and giving everyone such a scare!

We didn't come through completely unscathed though, as there's plenty of minor damage, but luckily nothing bad enough to stop us. Actually I think it's a huge credit to our rigger, David Lambourne, that the mast is still standing and appears in perfect working condition. So other than the wonky-looking targa, the starboard solar panel is all bent up and the windvane is now sitting on a bit of an angle, but amazingly and very luckily, it still works fine (go Parker!). There are also a few tears in the mainsail and one of the stanchions is bent in.

Down below, the cabin was a total disaster zone, everything is still wet or damp. The dunny, which fell apart, was in pieces spread from one end of the boat to the other, along with other equipment. The meth stove won't light, but will hopefully fire up when it dries out a little more.

After clearing up the worst of it and despite finally managing some good sleep, I still feel like a giant marshmallow. Physically, my arms and legs are all heavy and pathetic and of course I have a lovely collection of bruises! Mentally, I feel like I've aged a good ten years, but I'm back to normal now and in good spirits as we approach the halfway mark.

When the wind had finally calmed down, I was treated to a pretty incredible sunset and as I was clearing things up on deck, a couple of dolphins stopped by, as if they were checking that we were all okay.

I owe a huge thanks to Bruce, who was completely perfect, saying just the right things on the phone every time I called in and also to Bob who stayed up through the night to keep me updated on when the wind could be expected to ease.

I could go on forever, but better finish up as this has turned into a novel of a post and there's plenty still for me to do here!

I wasn't that worried as the weather started picking up but when the wind instruments showed gusts were coming through at over 60 knots I started to realise this wasn't just another gale. I hadn't expected it, so by the time I lashed down the mainsail it wasn't done quite as well as I would have liked. I would come to regret leaving this so long.

As the waves were still building, I spent the first part of the storm out in the cockpit, hand-steering and then when it became too wild I sat watching over the electric autopilot as it fought to keep us running down the waves. The wind was freezing and thick with spray and it hammered in. It bit into any exposed skin and hurt.

As the storm got stronger I was completely mesmerised by the waves. I was just completely awestruck. I'd seen big waves before but this was very different. They were huge walls of water. I'd visualised them for years, pinned up pictures of fierce Southern Ocean waves on the bulkhead on *Home Abroad,* but nothing had prepared me for their power and their beauty.

Ella's Pink Lady handled herself as well as could be expected with just the little storm jib up but after a few hours my nerves were jangling. The storm kept building and I was yelling almost constant encouragement to the boat and the autopilot. If a particularly big wave reared up behind us I'd loudly call out a warning so I could be heard over the howling wind, 'Okay girls, here's a big one coming, get ready!'

As the wave's crest knocked us sideways I hung on to whatever I could and kept yelling, 'Hold it, hold it, come on, you can do this!' I'm not sure now if I was talking to *Ella's Pink Lady* or myself. As the wave picked up we'd surf down the face with me yelling, 'Steady, steady.'

We'd hit the trough and for a few seconds it would be quiet (at least quieter) as the wind was muffled by the mountains of water on both sides of the boat. I wouldn't have to yell as loudly as I said, 'Good job girls, good job team.' As I felt the boat start to ride up the next wave I'd shout, 'One more, just one more. We can do this!'

I'm sure the yelling did more for me than *Ella's Pink Lady* and the autopilot but by keeping my voice strong and sounding so positive I *almost* tricked myself into thinking I was cool, calm and collected rather than completely freaked out.

It was like that time under the table with Maggie, our pet bird. I was reassuring myself by putting all my nervous energy into reassuring someone else. Does that sound totally crazy? It might, but it worked. There's nothing like a good bluff and pretending to be in control when really everything is out of control.

After a few hours the wind kept growing stronger and the waves had become massive dark mountains with faces completely streaked white. The white tops were foaming and curling like they do when breaking on a beach. There was nothing else I could do on deck, and I was getting really cold so I decided it was time to strap myself in below to wait it out.

Down below, I actually thought the weather was dying down a bit so I figured we were through the worst of it. I called Mum, Dad and Bruce and was quite upbeat and chatty. I was nervous but also excited that we'd done so well. But then, after a bit longer, I realised things weren't improving and I arranged to do skeds throughout the night. With one eye on the instruments, all I could do was settle in and let whatever was going to happen, happen.

I didn't have to wait long. The first knockdown wasn't a bad one and *Ella's Pink Lady* was back upright really quickly. She seemed to shake herself off and then raced off down another wave before I even realised what had happened.

A few more hours passed between that first knockdown and our second. I cursed myself for not having the boom lashed down more securely and for not having checked the latches on some of the lockers better. They came open and spilled out objects, including the brick-like Toughbooks, across the floor. I wasn't worried about the Toughbooks (they are *really* tough), just myself and the boat!

The second knockdown was much more powerful and I had to really scramble to wedge my legs somewhere so I could brace myself and stop from tumbling around the cabin. The mast dipped well below 90 degrees and stayed there for what could have been less than a second but felt much, much longer.

The third knockdown was the one that freaked me out. I was at the nav table at the time, filling in the log book and trying to keep myself occupied when I heard a huge thundering roar. The closest thing I can compare it to is an aeroplane engine, only throatier and scarier. I just had enough time to prop myself before

Ella's Pink Lady was picked right up, turned and then thrown upside down into the trough of the wave. I was clinging on to the handholds and my feet had inched up the wall then onto the roof as we went over. Things were flying around the cabin even though I'd tried to get everything secure. I kept yelling out to *Ella's Pink Lady* to hang in there and that she'd be okay.

I would love to be able to tell you what was going through my head right then but I can't because there wasn't anything! I was in a numb state of complete disbelief. Once we were back upright I risked a quick glance out the companionway slide. I couldn't see that much and there was no way I could go too far outside to have a proper look but the cockpit was a complete disaster zone. The solid steel frame of the targa and its inch-thick tubes were dented out of shape and Parker was sitting on a strange angle. The boom had moved and had knocked big chunks out of the dodger. That wave had to have been incredibly powerful to do damage like that. I didn't stay looking for long, just in case there was another with the same force close by.

To say I was pretty worried after that third knockdown is probably an understatement. I wasn't crying or getting hysterical. I went into this very sombre, rational mood and started running through different options to the possible outcomes. I was planning what I had to do if things got even worse.

When I talked to Bruce it was the only time in the whole trip that he asked me how I was and I replied, 'Not good!' I told him things were under control but we agreed it would be a good idea to contact the local rescue authorities so they were aware I was dealing with huge waves and bad weather and the situation could get worse. After feeling the force of that last wave and seeing what it had done I couldn't believe that *Ella's Pink Lady's* hull and rig were still sound. I stopped myself from telling Bruce that the life-raft had broken out of its lashings in the cockpit. I'd managed to get it below, knowing that I'd never see it again if there was another knockdown, so didn't see the point in worrying him more.

Bruce had spoken with Bob (it was the middle of the night in New Zealand so they were really looking after me!). Bob had a forecast update and when I heard it my heart sank. According to his computer models the worst of the storm was still to come. I couldn't believe it could get worse than it had already been! I didn't want to dwell on exactly how bad it could get but they'd worked out if I gybed over and changed course I might be able to clear the worst of the storm faster. Sounded good to me!

Once I'd gybed, I strapped myself back into the wet seat to try and get a few minutes' sleep. I was cuddling the sat-phone so I'd have it close in an emergency. There was one more knockdown but it was more like the first than the last and didn't pack the punch I was dreading. After some time I was sure that the conditions were slowly dropping off despite Bob's forecast. The roar of the wind and thump of the waves weren't as loud or as strong. Thankfully I was right. I managed a little more fitful sleep as the gale slowly petered out.

The way *Ella's Pink Lady* came through those four knockdowns was incredible. It just shows what a great boat the S&S 34 is.

Tuesday, 26 January 2010
Australia Day!

Every year at school we used to get asked what Australia Day meant to us, this year I couldn't be much further from Australia. There's none of the things that make a typical

Australia Day celebration out here, no sunshine, no beach, no public holiday or barbecue. But this year I really can say I'm proud to be an Aussie, and how great it feels to have the support of the country behind me.

I've still got a lot of the world to see (a lot of Australia too actually) but the things that are special to me about Oz (other than all the cool scenery) is our relaxed positive attitude and 'can do' approach. I'd like to think that we're a country that's capable of coming together to tackle challenges, one that's capable of showing the world that we can achieve the things that we believe in.

So how am I celebrating? Well, last night I was pretty thrilled to get a call on the sat-phone from Prime Minister Kevin Rudd who offered to pass on a Happy Australia Day message to everyone from me. That's about all I need to make my day!

In other news, I'm pleased to report that the dunny is all back together (thank goodness!) and that the stove fired up again after drying out a little. Can I just say that, after enduring a few days without a stove, my respect for James and Justin (the guys who kayaked the Tasman) and any other sailor or adventurer whose main food source was self-heating freeze-dried meals has just gone up about a million notches!

So getting *Ella's Pink Lady* back into shape after our little battering has been going well, not helped by another front that passed yesterday, but luckily it didn't give us any more than 40 knots of wind. I'm currently waiting for the wind to ease a little more so that I can finish patching the mainsail and pull it right up again. *Ella's Pink Lady* looks a little worse for a few battle scars but more importantly is still as strong as ever. I shouldn't really be surprised as this is what we set her up to take and why we picked the S&S 34. Still it's nice to know.

I certainly can't complain about the miles we've been covering lately, we're flying across the Atlantic. I'm starting to worry that it's all going to be over and we're going to be home before I'm ready.

Well, I'm going to sign off and have a go at making meat patties with tinned mince for a hamburger. Then maybe even some cake or muffins just because I'm so thrilled about the stove working.

Happy Australia Day!

P.S. Congratulations times a million to Abby Sunderland for departing on her voyage last Saturday, I know what a challenge it is just to get to the start line. Despite the fact that there seems to be a lot of adults determined to see Abby and I pitted against each other as rivals, I only wish her the best of luck and am totally thrilled that there's another girl going for the record!

Thursday, 28 January 2010
Eastward

The temperature is hardly cold anymore and *Ella's Pink Lady* and I are now far enough north to avoid the worst of the nasty weather systems to the south (not that we couldn't still cop a storm anywhere). So it's time to start making some serious ground to the east. Go too much further north and we would risk losing the prevailing westerly winds that mean easy sailing and good progress.

With only 2300 nautical miles till we pass under the Cape of Good Hope and Africa we're getting pretty close to being halfway across the Atlantic already. Time flies when you're having fun!

There's really not too much new and exciting to report from out here, just that all's well. I'm still loving every moment and enjoying all the little things. I've been finishing up a few jobs from after the storm, and yesterday I made the most of some sunshine to catch up on some washing – the rigging and lifelines make a great washing line!

With everyone back home back to school (sorry guys!) it's probably time that I have a go at finding where I stowed my schoolwork too.

It looks like I'll be in this calm patch for a while longer so we should have quiet sailing and hopefully good progress.

 Jessica Watson's Video Diary – Day 103
http://www.youtube.com/jessicawatsonvideo

Sunday, 31 January 2010
Sunny, foggy and flat

I know sunny and foggy isn't your normal combination and up until yesterday I had no idea that the two could exist together either. It was certainly very strange, as one minute I had perfect sunny conditions and the next the sun was still shining, but through a thick layer of fog. A bit odd. The fog hung around for the rest of the day and night, reminding me of the foggy conditions we had at around this latitude heading south in the Pacific.

We've also had really gentle sailing conditions, I can hardly believe how little swell there is and how flat it is, which makes life nice and comfortable. We haven't been making the most amazing speeds with the light winds, but *Ella's Pink Lady* has been able to keep up a steady pace to the east. All this warm sunshine and easy sailing reminds me of the tropics and feels like a holiday!

It's amazing that after only a few days of quiet conditions so many of my habits have changed. Mostly little things, like leaving stuff out on the bench and sleeping out in the cockpit. It's actually quite a thrill to be able to sit a cup down for a moment without it flying across the room. I have to keep reminding myself to keep everything tidy and shipshape, as I know that this will only last so long.

Only 2000 nautical miles to the Cape of Good Hope. That's going to be it from me today as I'm keen to get back outside into the sunshine!

Monday, 1 February 2010
Life goes on as normal out here

Still more nice sailing for me and *Ella's Pink Lady*. Yesterday was particularly great with our speed sitting on an almost constant 7 knots all day. The wind has mostly been between 12 and 17 knots. Well, that's my best guess anyway, because since losing the wind instruments, I've had to resort to the oh-so-primitive methods of looking out the window and tying a piece of string to the rigging to determine the wind speed and direction.

These are just the sort of conditions *Ella's Pink Lady* and I love. Does anyone object if I give Sydney a miss and go around for a second lap? No, don't worry, I wouldn't do that to you. I might still be having the time of my life out here, but there's also things back home that I miss. There's no way that I'd be able to sail past a hot shower and I'm worried that if I'm away much longer I won't be able to recognise my brother, who is apparently getting taller by the minute!

We've also had more of the weird foggy–sunny combination. It seems a bit strange to record zero per cent cloud cover next to 'very poor' for visibility in the log book. But I do come from Queensland, so fog will probably always be a bit of a novelty to me!

Also, you may have noticed that we're heading north-east, rather than east again. Bob's got me sailing north some more to avoid a particularly nasty system passing to the south.

It's crazy to think that not so long ago it was a battle to keep warm, particularly my feet, layered in socks and tucked away at the end of my sleeping bag. Now I'm constantly being irritated at being woken up with hot feet! The fact that a little thing like this is annoying me gives you an idea of how nice things are out here at the moment.

So, life goes on as normal. Yesterday was a house-work (boatwork) day and there's always the odd bit of maintenance to keep me busy, like tightening the fanbelts on the engine and re-taping a few chafe points. I also seem to be able to spend (or waste) a pretty huge amount of time cooking. My powdered-egg omelettes are steadily getting better but my attempts to change or add to my Easyfood meals are failing miserably, along with most of my other food experiments. It's a good thing that there's no one else to complain about some of the meals I manage to ruin!

There is no shortage of ruined meal stories I could tell you about, but nothing tops the time I managed to make myself a packet pasta meal using diesel instead of water. Yes, diesel fuel!

I was humming away to my music, busy daydreaming while making dinner so not really concentrating as I should have been and I didn't notice that I'd taken liquid from the wrong jerry can and was mixing diesel into my powdered milk. I didn't register the strange smell or notice a weird consistency and once all the powder had dissolved I added it to the pasta and heated it until it thickened. You'd think I would have twigged but it wasn't until I dipped my finger in to have a taste . . . YUK!!

In fairness to myself, just before I started cooking I'd been transferring diesel and I'd had a slight spill so my nose was probably immune to the smell. It was still a stupid thing to do and I snapped out of my daydream pretty quickly once the taste of diesel hit my tastebuds!

Tuesday, 2 February 2010
Cruising along

It's almost starting to feel a bit 'same old, same old' out here at the moment, which is probably a silly thing to say, because now that I've said it, Murphy's Law says something's bound to happen! And it's not as if no action is a bad thing. No news is good news right?

It also looks like my quota of sunshine is up, which is particularly annoying, as when I was going through some lockers the other day, I came across the sextant (an instrument used for finding your position from the sun or stars) and I'm itching to get the books out and see what I can remember – that would be much easier if I could actually see the sun.

But that's enough complaining, on the upside, progress has been good still with lots of 6s and 7s on the speedo. There's a lot more birds around too, maybe because we're getting close to islands. I'm seeing some different types as well. The birds up this way seem to be smaller than the ones down south and I sure miss seeing those albatross!

Even though it's looking like we'll miss the worst of that nasty weather to the south, we're expecting to see some pretty strong wind in a few days. I'll be glad when this front is all over and done with so we can go back to heading directly east again.

P.S. It looks like I spoke too soon! I'd just finished typing and was sitting here at the nav station staring out the porthole (one of my more glamorous hobbies!), when I got a huge fright as a great big orange object floated past less than a metre away. It turned out to be some sort of fishing buoy complete with aerial and just avoided getting into a tangle with Parker!

Saturday, 6 February 2010
Bouncy and dolphins

Yesterday was a bit bouncy with the wind up a bit as we just clipped the edge of that nasty weather system to the south. My best 'Jess-timate' (this is what Bruce calls my often slightly vague descriptions of what the wind is doing) would be 40 knots in the gusts.

The sea is still over 4 metres which isn't particularly huge, but the waves are a bit messy and really rolling through with a lot of punch behind them, so *Ella's Pink Lady* is being knocked around a little.

The wind went up and down just as expected and with everything ready well beforehand, there wasn't much to do other than hold on and roll with it. Now that we've been through a few gales out here, handling 40 knots of wind has become pretty routine, just like the way tacking, gybing or reefing has almost become an automatic reflex too. But if anything, it's only made me more cautious than ever. Knowing that everything has been double-checked is the only way to get any peace of mind.

Before the wind started coming up I was treated to a visit from some dolphins – actually, hundreds of dolphins! There were dolphins everywhere, in every direction right off to the horizon. Long lines of dolphins leaping out of waves, dolphins shooting off down the swell, dolphins playing on *Ella's Pink Lady*'s bow and dolphins quietly swimming along chatting away to each other in small squeals and squeaks. I didn't know where to look and their visit came just at the right time too, as I'd been feeling a little bit mopey and frustrated, but the dolphins sure put the smile back on my face!

The dolphins haven't been my only company lately, I've also been seeing a bit of shipping recently. By that I mean three ships in the last two days, which is a lot by my standards.

When doing a galley re-stock from the stores in the bow the other day, I discovered that I'm running short on Pringles (I'm down to my last pack!), getting low on tomato sauce and fast running out of tinned fruit. On the positive side, I did come across a hidden stash of Nutella (chocolate spread)!

So just over 1500 nautical miles to go till the Cape of Good Hope, but we'll be passing well south and clear of land.

When I said mopey, it's not that I was full-on feeling rubbish. I was just having one of those days when I couldn't be bothered dragging myself out of my bad mood. When I was like this I'd neglect the sailing side of things and any maintenance or non-essential jobs would be put off. I would leave a reef in when, with a bit of effort, I could have had more sail up and I wouldn't call or email anyone except for quick essential skeds.

Suddenly being surrounded by hundreds of dolphins was a perfect pick-me-up and there was no way I could keep moping while they were around. It's impossible not to smile and laugh watching dolphins play and ride *Ella's Pink Lady*'s bow.

Tuesday, 9 February 2010

Flying fish, rubbish, no wind then lots of wind

We've had both very little wind and plenty of wind in the last few days. All made much more pleasant because of the tropical-feeling temperatures. I actually found a few little flying fish (which are mostly only found in warmer waters) on deck and got wet inspecting them. But I don't squeal half as loud these days when an unexpected wave gives me a drenching!

Along with the flying fish I've been seeing quite a bit of plastic and rubbish floating past recently, it looks so out of place and ugly drifting by on the swell. So, I've resolved to put a lot more effort into refusing plastic bags and using less plastic when I get home.

Yesterday and again last night, the wind was up to 35 knots which kept *Ella's Pink Lady* moving nicely, reefed down and flying along. Sunday started out being extremely frustrating when the wind dropped right out to nothing. It wasn't so much the fact that we were making no progress that had me on edge, but the horrible rolling motion. With a big 4-metre swell left over from the latest weather system and no wind to hold the sails steady, the rolling was extremely unpleasant and really had me in a bad mood till the sky cleared and the sun came out. That one little thing made all the difference!

I spent the rest of the day having a great time in the sunshine going through my extensive stash of Ella Baché products, giving myself a total pampering and ensuring that my skin got its share of attention too!

By the time the wind started coming in again I was feeling better than I had in a long time, definitely ready to take on the rest of the world!

Another ship passed last night and, as I often do, I gave them a call on the VHF radio to check that they were aware of our position. Despite the fact that I'd rather have been asleep, the ship's watch-keeper sounded really friendly, it was good to chat to him till the conversation came to a bit of a dead-end when I explained what exactly I was doing out here. I get that reaction quite a bit, apparently it must be a little too much for them to take in or something?

But to be fair to them, I suppose it's a bit out of the norm to come across a little pink yacht in the middle of nowhere disappearing in and out of the swell on a dark windy night. And well, I suppose it would be quite unexpected to be casually told by a girly sounding voice that her next port of call is Sydney!

So, time for a long-awaited update on this fishing stuff. No good news I'm afraid. I've been putting the line out every now and then but after a bird went for the lure and got himself tangled in the line a few weeks back, I've been a bit timid about it all. The bird got himself free but I felt so bad that I spent the rest of the afternoon feeding the other birds chocolate biscuits (I'm pretty into my chocolate biscuits so I think that gives you an idea of how bad I felt!). Seeing as I've only got so many chocolate bickies onboard, you could say I've been a bit scare-easy about putting the line out recently. But we've still got plenty of miles to go, so I'm sure I'll get my confidence back sometime soon.

That's it for me today, the wind has dropped off to 15 knots, so it's time to go pull another reef out of the mainsail to keep us moving.

Saturday, 13 February 2010
Outdoor office

Flat seas and sunshine for the last few days and I'm loving it, even if *Ella's Pink Lady*'s speeds are a bit on the slow side. There's been a few too many 3 knots on the speedo, not exactly glamorous but we are moving and with the sun shining it's a bit hard to worry about anything too much.

This is definitely an attitude I'm going to have to put some serious effort into changing if I ever decide to have a go at racing. Otherwise I'd be left at the back of the fleet every time the sun came out!

The other day I finally had the bright idea of unbolting the Toughbook computer from its place at the nav station and taking it out into the cockpit to get some typing done — don't ask me why I didn't think of this earlier! Sitting in front of a computer is a hundred times more pleasant when outside right next to the water. It's also far easier to persuade myself to actually sit down and get everything done. Apologies to anyone reading this while surrounded by four walls!

While sitting outside in my lovely outdoor office I had two cute bluefish join us. They spent the afternoon swimming around us, nibbling away at who knows what on the hull. It's good to know that someone's keeping the hull clean of weed. Sort of like a drive-through car wash really!

Ella's Pink Lady is moving nicely at the moment but we've got headwinds with the wind from the south-east which means that we're not quite making the course that I'd like to be on. Also, tomorrow or possibly later today, we should be crossing over the prime meridian. I can't wait to be back in the eastern hemisphere, then it really will feel like we're on the way home.

If the sun was shining I coped really well with no wind and I would take the chance to get things done on deck, check for wear and get on top of any maintenance. The whole way around the world I was constantly writing myself new lists and ticking off the jobs as I went.

Here is an example of a job list I wrote on 12 February:

- Re-stitch mainsail
- Top up fuel tank
- Tighten fanbelt and look over engine
- Re-stow bow
- Tidy cabin [this was always on the list!]
- Top up metho in the stove
- Tighten tiller nut
- Tighten autopilot nut
- Spray electrics panel
- Spray and check windvane
- Run engine until batteries right up and volt meter showing 'F'
- Work on book stuff

Monday, 15 February 2010

Drifting around

We haven't actually been doing a lot of sailing over the last few days, more just sort of drifting and rolling, sometimes backwards, not particularly exciting stuff. So we still haven't quite crossed over the prime meridian. We're sitting just a few nautical miles away from the eastern hemisphere and not able to get there because there isn't any wind!

I've been spending my time either in the cockpit hand-steering or buried in a book trying to ignore the rolling and it's pretty frustrating – very frustrating actually!

Not making any progress makes it feel like we're just wasting time out here. I've discovered that the best way to stop from pulling my hair out is to apply the 'refuse to let it get to me' strategy like I do for storms. Isn't it great that teenagers are good at being stubborn? Oh, and chocolate, that helps too!

The good news is that the wind is forecast to start picking up soon, so looking forward to that.

I was going to give you all a more detailed rundown on how *Ella's Pink Lady* is holding up, all the wear and tear, etc. But I'll save that for tomorrow.

The prime meridian is the longitude (vertical line) that marks out zero degrees longitude on a chart of the earth. This prime meridian line begins at the North Pole and ends at the South Pole and when combined with longitude measurements can pinpoint exactly where you are on a chart.

We were quite a long way north at this point, some might say further north than we needed to be, but the reasoning for taking the slower route and heading up north was that the chance of hitting a nasty storm was much less. It all came down to comfort and safety over speed. Oh, and the sunshine and warm temperatures didn't hurt. I needed a bit of a recharge and as a Queenslander I find lack of sunshine hard to deal with. The slow progress was a little on the painful side but if I had to choose between that or gales and cold I'd take this slower progress any day.

Wednesday, 17 February 2010
Going places and wear and tear

It wasn't too long after I'd sent the last blog that we started getting some wind and sailed across the prime meridian into the eastern hemisphere – thank goodness! After that, the wind sat at around 30 knots for most of yesterday, so *Ella's Pink Lady*'s been flying along, covering lots of lovely miles to the south and east.

I'll admit I'm not really all that thrilled about the south part, after having temperatures between 20 and 26 degrees for so long. I can't seem to get enthusiastic about heading south back into cooler waters, I don't think *Ella's Pink Lady* and Parker like the idea of the cold anymore than I do. It's taking a lot of correcting from me to keep us heading south-east rather than east. But unless we do head back to a more southern latitude it's going to take us much longer to get back home. So south and cold it is, reluctantly!

Anyway, I promised a condition report on how *Ella's Pink Lady* is holding up. Overall it's pretty good considering the miles she's covered. I mean, how would you feel after almost four months hard work without a day off?!

To start with, I suppose you could say that along with the bent-up targa frame, a few other scars and the odd rust spot on the deck and stainless steel, she is looking slightly weather-beaten. But the rigging, sails, sheets, etc. are all doing pretty well, with only a few signs of chafe and wear.

Parker, the now slightly crooked Fleming windvane, is doing as good a job as ever steering us, although he does have a bit of a habit of chafing through the lines that link him to the tiller, which means I'm constantly end-for-ending, or shortening them.

The little Yanmar engine has really proven itself and has never once not fired up first go, when I start it up to give the batteries an extra charge (out of gear of course). The only maintenance it has needed has been a quick tightening of a fanbelt, the occasional squirt of grease on the stern gland (where the prop shaft goes through the hull) and I had to drain a little water from the fuel filter last week. One of our local mechanics (Jim) fitted a special filter that separates water from diesel (we actually got some water in the fuel tank during one of the knockdowns, when we were upside down). So thanks Jim!

Since the starboard solar panel got a little bent up during that storm, it's rudely stopped contributing any power to the batteries. But as the other panels and wind generator are still doing their share and because we've still got plenty of diesel, this isn't too much of a loss.

Fresh water supplies are doing okay. I've got enough to last till home, using close to two litres per day, which is plenty for drinking, along with my juice. But it doesn't leave a lot to spare, so the fresh water is strictly for drinking and cooking unless I get some good rain and manage to collect some more.

Most of the electrical equipment is holding up pretty well against the damp and wet. Well, apart from one of my Panasonic hand-video cameras which got a little wet while filming some dolphins a while back, ouch! But the Toughbook laptop has more than proven itself to be super tough, after copping a lot of salt water and mistreatment. I'm down to using only one burner on the meth stove and have more meth than I'd be able to use in about three circumnavigations, so it looks like we over-catered a little on that one!

And the skipper, well her hair has grown quite a bit longer and as far as I can tell, she's as healthy as ever. Although I do wonder if my legs are a bit thinner. I still do various exercises for them most days, but I'm thinking that maybe I won't be running any marathons right after getting home!

Before I left I had a complete medical examination, went to the dentist and had body composition scans and blood tests. It is interesting to compare the before-and-after results of the body scans (thanks to Body Composition Australia). Overall, really not much changed during the voyage. As far as I was concerned I left normal and came back normal! I did lose the slightest bit of weight and, yes, my legs were the slightest bit thinner.

Date of scan	Bodyfat Percentage	Total Body Weight (kg)	Fat Mass (kg)	Lean Body Mass (kg)	Fat Free Mass (kg)	Change (+/−) in Lean Body Mass	Change (+/−) in Fat Mass	Total Weight Change to Date	Total Body Fat Change to Date
13/10/2009	24.1%	50.0	12.0	36.2	37.9				
20/05/2010	23.6%	49.2	11.6	35.8	37.5	−0.4	−0.4	−0.3	−0.4

Regional changes in Fat Mass	13/10/2009	20/05/2010	Change (+/−) in Fat Mass (kg)
Left Arm	0.57	0.53	−0.04
Right Arm	0.46	0.40	−0.06
Trunk	4.42	4.26	−0.16
Left Leg	3.00	2.87	−0.13
Right Leg	2.90	2.78	−0.12
Central Fat	0.27	0.27	−0.01

Regional changes in Lean Body Mass	13/10/2009	20/05/2010	Change (+/−) in Lean Body Mass
Left Arm	1.90	1.91	0.01
Right Arm	2.00	2.04	0.04
Trunk	17.80	17.08	−0.72
Left Leg	5.92	5.91	−0.01
Right Leg	6.10	6.14	0.04

Thursday, 18 February 2010

Four months at sea

Four months at sea today, but it still feels like only yesterday that we were leaving Sydney! It's almost a bit scary how fast the time has flown and how completely I've settled into everyday life out here. But I'm also really looking forward to all things land and home.

We've got pretty rubbishy, overcast and drizzly weather at the moment but no complaints as progress is good.

The wind is about 25 knots and because we're running pretty close to directly with it, *Ella's Pink Lady* is rolling and surfing a little uncomfortably. Not long now till we're back in the Forties and with the temperature dropping a little more, it looks like my nice, sunny Atlantic holiday is over. But on the upside, hopefully I'll start seeing a few more albatross again.

There's still the odd ship around. Another one passed pretty close last night, they were really friendly again and when I mentioned over the radio that I was a little uncomfortable with how close we were set to pass each other, they immediately offered to change course to give us a little more room.

Something I forgot yesterday was to give you an update on how the food is going. Apart from those few tragedies with the Pringles and tomato sauce, overall it's all going really well. I'm eating a bit less than what Mum planned for, which means there's quite a bit left over in each food bag, and I'm able to pick out my favourites and leave the not-so-good stuff. The dried fruit, chocolate, pasta, tinned pie, mixed Chinese vegetables and tuna are the first things to go and by the end of the fortnight, the pile of leftovers normally includes crackers, banana chips, dried peas and tinned beans. Which gives you a pretty good idea of my likes and dislikes. Anyway, to cut a long story short, it looks like I'll be returning with enough food to feed a small army!

We've got just under 600 nautical miles sailing to do to pass under the Cape of Good Hope. So that's going to be it for today.

Seeing ships after so long was such a novelty it was worth losing sleep while waiting for them to pass safely by. I'd often call them on the radio just to make sure they were aware of our position. The collision has made me extra cautious, possibly even over-cautious, around ships.

The watch-keepers all sounded very surprised when they replied after hearing my 'little girl' voice come over the radio. I'd politely request that they change their course and they never seemed to mind.

Stage Five

ROUNDING SOUTH AFRICA

Sunday, 21 February 2010

Quick update on some fast sailing

Lots of nice, fast sailing over the last few days. Now only 250 nautical miles until we pass under the Cape of Good Hope!

Ella's Pink Lady has been surfing off down the waves, keeping up a great pace in 25 knots of wind. Despite the wet drizzly conditions, I've been spending a lot of time on deck watching us fly along.

I decided to give Parker a bit of time off yesterday and spent quite a while hand-steering, which I really enjoyed. I still get a kick out of feeling us take off down a wave and I don't think watching the waves and birds will ever get boring!

 Jessica Watson's Video Diary — Day 127
http://www.youtube.com/jessicawatsonvideo

Monday, 22 February 2010
Almost around the cape and why I am sailing around the world?

I'll start with the good news, or I should say the best news, as there isn't any bad news today. Now only 120 nautical miles till we pass under Cape Agulhas (I've been saying the Cape of Good Hope but the most southern point of Africa is actually Cape Agulhas) and can officially tick off another cape!

The wind dropped off a little today and with it *Ella's Pink Lady's* great pace too. But we are moving nicely still and for the first time in over a week it was warm and sunny. After misty drizzle and grey skies for so long, sunshine feels particularly lovely! As there's a high pressure system passing over us at the moment, it looks like the calm sailing (fingers crossed that it's not too calm!) will last for a while yet.

So, anyway, while sitting out in the sunshine and hand-steering today, I did a bit of thinking (dangerous thing to do I know!). Seeing as we're now over halfway around the world, I thought it might be a good time to have a bit of a re-think about exactly what I am doing out here and whether or not my expectations have changed at all.

When I first dreamt of sailing around the world [as I told you earlier] the first thing that caught my attention was curiosity about whether or not it was even something that was achievable. I wanted to challenge myself and achieve something to be proud of. And yes, I wanted to inspire people. I hate that so many dreams never actually become anything more than that, a dream. I'm not saying that everyone should buy a boat and take off around the world, but I hope that by achieving my own dream, I'm showing people that it is possible to reach their own goals, whatever they might be and however big or small.

Now that I'm out here, I'm also finding that a big part of it is just about having fun and making the most of every day. And the other amazing thing is that it's no longer just my dream or voyage. Every milestone out here isn't just my achievement, but an achievement for everyone who has put so much time and effort into helping get me here . . .

. . . Also, because I always hated being defined by my appearance or my age, I hope that part of what I'm doing out here is proving that we shouldn't judge by appearance and our own expectations. I want the world to know exactly what 'little girls' and young people are actually capable of!

But enough of that, on another subject I managed to cut my knee on something today. A little bit of blood (pink and red do not look good together!), but nothing at all too serious, which made me realise how well I have done so far on the health and injury side of things (touch wood). All the salt water has never once given my skin any grief (not hard to guess why not – thanks Ella Baché!) and as time goes on I'm even managing to give myself less bruises.

Everyone's been telling me about Torah Bright and her amazing gold medal effort in snowboarding for Australia at the winter Olympics. I know I'm a bit behind the times, as news sometimes takes a while to reach me out here, but I'm just going to say wow and congratulations to Torah!

I spoke to Mike and Don that day – it was the most ridiculous conversation and they both teased me a bit too much! Chats like these were pure gold because it was a chance to have a mindless laugh and take my mind off what I had to do on *Ella's Pink Lady*. We'd chat about the silliest things. Once Mike and I spent quite some time discussing and comparing the features of our kettles and another time Don spent close to half an hour trying to teach me a rhyme to remember how many days each month has. Not exactly the conversations you'd expect between fellow circumnavigators.

Mike was planning to team up with Don to re-create Captain Bligh's famous epic voyage after he was cast adrift from his ship the *Bounty* by a mutinous crew and then had to sail from Tonga to West Timor. They were going to sail a replica open wooden boat similar to the one Bligh used and were taking no modern equipment with them like charts, a compass, lights or even toilet paper. It was an amazing and incredibly challenging thing to do and Don was using it as a fundraiser for research into motor neurone disease, Parkinson's disease and Alzheimer's disease.

It turned out that Mike had to have his appendix out right before the start of the trip so he wasn't recovered enough and had to pull out but Don left on 19 April 2010. In a remarkable triumph of endurance and the power of the human spirit he arrived in Timor with his three crew, David Pryce, David Wilkinson and Chris Wilde, on 15 June. Apparently Don lost 18 kilos during the re-enactment. And you should have seen his beard!

Wednesday, 24 February 2010

Another cape down and into the Indian!

Well that's it. Another ocean and cape down! It took a while with light winds for the last few days but *Ella's Pink Lady* has passed under Cape Agulhas, but being 400 nautical miles south of land I couldn't quite see it this time. A bright orange half-moon and a spectacular sky of stars was enough of a celebration. But of course, I also put a bit of a dent in the chocolate supplies and let off a few party poppers!

There's still so many miles to cover across the Indian and then around the bottom of Australia, but it really feels like we're on the homeward leg now. Only 4200 nautical miles till Cape Leeuwin and Australia, a very exciting and slightly scary thought! The lovely weather over the last few days has more than made up for our slowish speeds. As a high pressure system passed over us, we've had perfect clear skies, warm sunshine, gentle seas, plenty of birds and the odd albatross for company. In between a lot of enjoying the sunshine and contemplating how perfect it all was, I also used the quiet conditions to keep up with a few jobs and give everything a good double-check over. I made a total mess re-applying Sikaflex to the odd persistent leak. Also snapped another two needles and put a few holes in my hands re-stitching one of the tears in the mainsail, then threaded on new windvane lines after finally giving up on the chafed and scruffy old set.

. . . As always, good things can't last forever and with a front and some nasty weather expected tomorrow, my quiet few days are over for now. Back to reality and more typical Southern Ocean sailing. Hopefully we can use the strong winds to make a serious dent in the Indian Ocean!

Rounding South Africa was another important step in the voyage but it couldn't compete with the excitement of rounding Cape Horn. I'm sorry, the name just doesn't have the same zing and it isn't as steeped in sailing mythology as Cape Horn.

On the chart it is an impressive milestone but on *Ella's Pink Lady*, so far offshore, I had to work hard to create any sort of atmosphere and sense of occasion for the moment. It was mostly just another day's sailing . . . but a good one!

Thursday, 25 February 2010
Speeding, surfing and dancing along

It's my sister's eighteenth birthday today so first off, happy birthday Emily!! It's the second year running that I've been away, so I'll have to find a special way to make up for the late presents next year!

Loving the fast sailing at the moment. It's a bit breezy and the sea is up enough to give *Ella's Pink Lady* something to surf. She's really dancing along, climbing up each wave, surfing down and rolling with the gusts of wind. But it's not too uncomfortable with the wind gusting to just over 30 knots and the third reef in the mainsail. The sun is out again after a drizzly overcast night and morning, which means the waves are a lovely shade of turquoise blue and the streaky whitecaps look pretty, rather than menacing. I'm finding it a bit hard to concentrate on anything much at the moment, because of frequent glances at the log displaying our speed. I keep catching myself watching it, as our speed ranges from 6 to 9 knots and occasionally shooting higher as each wave rolls past. I think I may have confused a few people yesterday saying that there are only 4200 nautical miles till Australia, that's only till we're under Cape Leeuwin in Western Australia. Sydney's still a long way after that and that's not accounting for any of the likely zig-zagging around weather systems.

Stage Six

SOUTHERN OCEAN
TO HOME

Tuesday, 2 March 2010

Time flying by and heading north

Time seems to be passing very strangely at the moment – flying by in great chunks at a time, but then occasionally dragging minute by minute. But fast or slow, I'm still enjoying every minute of it all.

Right now it's perfect sailing, with 20 knots of wind and sunshine. Life onboard is same old, same old with the little ins and outs keeping me happy. As much as I'm looking forward to it, getting back home is going to be quite a shock, as I've really worked myself into my own groove out here.

One exciting thing that happened lately (exciting in my book anyway!) is that we've sailed onto the Indian Ocean chart that shows Australia on the far side. It looks so far away, yet so close at the same time. We'll also be passing a surprising number of little islands way down in the bottom of the Indian. I had no idea that there was anything down there other than endless waves.

Well, I'm off to re-stow a few things and do a bit of tidying up. As always, after a quiet few days sailing, the cabin has become a bit unruly. But a bouncy-weather forecast is far more effective at forcing me to tidy up than Mum ever was!

Friday, 5 March 2010
Day-to-day ins and outs

The last few days have seen a bit of everything. The weather hasn't exactly been all that strong, but it was a little uncomfortable for a while there as *Ella's Pink Lady* was reaching (taking the wind side-on) in a pretty big sea (5 metres or maybe a little more). And right now we're back to calm, sunny and slow conditions.

It probably sounds a bit strange and most people think it's the other way around but, believe it or not, light winds can often be one of the busiest times for a sailor. When the winds are light, it's normally very shifty, meaning that there's a lot of course changes and sail tweaking needed to try and keep the boat moving. When the weather is up, *Ella's Pink Lady* normally just powers along without needing much attention – and as the bouncy motion makes doing even the simplest things a million times more difficult in those conditions, I often just resort to reading a book while wedged in my bunk, in-between the few jobs that are necessary (like feeding myself!). When just opening a locker can mean the entire contents being emptied all over the floor, I find that it's often best just to sit tight and do as little as possible!

Seeing as there's nothing particularly glamorous and exciting to report just now, I thought it might be a good idea to describe my daily routine in a bit more detail. But when I started thinking about it, I realised that it wasn't actually such a bright idea, as I just don't have much of a routine to describe. With a few exceptions for things like daily call-ins, there's absolutely nothing routine about my life. Strange sleeping habits, strange moods, my 'eat when hungry' policy and – most of all – the changing weather, mean that no two days are ever the same out here.

Some days I'm all motivated and really get into maintenance and cleaning. Some days I hardly look up from the book I'm reading. Sometimes I'll be really chatty, make a few phone calls and spend lots of time sending emails, then there's the days on end when hardly anyone hears from me. One day I might sleep lots and the next hardly at all. Sometimes I'll really get into my cooking and sometimes I survive on Cup-a-Soups and biscuits. I don't even write in my diary regularly, often skipping a few days then making up for it by writing lots all at once. I suppose you could call me a little random! But more than anything, the weather has the final say and takes priority over everything.

So that's a description of my days. I'm still in great spirits and totally loving it out here. But I did manage to make myself feel pretty homesick and land-sick yesterday, by going through some pictures. It's not that the waves,

birds and the sky are ever boring, it's just that every now
and then I'd really love something new to look at!

People always ask me what I did with my rubbish out there
and the answer is simple, it all came back with me. Each time
I filled an empty food bag with rubbish I'd jump on it a few
times (weather permitting), tape it up and store it either in the
back locker or the bow. Two hundred and ten days of rubbish
sounds like there'd be a lot but there wasn't as much as you'd
expect because when Mum was collecting and sorting the food I
was bringing with me she stripped all the excess packaging off. I
couldn't believe the huge pile that discarded packaging made. It
really made me think about the waste that is built into so much
of what we buy.

I saw plastic and rubbish during my voyage but not a lot
because I was sailing so far south. Ian Kiernan, the famous
yachtsman and environmentalist, had been horrified by the
amount of rubbish he saw in the ocean while he was competing
in the 1986/87 BOC Challenge solo around-the-world yacht race
and when he got home he decided to try and make a difference.
With friends he formed a committee and they organised a Clean
Up Sydney Harbour Day in 1989. It was a huge success and over
40,000 people turned out to help. From there the idea grew and
the first Clean Up Australia Day was held in 1990 with 300,000
people involved. Ian Kiernan has shown what one person and
'people power' can do. His idea has now become an annual
national event and has also become a worldwide campaign that
according to www.cleanup.org.au 'annually attracts an estimated
35 million people from 120 countries including from Micronesia
to India in Asia Pacific; from Argentina to Venezuela in South

America; from Turkey to the United Arab Emirates in West Asia; from Aruba to Zimbabwe in Africa; from Greece to Poland in Europe; and USA and Canada in North America.' From little things big things grow!

Monday, 8 March 2010
Smooth sailing

Yesterday was just about perfect sailing, with 15 knots of wind, great speeds, clear skies, gentle sea and a lovely sunset to finish. Better still, today is more of the same and the forecast for the next few days is also good, as a slow moving high pressure system moves away. With the speeds that *Ella's Pink Lady* has been doing lately, I'd say that I'm not the only one keen to make some miles to the east. The temperature is a lovely 25 degrees in the sunshine so I'm getting about in a singlet and pulling on a light jumper during the night. I feel a little spoilt!

So it's all smooth sailing at the moment. Well actually, not quite. The dunny is giving me a bit of grief. Despite spending yesterday afternoon pulling off and replacing various pipes, it's still refusing to work, which really has me stumped as it's not exactly the most complicated or high-tech piece of equipment. Definitely not the most glamorous or pleasant job, but I can only keep trying!

Other than that, I treated myself to fresh sheets and a new towel today. Not exactly something to get excited about, but the thing that really hit me when I cut open the plastic packaging was the fresh and faint smell of detergent. It made me realise how few different smells there are out here. It's mostly just all fresh and salty sea air. I imagine that when I do get back to land, all the different smells will really stand out.

On a completely different subject, something that I've been working on lately with all the team back in Australia, is coming up with a title for the book (we originally had *Around the World* as a working title but it wasn't quite right). Finding a title that really fits and we all like is turning out to be quite a challenge. So we wondered whether you guys might have any suggestions as the time has now come where we have to pick something. I'd love to hear from you if you have any ideas!

Yesterday was Clean Up Australia Day, I hope it all went well. There's not much that I could do to help the cause out here, but I did make an extra effort to tidy up the cabin!

I had so many book title suggestions from all the bloggers, it was fantastic to have this feedback but it was still really hard to choose. I wasn't really sure what I wanted. I'd already had heaps of suggestions from friends and family but nothing had jumped out at me. One that everyone else liked was *Fearless Spirit* but I was anything but fearless and so had to say no. Of course I had fears. One of the messages I hoped that would come out of my journey was that it is normal to have fears, what's important is managing them and making sure fear doesn't stop you from experiencing things and pushing yourself. The notion of being fearless was all wrong. There was no way I wanted people to think I was some kind of adrenaline junkie, that wasn't what this voyage was about. When another title,

True Spirit, was suggested to me I didn't like it either. I felt it would be like bragging and saying that I was an example of true spirit. But just like the way Jesse Martin hated *Lionheart* at first, it grew on me. I wanted something strong and inspiring and couldn't come up with anything better myself. I'm glad now that I didn't reject it because even though there's no way I'd ever use the words 'true spirit' to describe myself, it is a great fit for the voyage.

Thursday, 11 March 2010
Sunshine, stars and sunsets

First off, a huge thanks for all the book title ideas. That was a pretty amazing response and certainly gave us plenty to think about, as well as a lot of laughs! So, thanks again.

Ella's Pink Lady hasn't been breaking any speed records lately but we are sailing along steadily. Yesterday was pretty slow but today's been better. The sunshine and calm seas continue, so we're not exactly doing it too hard. But when the speedo drops below 3 knots it becomes a bit of a test of my patience. It's not that I'm in any terrible rush, because I'm having such a good time still, it's just that it feels so much more purposeful to be going somewhere. The warm sunshine, amazing starry nights and lovely pink sunsets put me in a great mood, but add speed as well and I'm one happy girl!

Another great thing about the quiet conditions is that I've been able to leave the front hatch open, which is doing wonders at giving the cabin a nice freshen-up. It is really helping my efforts to keep the mould and damp at bay.

You wouldn't believe some of the places I'm finding little patches of mould. The damp works its way in everywhere, for example all the zips on my jeans have corroded into place which is a little annoying!

Finally, I'm relieved and pleased to be able to report that the dunny is back in action, the problem was some tiny bits of grit stuck in the pressure relief/air valve.

If I had to pick a favourite part of my trip it would be this week. Only a short time before I'd been feeling pretty homesick, but that week I couldn't have felt more different. After days of slight seas, easy sailing, warm sunny days, breathtaking sunsets and clear nights with endless starry skies I was in great spirits. It was my longest period of stable, comfortable weather and I loved every minute of it.

I never tired of clear nights watching the glimmering faraway stars but one of the most amazing things I saw at night on the voyage was during a squall back in the Pacific.

Ella's Pink Lady and I were flying along on a breezy night with a luminous full moon disappearing and then reappearing behind the dark patches of cloud.

It was very dramatic as the world went lighter, then darker and then the moon peaked out a bit more and I saw a silvery, multi-coloured rainbow appear. I had to blink a few times to be sure that I was really seeing . . . a rainbow at night! A moonbow.

There was no mistaking the perfect arc of colours caused by the brilliant moon shining through the edge of the rain squall. Since I've arrived home I have learnt that a moonbow is a recognised phenomenon. I'd seen rings around the moon before but never anything as beautiful as this.

I was never bored and kept busy with little jobs and maintenance during the day and then as the sky started to turn pink I'd drop whatever I was doing and settle myself into the cockpit with a pillow and something to nibble on, like a cheese stick, packet of dried fruit or bar of chocolate (or maybe all three) and watch the sky slowly change colour then darken. I'd sit there for hours taking it all in, looking up at the stars or out at the speckles of phosphorescence in *Ella's Pink Lady*'s wash.

I'd lose myself in re-living family holidays, adventures with Emily and my friends and make myself laugh remembering something funny Tom or Hannah had said or something we'd done; or dreaming about the future. During that week I really appreciated how lucky I was. I was living my dream and loving my simple life aboard *Ella's Pink Lady*. I have an amazing family, an exciting future and knew when this trip was over that there was a lot to look forward to back home. But for this week, I was content to be exactly where I was and enjoy every second.

Sunday, 14 March 2010

Still calm weather and some company

Nothing much new about the weather to report. It's still calm, warm and sunny. Lovely clear days followed by amazing sunsets. Our speeds have been slightly on and off as *Ella's Pink Lady* sometimes flies along on the flat water and sometimes just sits there, drifting forward ever so slightly.

Yesterday we found a flock of 'groupies'. These birds spent the day landing in the water next to us, watching us sail past, drifting off behind, then taking off to fly around in a big circle, landing next to us again. The birds' fascination with *Ella's Pink Lady* may have had something to do with the crackers and tinned vegetables I threw to them (yes, I'm very pleased to have finally found a use for vegetables!). But whatever it was that had them coming back, it was nice to have the company.

Talking of company, for the first time in quite a while the AIS alarm went off yesterday, warning me of an approaching ship. Our paths looked set to pass pretty close and as it was a lovely clear day and I didn't happen to be sleeping at the time, I actually welcomed a bit of excitement. I pulled the washing down, brushed my hair and turned the stereo down in anticipation, so I was a bit disappointed when they ended up passing too far off for me to make out the crew. Still, I had a nice conversation over the VHF with the watch-keeper who told me that they were also headed to Australia, to Port Kembla which is only just south of Sydney. They wished me luck before quickly disappearing again.

Later the wind dropped off and the sea glassed right out as the sun was setting, which was totally spectacular. The water was just like a mirror reflecting firstly the pink of the setting sun, then when it was dark, the stars. The silence was amazing. It was one of those 'OMG this is really happening' moments. But I could only enjoy it for so long before it became a bit eerie, so I turned the music back on.

Later in the evening I had a chat to Seamus, the pilot of a passenger plane passing close overhead. With all their cabin lights on I was hoping to be able to see them, but in the end our paths didn't quite cross close enough.

On another subject, I've been discovering that despite being thousands of miles away and in the middle of the ocean, my brother Tom is still finding ways to annoy me. On top of the usual collection of terrible jokes written all over my food packets (if you'd heard Tom's jokes you'd understand!), this week I found that he had replaced some of the usual treats in the food bag with a stash of salty plums, which he well knows is my least favourite food ever! He then responded to my complaints by sending me some not so lovely pictures of a recent operation to his toe. Aren't brothers just wonderful? There are definitely some things that I don't miss about home!

Our progress across the Indian Ocean chart is starting to look quite impressive. There's still a lot of them to go but the days and miles until home are really starting to disappear. I'm also expecting to tick off a lot miles over the next week, with some lively weather expected.

Well, I'm off to have lunch which happens to be self-saucing chocolate pudding (with cream and custard of course!). Then, as always, I've got a list of jobs to do before the wind starts getting up.

Wednesday, 17 March 2010
Not exactly comfortable

It looks like my quota of sunshine and calm sailing has run out. In fact, I don't think the conditions right now could be any more different to just a few days ago. We've got pouring rain, 4 metres of steep sea and gusts of 40 knots. Nothing too dramatic but as we're close reaching (sailing at about 80 degrees into the wind and waves), the motion isn't exactly comfortable and we're heeling (leaning over) quite a bit.

Sticking my head up above the dodger means a face full of stinging rain and spray and typing this is more an act of acrobatics than anything else, as I've got my legs up around my ears to brace myself, leaving my hands free to type. Okay, that makes it sound far more impressive than it really is. With three reefs in the mainsail and the little orange storm jib flying, *Ella's Pink Lady* is handling everything beautifully, climbing up and over each wave.

The weather is expected to stay like this for another six to twelve hours before easing again. So plenty of time to finish my book while safely wedged in my bunk! It's funny that every time Bob's weather forecast is for some unpleasant stuff, I still get a little hint of nerves. But once we're in the thick of it with everything as ready as possible, I'm back to being as happy as Larry. (I often wonder who Larry was, and why was he so happy anyway?)

This time particularly, waiting for the wind to build up had me a bit on edge, as yesterday we had the most brilliant bright red sunrise and you know how the saying goes; red sky at night is a sailor's delight, red sky in morning is a sailor's warning.

As well as the usual trashy, girly novels, I've really been getting into the travel books lately, which probably isn't the best idea, as the list of places I'm itching to visit just keeps getting longer and longer! I also came across the 'learn to drive' book, so I've started trying to memorise various

The damage to the stainless steel targa frame, the torn sail and my exhausted expression tells you how fierce that first storm was.

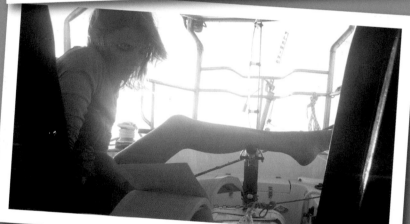

I was never bored on the voyage – there was always something to do. Things like watching amazing sunrises or sunsets, reading, talking to my fabulous crew, stitching up sails, cooking muffins and cupcakes and trying to catch a fish (I did, finally!), as well as everyday tidying and maintenance, kept me very busy.

Sailing through the Southern Ocean under Australia was probably my toughest time. Front after front came through, so there was some very challenging sailing. I made sure to really enjoy things like this sunrise and kept negative thoughts out of my head.

Once I rounded Tasmania I was on the home run, so I had fun sailing through the wild weather. The only bummer in that last week was the constant smell of diesel from my modified fuel line repair.

What can I say about my homecoming but...thank you! Never in my wildest dreams did I imagine I would receive such a welcome home. I was overwhelmed by it all but very grateful.

On my first night home, we had a get-together for friends and family. Also present were some of the biggest names in solo circumnavigation. Here I am with Mike Perham, Jesse Martin, Brian Caldwell, David Dicks and Jon Sanders.

My seventeenth birthday party. A room full of amazing people and a special night.

Now that I'm home I am looking forward to catching up with my family and friends, like Pamela (LEFT) and Mike (RIGHT), learning to drive and enjoying not worrying about the weather...until my next adventure.

road signs. It's not something that's particularly relevant out here (with a capital 'R'!) but getting my learner's licence is one of the first things on my list of things to do when I get home.

Well, as I wedge myself back into my bunk to avoid any more bruises, I just wanted to finish up by congratulating Shaun Quincey who arrived in New Zealand the other day, after rowing from Australia. I know I've said it before, but I'm a bit behind the news sometimes. Following Shaun's voyage has really made me appreciate all my luxuries aboard *Ella's Pink Lady*!

On 14 March 2010, twenty-five-year-old New Zealander Shaun Quincey became the first man to row solo from Australia to New Zealand. A sense of adventure definitely runs in his family because his father, Colin, had rowed the other way, from New Zealand to Australia thirty-five years before. Shaun spent fifty-four days at sea and I read on his blog he 'lost seventeen kilograms, went backwards for around twenty-two days out of the fifty-four and rowed nude four times (slightly overrated) and my favourite visitor was a Pilot whale'. What is it about boys and sailing or rowing nude? Jesse Martin talks about being nude while sailing *Lionheart* in warmer temperatures. What's wrong with togs?

Thursday, 18 March 2010
A bit of everything

Looking at the chart today I actually got a bit of a scare when I realised how close we are to being halfway across the Indian Ocean. All going to plan, as of tomorrow we should be closer to Cape Leeuwin, Western Australia, than Cape Agulhas, South Africa!

I keep telling myself that there's still such a long way to go but at the same time I can't help feeling excited about so much HVP (high visual progress). More and more of the familiar shape of Australia is sliding into view on the chart plotter screen as *Ella's Pink Lady* slowly sails closer.

The weather has calmed down since Tuesday and after dropping right out to hardly anything for a few hours the wind has settled into a nice steady 20 knots from the north-west. It's always slightly frustrating when the wind dies out right after a gale, because there's normally still a big swell left over. Trying to keep us heading in the right direction with not a lot of wind and quite a lot of waves means a lot of disrupted sleep.

I talked to Captain Nick of the *Queen Mary II* over the satellite phone today as they passed well to the north of *Ella's Pink Lady*. They were headed from Perth to Mauritius and Nick passed on the best wishes of all the Aussie passengers and left me thinking a little longingly of all the luxuries on board the *QMII*.

Mike Perham's book about his voyage titled *Sailing the Dream* was launched today in the UK and Australia. I was lucky enough to be sent one of the final drafts to read (I read the whole thing in a few hours then went straight back to complaining about not getting enough new reading material!) so I can tell you that it's definitely worth a read.

Oh, and I've just heard that Jesse Martin has been nominated for *Cleo*'s Bachelor of the Year in Australia. So for all the girls out there, come on, we need your votes on this one!

Jessica Watson's Video Diary — Day 154
http://www.youtube.com/jessicawatsonvideo

Monday, 22 March 2010
Sailing Ella's Pink Lady and islands

On Friday there was another front that came through, bringing with it close to 40 knots of wind again, but that passed pretty quickly. After four days of overcast sky, today we've got lovely sunshine and a comfortable 15 knots of wind.

The good progress means that we're now not far away from two little islands, Amsterdam and Saint Paul. So I've got my fingers crossed that the weather stays good so that I can pass close by and possibly even get a bit of a look at them.

All's well out here with one tragic exception. The lolly supply is running low. Sure there's still plenty spread out through the fortnightly food bags, but my additional stock for when I eat all the good stuff in the first few days (which is fairly often!) is down to just a few lonely packets. So now in the second part of the fortnight when I need a sugar hit, the only thing left to satisfy my craving is a sorry little pile of lollies called Goo-hearts, which taste about as good as you'd expect from the name!

A few people have mentioned that I don't talk about the ins and outs of actually sailing *Ella's Pink Lady* very often. One of the reasons for this is because quite often there isn't actually all that much to talk about. Because of her simple rig and because this isn't a race, more a sort of marathon cruise, it's a very simple boat to handle. To give you an example, I can pull all three reefs in and out of the mainsail (meaning that I can increase or decrease the size of the mainsail) without even leaving the companionway, and pretty much everything else can be handled from the cockpit. In fact, because I have an over-cautious habit of pulling up the storm jib on the inner-forestay whenever the weather forecast is bad and the wind rises above about 25 knots, I can actually claim to have left the safety of the cockpit in over 35 knots of wind only once. In an unexciting and not very dramatic way, that's actually quite amazing.

So, sorry to spoil all those dramatic ideas about me heroically battling with sails on the foredeck in monster seas and high winds, but this particular voyage is more about cutting down on risks, lots of preparation and sticking it out for a (very!) long time rather than edge-of-your-seat action sailing. That comes later!

Speaking of risks: Apart from a bit of zig-zagging north to avoid numerous passing fronts *Ella's Pink Lady* and I pretty much sat at about 38 degrees south latitude the whole way across the Indian Ocean. It was a fairly conservative sailing position but we were putting safety and comfort ahead of speed (I think you know by now how much I like my sunshine!).

Also, despite all the speculation and even a few of my own doubts before departure, there hasn't been one time out here (so far!) that I've wished I was stronger. I'd really like to say that's because of my huge muscles and super-human strength, but sadly that wouldn't be true. In fact it would be a very, very long way from the truth. The reason I find *Ella's Pink Lady* so easy to handle is because of the time and thought we put into setting her up and because of the kind of boat *Ella's Pink Lady* is. The S&S 34 isn't a big boat and its design is pretty conservative. The things you have to do (sigh) in the absence of super powers!

Anyway, having some sunshine again has been a good chance to get back to work at my de-moulding efforts. This time, I've been attacking the insides of various lockers, which has actually been quite good fun as I've been finding all sorts of bits and pieces that I'd lost or had forgotten about. The best find of all was my iPod, which went missing some time ago. It's almost like having 8GB of new music!

Wednesday, 24 March 2010
A bit of excitement and a noise in the night

Well, things did get a bit exciting the other night when the wind suddenly picked up with a huge swing in direction. One minute it was a quiet, starry night and *Ella's Pink Lady* was sailing along comfortably under full sail. The next minute the wind was gusting well over 35 knots with *Ella's*

Pink Lady heeling right over and taking off in the wrong direction. Getting soaking wet at two in the morning isn't exactly all that out of the ordinary, but this time with the southerly wind, the waves and icy rain were particularly cold and unwelcome.

After gybing us over, and once everything was under control again, I went back below and heard a strange electrical noise. It was the kind of noise that instantly has you thinking 'not good'. After a desperate few minutes emptying lockers trying to find the problem, all the while imagining all sorts of critical damage, I was very relieved to discover that the noise was coming from the little hand-held vacuum packer which had switched itself on. I had a good laugh at myself over that one!

The weather stayed windy and squally with the sea building up to 5 metres, so as we approached Amsterdam Island, sightseeing wasn't at the top of my priority list and we ended up passing well clear to the north during the night.

Maybe next time I'll get a better look. Both Amsterdam Island and Saint Paul Island sound like they have pretty colourful histories. All these little islands in the middle of nowhere seem to come with stories of shipwrecked sailors surviving for years, before being picked up by other ships. But the story about these islands that really caught my attention was one about a company that set up a lobster cannery on Saint Paul before going bankrupt, leaving seven of their workers stranded on the island. When someone eventually remembered the poor guys and came to pick them up three years later, there were only two survivors.

Imagine being forgotten and abandoned on a little island completely in the middle of nowhere!

The wind and sea have now dropped off again. Actually, I wouldn't mind a bit more wind right now, as we're not exactly going anywhere too fast. So it's time to pull out the patience hat till things do pick up a little more. Talking of wind, I was sorry to hear about the damage from the cyclone that crossed the Queensland coast last week and hearing about all the boats washed up and wrecked in Airlie Beach.

Saturday, 27 March 2010
Kelp and a seal

Mostly the wind has been sitting on a pleasant 15 to 20 knots pushing *Ella's Pink Lady* along nicely. But it has dropped off again and so has our good progress with it. There's also a big swell rolling through making the motion pretty uncomfortable and knocking *Ella's Pink Lady* off course. Just keeping us pointed vaguely in an easterly direction is taking constant adjustments by Parker (windvane). But the good progress over the last few days more than makes up for today's painful sailing.

We've been sailing past lots of little clumps of kelp in the last few days which I haven't seen since near the Falkland Islands.

Yesterday I glanced out the porthole in time to see a very strange fin sticking up in the air. I rushed up on deck in time to see that it was a seal lying on its back with one of its flippers in the air (sorry, I didn't manage to get a picture!). It's the first seal I've seen since being out here and I was quite surprised to see it so far from land. But then again, I don't really know much about where seals like to hang out.

Today's been an engine maintenance day but because there wasn't much in the way of maintenance needed, it mostly meant that I spent a bit of time cleaning and getting nice and greasy myself.

Less than 1400 nautical miles to go till we're under Australia now!

Tuesday, 30 March 2010

Big seas

We've had lots of good progress in the last few days but not towards Australia. We've been heading north again to avoid the worst of a passing front, it's safely past now but did give us – and is still giving us – some pretty big seas with some of the bigger ones reaching maybe 7 metres. Mostly, *Ella's Pink Lady* takes it all in her stride as always but the occasional breaking wave is a little hard on my nerves and makes for some pretty bouncy sailing.

When the wind started easing a little this morning, I finally put my head down for a few minutes' sleep and must have been pretty tired because I slept through my ear-splittingly loud alarm (well that's a bit of an exaggeration! After all, my head is still in one piece but believe me it's very loud) and didn't wake up till over an hour later to find that *Ella's Pink Lady* was rounded up into the wind (pointing into the wind) and drifting off course. One of the bigger waves must have snapped the windvane blade while I was sleeping and without it, Parker wasn't able to keep us sailing in the right direction. Luckily, I've still got a few spares so it was a nice easy fix.

Most of the time getting plenty of sleep isn't too much of a problem even if it is only in short amounts. Normally I wake up at least once an hour to glance at the instruments and check on everything, but when you add a bit of strong wind, any sort of unstable weather or approaching land it sometimes gets a bit hard to catch up again. I always know when I'm getting a bit run down because I start getting a tickly throat just like you do before getting a cold but seeing as there aren't any germs out here I never do actually get the cold which is definitely a plus!

When the sun came out today, the whole cabin was steaming as all my wet-weather gear and everything dried out. The wind and waves are still pretty big and strong through the day. Just hanging on has been enough to keep me busy.

I'm sure there's still plenty more weather to deal with and there's a lot of miles to cover yet but I can't help thinking about getting home more and more. Kinda strangely, the closer to Australia I get, the more I'm missing everyone. I'm already getting excited but just a tad nervous too! Did I mention how much I'm looking forward to going for a walk!

It's dark again now and there's enough light from the full moon to see the white tops of the bigger waves, feeling *Ella's Pink Lady* take off down the bigger ones is something I'll never get bored of.

It probably seemed odd that I was nervous about getting home but I was a little. I was told there might be a big homecoming planned and that was enough to give me a few butterflies. Then Andrew said a couple of times that my life would be very different once I was back. Just the fact that I'd spent the two years before I left concentrating completely on the trip meant it would be strange not to have that focus anymore. But there was another aspect to how I was feeling that is a little harder to explain and I hope I don't upset Mum and Dad by mentioning it. I was really looking forward to seeing everyone but sometimes, when I thought about it, I felt claustrophobic. I wasn't sure how I'd go settling back into living at home after having so much independence out on the water. I might not have been able to stray from the boat but I could do whatever I wanted to do, at whatever time I wanted to do it and was totally in charge of my own routine. Going back to sharing a house with my family was going to mean giving up this independence, for a while at least.

Though having Mum and Dad around would definitely mean my eating habits would get better. I'd become seriously lazy with my cooking and I was going through a bit of a corn and chocolate faze. Instead of bothering to make an omelette or cook up some lamb shanks when I was hungry I just opened a can of corn and then I'd finish off with a bar of chocolate. Sounds terrible, I know!

Wednesday, 31 March 2010
Too much or too little!

I still can't report any great progress towards Australia. This time it is light headwinds that are stopping us making any real progress east. I hate to be one of those people who are always complaining about either too much or too little wind, but it's starting to feel a little like that.

Last night when I gave up adjusting the tiller every few minutes to keep us on course, *Ella's Pink Lady* actually drifted around in a big circle. I'm not sure it's something to be proud of, but if this was a synchronised loop-drawing contest, we'd have easily taken first prize. It was quite a loop! Maybe there's a future for me being one of those pilots who draw and write things in the sky? Jokes aside, I'd really love to be flying towards Australia right now, but the weather has other ideas. So there's not much I can do other than wait it out and go with the flow.

As always, the calm conditions have been a great chance to keep up with maintenance.

Yesterday I got stuck into a bit of de-squeaking and while going over *Ella's Pink Lady* with a spray can, I found a few shackles that had worked themselves loose. So it was good to find them now while it's nice and flat.

I also treated myself to a whole bucket full of hot water for a bath yesterday, rather than just the normal kettle full. Talk about luxury, even if it did take forever to heat it all up. *Queen Mary II* has nothing on *Ella's Pink Lady*! There was even leftover hot water, so I was able to sit with my feet in it while brushing my hair. Then, of course, I finished up by turning the heater on to blow dry (I'd finally fixed the heater but my 12-volt hair dryer sadly stopped working back before Cape Horn, a total tragedy!).

The other day when things were still a bit bouncy with those big seas, I was talking to Dad over the satellite phone and he asked me to describe what the motion was like. It made me think about how best to describe it to all you non-sailors out there. I think the main thing is that you're not just moving in one direction and that the motion isn't in the slightest bit consistent. First there's the rolling, maybe like swinging in a hammock. Then add pitching (like on a swing), then there's the occasional acceleration as we take off surfing down a wave, just like you do at the beach. Add a few sudden drops and rises like a hyperactive lift and finish by tilting your whole world on a 45-degree angle. (Sorry, I'm struggling to come up with an everyday comparison to that one!). So sort of like living on a roller-coaster (well I think that's what a roller-coaster is like, but who knows because I've only been on one once and hardly remember it because I was completely terrified!). But a roller-coaster with sudden stops and random sideways jerks, add a bit of noise and a lot of water and that's sailing in 40 knots of wind and big seas.

And talking of the satellite phone, I wanted to put a quick word in for the guys at SatCom Global, who sponsored my Iridium satellite phone and also the Sailor 250 that I use to send my blogs, pictures and video. I mean you have to admit, taking on a sixteen-year-old girl's phone bill is a pretty brave and amazing thing to do. So thanks heaps guys!

Anyway, I'm going to finish up with some good news – I've got some wind again!

While I've been typing this, a nice steady breeze has slowly picked up and *Ella's Pink Lady* is moving along at over 3 knots in a south-easterly direction.

Australia, here we come!

Friday, 2 April 2010

Quick update and pictures

We're still not breaking any speed records, but *Ella's Pink Lady* is getting along reasonably well again. So all's well and the sun joined us again today which also did wonders for brightening my mood. It won't be long now till the high pressure system that's giving us these light winds moves off and we get some decent wind to give us a nice shove along.

I've had a busy day – making the most of the lovely weather to get stuck into some washing. In fact, I did so much scrubbing and cleaning that I actually snapped the scrubbing brush in half. Maybe I was wrong about not having super-human strength! And not to worry, I've also got a spare one of those.

I know washing isn't the most thrilling pastime, but seeing as I can't go for a nice long jog on the beach to vent my excess energy, I don't have a choice but to take it out on my clothes and *Ella's Pink Lady*. And even doing the washing isn't that bad when you're sitting in the cockpit surrounded by blue water, with warm sunshine on your back, a gentle breeze and a mix of music!

It was great to hear that Abby Sunderland rounded Cape Horn yesterday. I'm really thrilled for her. It brings back lots of memories of when I was down there. Go Abby!

Wednesday, 7 April 2010

A few ups and downs

Really sorry I've not updated you all in so long. It's been a bit of an interesting few days weatherwise. Also, a late happy Easter to everyone. It turns out that no one remembered to pack any Easter eggs for me but it wasn't the end of the world, because I've got more than enough chocolate and Mum challenged my brother Tom, sister Hannah and I to an egg-decorating competition via emailed pictures. I'm not actually sure who the winner was in the end, but it certainly wasn't me!

The sea never really got that big with the latest bad weather, but it made up for its lack of size by being short and messy, meaning an uncomfortable ride for me. This time, rather than just clipping the edge of a front like normal, the middle of a low pressure system passed right over the top of us, firstly giving us strong northerly winds, then dropping out to nothing, before hitting with a bit of a punch from the south. A change of wind direction like that makes for a pretty ordinary sea state.

Even though the conditions weren't at all the worst we've been through, for some reason or another, the uncomfortable motion and my damp bunk really got to me, making me pretty moody and a little homesick. Normally I can pull myself out of a bad mood in a few hours tops, but this time I didn't have the energy and managed to be grouchy for a full few days, a voyage record!

But it only took a proper meal and some good progress to get me back to my normal self and singing away (very badly) at the top of my voice to my current favourite song, 'Forever Young', while I was out on the deck in the rain with *Ella's Pink Lady* rolling along in the dark.

I haven't been the only one copping a bit of weather lately. The solo Trans-Tasman race fleet, including one of my biggest supporters, Bruce, on his 46-foot multi-hull *Big Wave Rider*, had a bit of a bouncy ride the other night off the other side of Australia. So far Bruce is holding the lead and sitting on speeds at least twice as fast as *Ella's Pink Lady*!

Today, I've been pulling reefs in and out a lot as it's been quite squally. With each line of cloud comes a gust of wind, then a quick dumping of rain before the sun peeks out again for a few minutes. Even though I've been getting lots of rain in the last week, today's been the only real time when I've been able to collect much water. Every time it's rained lately there's also been a lot of spray around, making any water I collect brackish. But I managed to get so much water that I treated myself to a full fresh-water wash. Having unsalty decks is also quite a novelty!

Australia's sure creeping up on us now. Less than 400 nautical miles and only a few more days till we're under Cape Leeuwin!

It wasn't so much the weather that stopped me writing a blog for so long, it was my mood! Looking back, that was the toughest time for me mentally during the whole voyage. I'd completely let myself fall into a black hole and unlike earlier instances, where I'd been able to have a cry and a short wallow for a few hours and then move on, I couldn't snap myself out of it. This time I was moody and blue for three days straight. Lucky I was by myself! I eventually got through it and started to feel better and I put this depression down to the wet and painful weather, which was complete rubbish. It was either that or the moon!

Thursday, 8 April 2010

Grey and overcast but smiling

Some bad news today. Something that has been threatening to happen for quite some time has finally happened. The handle has fallen off my only kettle! But it won't be too long now till I'll be able to pop down to the shops for a new one.

We're down to being just over a few hundred nautical miles away from passing under Cape Leeuwin, so sometime during the weekend we should be under Australia! The weather's been grey and overcast again today with a bit of a swing in the wind direction and a little more rain. Nothing too out of the ordinary just more sailing.

I really enjoyed speaking to Jamie Dunross today who's not that far ahead of us in the middle of the Great Australian Bight, sailing a bright yellow S&S 34 and aiming to become the first quadriplegic to sail solo around Australia. Apparently he had trouble getting people to take him seriously when he told them about his plans too. I know I'm a bit biased because he's sailing such a cool boat (go the S&S 34!), but if you ask me, what Jamie is doing really says that anything's possible.

I don't say it nearly enough, but thanks to all the bloggers, my huge adopted family! And everyone who leaves a quick message, I really appreciate all the support. Reading your comments every now and again always makes me smile, even if I do like to pretend that it's not me you're all talking about!

Am thinking about having chocolate muffins for dinner tonight, but that all depends on whether or not I manage to stop myself eating all the mixture!

I'm sure you would be interested so I thought I'd tell you a bit more about Jamie Dunross. Jamie started sailing when he was ten years old and he stayed involved until his early twenties. At twenty-two he moved away from the coast to Meekatharra in midwest Western Australia, 538 kilometres inland from Geraldton. He moved there for a career in gold mining.

On 24 August 1988, four days before his twenty-third birthday, he was just at the end of a shift and was cleaning out some equipment when a faulty valve gave way and released pressurised water that hit him in the chest. He was thrown into the air and landed badly. It was a moment that would change everything. He was diagnosed as a C5 quadriplegic.

Jamie's story is an absolutely inspiring one. He initially struggled with his rehabilitation and the suicidal depression that was part of grieving for his old self. Eventually, after some very hard years, he came to terms with what had happened and a big part of that was starting to sail again. He won a gold medal at the 2000 Paralympic Games in the Sonar Class and has competed all over the world.

Having already broken a number of Australian records, Jamie set out from Rockingham in Western Australia in his S&S 34 *Spirit of Rockingham* to become the first quadriplegic sailor to circumnavigate Australia. Jamie was in Sydney to welcome me when I got home, which was wonderful, and as I send this book to the printer he is about to round Cape York. You can follow Jamie's progress on his website: www.solo1.com.au, though by the time this book hits the shelves he should be just about home.

Jamie has an amazing attitude and says on his website: 'Life goes on. It's what you make of it that counts.'

Saturday, 10 April 2010
Australian waters and squid lunch

Today started with a lovely sunrise as *Ella's Pink Lady* sailed over the green line on the chart and into Australian waters. Hot chocolate in hand (yes, I managed to repair the kettle!), a light sprinkling of rain and an albatross circling above, it was one of those really special moments.

But we've still got a long way to go and over the next week we will pass under the Great Australian Bight and head south to Tasmania. It's very likely that I'll pass back over the green line out of Australian waters again. It's weird being so close, but still having so many miles to cover.

Even more exciting than being back in Australian waters was the fact that Mum, Dad, Tom and Hannah came out in a small plane that day to fly over me. They had Gary (the same photographer who was with them in Chile) there to try and get some photos. They weren't able to get as close as they had off Cape Horn because of some air-space rule or other but just knowing they were there was great. Chatting to them as they circled overhead felt just like a normal family get-together, which gives you some idea what we'd come to think of as normal!

At the time sailing conditions were perfect, with 18 knots of wind and a good-sized sea to surf. I was pushing *Ella's Pink Lady* a little harder than I normally would have, with a full sail up to show her off. On a broad reach we were flying along, almost dancing between the whitecaps. I was thrilled that Mum, Dad, Tom and Hannah got to see *Ella's Pink Lady* in her element (even if it was from a distance).

Mum kept saying how small she looked between the swells. It was a strange concept for me because *Ella's Pink Lady* was my whole world at that point. I was a bit annoyed that the plane couldn't get closer but I loved that most of my family were there. It was the perfect welcome back to Australian waters and the perfect way to celebrate the upcoming rounding of Cape Leeuwin.

I think a lot of people are wondering why I'm going south of Tasmania, rather than taking a short cut through Bass Strait. The reasoning behind this is that Bass Strait is full of shipping and islands which would mean a few days with very little or no sleep for me. Plus, Bob's long-range weather forecast also predicts light headwinds (also known as very painful sailing) if we take that route, instead of heading south around the bottom of Tasmania. So I'm just going to have to grit my teeth and put up with a slight drop in temperature again, before heading north for the last time.

I found a few squid on the deck again this morning. Another one jumped onboard just as I was thinking about lunch, so I got brave and decided to have a go at eating it. I opened a can of prawns (they could hardly pass as prawns, tiny little things!), sliced up the squid, all half a mouthful of it and made a sort of variation on garlic prawns. Then I finished up with Vegemite on crackers to celebrate being back in Australian waters!

Bruce and *Big Wave Rider* have struck light winds out in the Tasman which is pretty frustrating for Bruce, but I'm secretly thrilled not to be the slow one for once!

There's another exciting milestone coming up very soon too as we'll be passing under Cape Leeuwin at some stage tomorrow morning!

Monday, 12 April 2010
Lightning storm

... Things got pretty interesting for a while last night, when what I thought was just a light passing squall turned into a full-on electrical storm, the worst I've seen at sea yet. Even though I could hardly see it through the icy cold sideways rain, the lightning was striking the water nearby – much too close for my liking. The wind gusted pretty high too.

Ella's Pink Lady was already well reefed down at the time. But till I was able to furl almost all of the headsail away and pull the tiny third reef in, we were heeled over pretty dramatically. The wind soon dropped again and as it did, the rain really started. It was so heavy that you could hardly see where the water stopped and the sky began. A bit of thunder has never worried me, but alone at sea at four in the morning, it seems particularly menacing and it becomes a lot harder to keep your nerves in check!

Other than the lightning storm, the weather's still been really unsettled with almost constant rain, squalls and a messy sea. Luckily the wind hasn't been too strong though. Progress has been good and even with all this gloomy grey stuff, I'm happy as Larry and mostly staying dry thanks to my snug dodger.

Bob's forecast is for a bit of a blow tomorrow but after that things are looking a lot nicer.

It was really cool to hear that Bruce and *Big Wave Rider* held their lead right to the finish line at Mooloolaba and that the Sunshine Coast gave them a great welcome!

That's it from me as I've got a bit of sleep to catch up on. Fingers crossed that I can actually put my head down for more than ten minutes without something waking me this time!

Lightning at sea is really something . . . but not something good as far as I'm concerned! The flashes of light might look spectacular if you are safe inside your home but knowing that *Ella's Pink Lady*'s metal mast was the tallest, and only, thing around didn't help me relax whenever there was an electrical storm. I couldn't really do anything to safeguard the boat so I just had to stay in the cabin and hope for the best. In most storms I could be mesmerised by the waves and watch the rain and swell from the companionway but whenever there was lightning around I preferred not to watch.

Thursday, 15 April 2010
Headwinds and more lightning

The last few days have been a bit tough (yes, that's an upgrade from the usual interesting!), with strong headwinds, messy seas, lots of lightning and a few high-drama moments this morning.

The night before last there was a lot more lightning hanging around and it was much too close for comfort. This time there wasn't any wind and rain with it, which in one way made it even worse, because I could see how close the lightning was flashing into the water around us. One lightning cell after another rolled past, keeping my nerves on edge and stopping me getting any real sleep as I worried over it. Some of the flashes were so bright I felt like putting my sunnies on!

But after a few hours I decided that watching and fretting wasn't doing any good, so I dug out the most trashy novel I could find, put together a playlist of quite gentle music on my iPod and sat down to read with just one headphone in. (I hardly ever use both headphones so I can hear what's happening on deck. After so long at sea I pretty much sail *Ella's Pink Lady* by my ears, well not literally, but I'm constantly listening out for any little changes!)

After that, the wind picked up to 25 to 30 knots on the nose, along with a messy sea and pouring rain. That's not my definition of comfortable sailing.

Then, as I started to think things were improving, the wind suddenly started gusting like crazy, laying *Ella's Pink Lady* right over on her side and pinning her there. While I was having some serious fun (note sarcasm!) reefing in the cockpit (double-clipped on of course!), down below, water was flooding in up through the sink because of the crazy angle we were on. Normally I shut the sink seacock when the weather's a bit bouncy. But having thought that things were quietening down, I'd only just opened it again. The water flooded right through the galley then into the bilges. But *Ella's Pink Lady*'s pumps soon had it out again. I'm not particularly thrilled about my soggy mess of a galley. But far more annoyingly, before I managed to get enough of it down, the mainsail tore badly in two places. The wind didn't last long and when the weather improves a bit I've got a lot of stitching ahead of me.

Everyone's telling me not to let my guard down being so close to home. But believe me, with this weather keeping me on my toes, there's no way I'm relaxing in the slightest. I was beginning to think that I'd seen a fair range of different weather but this lightning has been something new. It's all part of the challenge though and will only make me appreciate finally being able to relax even more when we are safely tied up to a dock in Sydney. Oh, and a bed that's not damp, I'm really looking forward to that too!

I'm feeling much better for some decent sleep today and after a chat over the sat-phone to my sister, team and a few friends, I am feeling so cheerful that I'm not even too annoyed about the cabin being a soggy mess and the continued miserable weather.

Right now we should have a lot more sail up and could be going a bit faster but with lightning flashing in the distance again, the torn mainsail and all the drama of this week, I'm happy to just take it easy till things clear up a bit more.

Sunday, 18 April 2010
Slow sailing, stitching and fog

The weather's been much calmer again. Sometimes a little too calm, with the wind occasionally dropping right out. But the light conditions have been a good chance to get on top of all my latest jobs and have given my bruised and tender hands a bit of time to recover.

It's been a lot clearer today but the last few days have been quite foggy. Normally I don't mind a bit of fog because it's sort of pretty swirling and sitting in the troughs between the swell. But this time it was mostly just grey, damp and dreary. Is there any kind of bad weather I haven't had lately?! I'm starting to wonder what I did to offend the sun, it's hardly shown its face in weeks!

The mainsail is all stitched up again. I don't think I'm going to win any embroidery awards but it should all hold together. I didn't snap or lose a single needle overboard this time and only stabbed my hands a few times, pushing the needle through the thicker parts of the sail with my palm. The galley is also far more orderly again after spending yesterday afternoon emptying lockers and drying everything out.

Today I've been busy shifting a bit of weight around to keep us trimmed and sailing nicely. Now that I've used so much of my water and diesel, it's a job that would be a lot easier if I could step off to see if the bow or stern is sitting high in the water. Then I had a small mechanical problem to sort, a few other jobs to do and I swapped the headsail over to the spare because the old one was looking a little scruffy.

Ella's Pink Lady is getting along nicely with the code zero up at the moment. We're sitting on a nice 6 knots heading south-east. The wind feels a little cooler now that we're back south in the 40s again and I'm back to wearing my Musto mid-layers and socks to sleep again.

I was sorry to hear that Powderfinger have decided to break up. I got sent their new song 'Sail the Wildest Stretch' a while back and I have totally played it to pieces ever since.

Well, that's enough from me today. I'm headed back on deck with a cup of coffee and a jar of Nutella (don't worry, I'll be a good girl and use a spoon!) to see if there's any stars peeking out from behind the clouds.

My hands got really battered and sore during this last leg. They were almost constantly wet and the salt water stopped even the smallest cut from healing. It wasn't easy sailing so all the things I had to do to keep *Ella's Pink Lady* heading in the right direction meant I didn't get much rest and they were constantly tender. When I finally made it around the bottom of Tasmania a helicopter came out to find me so that a photographer could take photos. I was excited to see the chopper (though worried when it dropped down and hovered so close to the water, the pilot seemed to be cutting things a little fine!). I got out on deck and waved frantically, with a huge smile on my face. The next day, when the photos were published in News Limited papers, I was flooded with emails from Mum and my concerned aunties because they were worried about my hands. The bloggers were equally as concerned and when I finally saw the pictures when I got home I realised how sad and painful they looked. Not surprising really, it was a very full-on time sailing under Australia and around Tasmania and considering everything I was actually in great shape.

Monday, 19 April 2010

It wasn't a fly, it was a moth!

Every now and again when I can't think of anything new to blog about, I always get told that it doesn't matter. I could write about a fly landing on *Ella's Pink Lady* and someone would find it interesting.

Well, today a moth landed on *Ella's Pink Lady* and I don't know about you guys, but I got quite excited about it (sounds kind of silly I know!). I'm not normally into bugs, but this was the first insect I've seen in six months and seeing as the nearest land is close to 500 nautical miles away, I was pretty surprised to find a tiny grey moth sitting on the deck. Don't ask me what such a delicate looking creature is doing this far offshore.

Anyway moving on!

You might be more interested to know that yesterday 18 April marked six months at sea for *Ella's Pink Lady* and me, plus of course everyone else virtually tagging along! It's pretty amazing to think it's been six months since I've seen another person, but it still feels like just the other day that we sailed out of Sydney.

Time has really flown!

I certainly wasn't complaining about the way the voyage had gone. In that first stage I couldn't believe how quickly we had covered so much distance. Originally we'd estimated that I'd sail 23,000 nautical miles and be at sea for approximately 230 days. We'd projected that I needed to sail an average 100 nautical miles a day or 4.2 knots. By the time I got home we'd ended up sailing a total of 24,285 nautical miles and took 210 days so we averaged 115.6 nautical miles per day or 4.8 knots. I am really proud of how close our predictions were and of how the whole trip went. All our research and preparation paid off and it reinforced what James and Justin, the 'crossing the ditch' boys, had told me right from the beginning – preparation is two-thirds of the voyage. My trip was very different from theirs but the same principle applies: hard work and good preparation is the key to any success.

The wind has been really light still, so progress has been really unimpressive. Is it just me or is this last leg really taking forever? Not that I mind all that much. I still love it out here and as much as I'm looking forward to a million land things, I'm also going to miss so many things about being out here.

For most of today there's been no wind at all. So to stop myself from getting frustrated, I turned off the instruments so I couldn't see how depressingly slow we were going and decided to have a go at replacing the wind generator (which hasn't been working lately) with the spare one. I wasn't going to bother replacing it because I've got enough diesel to run the engine (out of gear), to keep the batteries topped up, but I was looking for something to keep me busy and I had plenty of energy to burn. It took all afternoon and manoeuvring it into place was enough of a challenge, that I hardly noticed the glassy water and the fact that we were hardly moving. The sun even came out for a few hours, so it was well worth the effort, even just for the scene at the end of the achievement.

I've still got to dismantle the old generator for stowing it, so I better finish up and get back to work!

Wednesday, 21 April 2010
Good sailing

I'm happy to report that yesterday we finally made some good progress and today's been a good day's sailing too. It's amazing how much closer Sydney looks when we're moving. And wow, we're starting to get close too!

So, nothing too new or exciting to report, just lots of flying along with the occasional patch of sunshine and life as normal on *Ella's Pink Lady*.

Something I'm not too thrilled about though is the forecast for the next week. It's not going to be the easy sailing that I asked for. Hopefully nothing too bad but not exactly walk in the park stuff either. Okay, 'walk in the park' isn't really the best expression to use, but you get the picture!

I had to give myself a good talking to after reading Bob's latest forecast. I'd been hoping that was the last of the nasty stuff. Oh well, I've only got to keep up the whole 'pretending to be tough' thing for a little while longer!

I hear someone (Granddad Chisholm!) has been stirring things up on both sides of the Tasman over whether I'm a Kiwi or an Aussie. Apparently New Zealand's trying to claim me! I don't think that anything I say will make the slightest difference on this one, but I will say that I do have both Australian and New Zealand passports.

Australia's home to me (sorry Granddad!) but my trusty first mate is a stuffed Kiwi!

Saturday, 24 April 2010

Knockdown, huge seas and a buzz from customs

Despite the fact that today started with a knockdown, a wet bunk, a headache and some pretty huge seas, I've had a great day. I know the words 'knockdown' and 'great' don't belong in the same sentence, but right now I'm feeling better than I have all week. And I don't mean that I've been feeling lousy all week, I mean that right now I've got sore cheeks from smiling all afternoon.

The wind started coming up yesterday and sat on about 35 knots all night with maybe the odd gust reaching close to 40, which isn't really a big deal with *Ella's Pink Lady* sailing under just the storm jib, because I was being extra conservative (i.e. my nerves weren't really feeling up to any fast surfing!).

It was the swell that got interesting. The big seas were from a nasty low pressure system passing to the south, and although we missed most of its wind, we sure copped some swell. Probably the biggest I've seen so far (the sea during that storm in the Atlantic was nastier though, because it was steeper and more closely spaced). These swells were 10-metre liquid mountains, rolling past with tumbling white tops. *Ella's Pink Lady* was handling it all beautifully though, and when we were knocked down just after it got light this morning, I'd actually started relaxing because the wind and sea had already started easing.

I was in my bunk asleep this time when we went over and was woken up when various objects and a whole lot of water landed on top of me. Seriously, whatever happened to gently shaking someone awake and handing them a cup of coffee?

Anyway it wasn't too bad as far as knockdowns go. I'd say the mast only just touched the water and there wasn't any damage. But having a whole lot of bilge water in my bunk didn't have me thrilled. Annoyingly, I'd only just turned the outside cameras off half an hour before. If the cameras had been on just a little longer, you could well have been watching this instead of reading about it.

After *Ella's Pink Lady* picked herself back up I figured there wasn't anything I could do till things calmed down a bit more, so I put my wet-weather gear on, pulled up the hood and climbed back into my soaking bunk. It doesn't compare to comfy PJs (pyjamas) and a soft double bed with fresh sheets, but I couldn't have slept better!

When I got up again, the sun was shining and the sea had dropped off some more but was still spectacular. Totally amazing to watch from under the dodger, which was what I was doing when the wind generator suddenly started roaring like crazy. I quickly climbed out into the cockpit to see that the roaring wasn't coming from the wind genny, but from a plane just overhead!

It was the Australian customs sent to investigate the suspicious looking pink boat. Nah, just kidding. They were on a routine flight and dropped by to say 'hi' and to remind me to check in with the appropriate authorities when I reach Sydney, which seems kinda strange, seeing as I haven't stopped anywhere. But I suppose it's regulation and my shore team has all that under control.

After that, with some more sail up as the wind kept dropping, I had a really fun afternoon hand-steering in the sunshine, surfing along and taking in the amazing sea. The rest of the week isn't going to be any easier, with another front and low pressure system expected, but unlike a few days ago, I'm not dreading it anymore. Just looking forward to getting down under Tasmania and doing some fast sailing.

It's Anzac Day tomorrow so I'll make a special effort to watch the sunrise, take a minute to think about all our soldiers away from home and maybe I'll have a crack at making some Anzac biscuits.

If I hadn't burnt the Anzac biscuits they would have been yummy. I still ate them though! Here's my recipe:

½ cup multigrain bread mix (instead of flour, because the weather was still too bouncy to go digging around in the bow storage – it worked surprisingly well)

⅓ cup shredded coconut

⅓ cup sugar

¾ cup rolled oats

4 tablespoons tinned butter

2 tablespoons golden syrup

½ teaspoon baking soda dissolved in boiling water.

1. Mix the dry ingredients together in a bowl with a rubber non-skid bottom!
2. Melt the butter and golden syrup together then add the baking soda liquid and mix.
3. Mix the wet ingredients into the dry.

4. Bake in a pot on a few layers of tin foil with the lid on and be sure to place only a small amount of mixture on each paper doily otherwise you'll end up with one big biscuit (actually, not such a bad thing if it isn't burnt).

Making the biscuits distracted me from the weather for a while but it was a bit of a balancing act at times. Opposite is a weather chart (courtesy of the Australian Bureau of Meteorology) that shows you the systems that were rolling around the bottom of Australia through the Southern Ocean at the time. The spiky arrows show the passing fronts and, as a general rule, where the curved lines (or isobars) are close together the wind is stronger.

Wednesday, 28 April 2010
Stalling and over again

Saturday's front went through with only 35 knots of wind and without a hitch, but this low pressure system passing down south is making life pretty interesting right now. Make that very interesting and very, very annoying!

With the forecast looking worse and worse on Monday and after a lot of umming and ahhing and discussion with Bruce and all the team, I decided to stall and stick up north for a few days till the worst of the weather has passed down under Tasmania.

Saying we were umming and ahhing is actually a bit of an understatement. The pressure of deciding whether to cut through Bass Strait or to stick to the plan and sail under Tasmania was

doing my head in. Knowing that the weather patterns were not going to make it easy, I was really tempted to go through the Strait, but once I thought about it properly there was really only one decision I could make. I'd always said I was going to sail under four capes – Cape Horn, Cape Good Hope, Cape Leeuwin and the South-East Cape of Tasmania. Despite the battering we were getting, I was going to finish what I'd set out to do. I knew I would always regret it if I had the ability and the boat was up for it and yet I took the easy way!

With Bass Strait right there in front of us, taking a short cut through it and out of the weather had to be considered too. But it was decided that the safest thing to do was to just hang about waiting for it to pass before heading for the bottom of Tasmania again. I don't think there was really any choice, it just took me a while to get over being annoyed and accept that I was going to have to hang about and wait a little while longer before getting to Sydney and having a hot shower!

And last night things sure got interesting. I put out the drogue (a parachute-like thing that you trail behind the boat to slow you down in really big seas) to stop us losing too much ground and to stop us being knocked down. The wind gusted at 55 knots and the sea was (and still is!) a total, gigantic mess, with 8- to 12-metre swells. Although the wind is easing now, the sea's still rising.

Riding out the weather with the drogue out was a lot like my first gale in *Ella's Pink Lady* because of the new motion and all the new noises. It didn't make for the most relaxing night as I played around with the bridle to try to get us sitting at the right angle to the waves. Then when I did put my head down for a bit of sleep we were knocked down again when the lashing came off the tiller and a big wave caught us on the side.

This time we went more than 90 degrees over, portside (left) down for a change. No damage again but this time my big bottle of dishwashing liquid worked its way out of the locker and went flying, emptying its contents absolutely everywhere! The whole cabin including the keyboard I'm typing on is covered in sticky, slippery, bubbly lemon-fresh washing-up liquid – lovely. Mum reckons that I have some sort of obsession with cleaning! And I'm starting to wonder why I bother drying and tidying the cabin anymore, as it never lasts.

It's still going to be some time before the sea drops off and we're able to head south, which is going to delay my arrival date back. But on the upside, these waves are just amazing. I spent years dreaming about what waves like this looked like and they are ten times more incredible than I'd ever imagined. I just can't believe I sailed the whole way around the world to see them when here they are right in my own backyard!

I was sorry to hear about Abby having to pull in to Cape Town for repairs. But like Abby said so well in her blog the other day, in one way it's great that we're now aiming for slightly different records, so that we don't have to be competing with each other. I'm also totally jealous that she's probably going to beat me to a hot shower!

I ended up with a fat lip, blood everywhere and a black eye after throwing the drogue out before that latest knockdown. I was always pretty sore and sorry physically for a few days after any intense weather. Just trying to stay upright was a complete workout.

After a knockdown I could always tell exactly how far we went over by the way the various flying objects ended up arranging themselves in the cabin once we righted ourselves. No matter how well I tidied up and prepared before a storm, things always worked themselves loose and ended up in the strangest places. During that storm in the Atlantic I could tell the exact angle we were knocked over to by the . . . well, I don't like to tell you because it is a bit gross! Let's just say there was a brown line on the roof above the dunny! Luckily this time it was only dishwashing liquid that ended up dripping from the roof and running down the walls.

Some of the random places I found things wedged really showed how *Ella's Pink Lady* was thrown around. She really was a tough boat!

During the Atlantic knockdowns a packet of yoghurt balls split open. They drove me crazy rolling madly around the cabin while I was strapped into the dry seat holding on tight and couldn't do anything about it. For weeks after that I kept finding yoghurt balls in the most obscure places. One had moulded itself to the struts of the stove where it swung into the cupboard below. I couldn't believe it when I found another one in a pile of socks stored in the bow.

I never got to see the actual waves that knocked us down and I kind of regret that. They must have been amazing, and who knows exactly how big they were!

Thursday, 29 April 2010

Taking it as it comes

The swell is still pretty big but overall conditions are much more pleasant today. The drogue got winched in at dawn which turned out to be a lot easier than I was expecting and since then *Ella's Pink Lady*'s been flying across the waves with only a little sail up. I've been catching up on a bit of sleep today, recharging my batteries while I can.

So that was the good news. The bad news is that there's MORE rubbish weather headed our way. After looking at the weather charts showing this new low pressure system expected over the weekend, I'll admit I had to dig real deep to stay cool about it all. Right now I've got more than a few bruises and sore muscles. Overall I feel pretty drained and would kill for some easy sailing, but seeing as that's not what I'm going to get, I'm just going to have to toughen up some more and deal with it!

It helps a lot knowing that *Ella's Pink Lady* was built to take this and having Bob's great weather updates. As long as I keep myself fed and rested, there's no reason that I can't take anything on. Also, for one reason or another, it really does help knowing that there's tonnes of people thinking of me out here, so thanks guys!

Things were pretty tough at this point. Ever since we'd reached Cape Leeuwin we'd been hammered almost non-stop by front after front as the nasty set of low pressure systems passed to the south.

When another forecast came through from Bob predicting yet another gale and possible gusts of over 65 knots and 11-metre seas I wasn't happy at all! I was already stretched thin and this felt like the final kick in the guts. If there'd been an easy option right then I might just have taken it. After I got that forecast I spent half an hour moping and let loose a few tears feeling sorry for myself. I just wanted a hug from someone and to be looked after. I was missing home and was completely fed up with the salty moist air that coated everything. After a while I started to get a bit annoyed and then I got angry at the conditions but mostly at the way I was letting it all get to me. I decided I wasn't going to finish my trip being miserable and that I just had to toughen up some more and deal with it.

There is a quote that I love from Bethany Hamilton. Bethany was an up-and-coming surfer when she was attacked by a 14-foot tiger shark at her home break in Hawaii. She was fourteen. She had her left arm ripped off just below the shoulder but was back in the water surfing only a month later. She is now twenty years old and is a professional surfer. Bethany is one gutsy woman and she says: 'Courage, sacrifice, determination, commitment, toughness, heart, talent, guts. That's what little girls are made of; the heck with sugar and spice.'

I was going to take Bethany's words to heart. I was still scared and still fed up and I would definitely have taken an easy option if there had been one but I knew I was tougher than anything the Southern Ocean could throw at me so all I had to do was get on with it. That meant pushing *Ella's Pink Lady* as hard as possible to try and get around the bottom of Tasmania before the worst of the low pressure system hit us.

Monday, 3 May 2010

The last cape!

Good news. *Ella's Pink Lady* and I have made it around the South East Cape of Tasmania and we're now headed north on the final leg to Sydney! We passed well clear of land, in the dark and with not the nicest conditions. But I still got a big kick out of it.

I never expected rounding Tasmania would be much of a big deal, but all of last week's struggles made finally getting around the cape ten times sweeter. (Insider's tip: Jumping up and down in a 5-metre swell isn't a good idea. Ouch!) There's no letting my guard down yet, but it's great to be back in more familiar waters.

I'm also thrilled to be heading north into warmer temperatures again. Okay, so it's not really that cold down here, mostly I'm just complaining. But when you're working on deck with a bit of water on your hands, this wind only takes a few minutes to make them go numb.

After all my worrying, this time we got lucky and the expected weather didn't get as bad as it might have. It's been pretty breezy for the last few days, but only gusted to not much more than 40 knots last night. The wind is sitting on about 25 knots at the moment and the swells are starting to die off as we pass into the lee of Tasmania.

Tuesday, 4 May 2010

A day off, headwinds and what next?

Yesterday I finally got the day I've wanted for a long time: clear skies, small seas and light winds. What a novelty not to have to hang on for dear life 24/7. Well, that's a slight exaggeration but, still, it was a real treat.

First off I had the best sleep I've had in a long time and was eventually woken up mid morning by a friendly voice over the VHF radio as another customs plane dropped by to say 'hi'. I spent the rest of the day being really lazy with the sailing side of things.

Instead, I caught up on a few jobs in the sunshine, got some washing done and gave myself a pampering with all my Ella Baché goodies. I'm not just saying this because they're my sponsor. Ella Baché really has some amazing products. It says a lot that after six months of salt and wind, my skin is better than it's ever been! I highly recommend their sunscreens and after-sun products.

I so needed that day off all right! Just like after Cape Horn, once I'd rounded the cape and cleared Eddystone Rock (a 30-metre high, strange-shaped island just off the South East Cape) I could hardly keep my eyes open. It wasn't a place where I could afford to let down my guard so I had to recharge quickly. This area of Tasmania is famous with surfers for the secret reef breaks that can see huge waves roll in from the Southern Ocean. After the wild seas coming under the Great Australian Bight *Ella's Pink Lady* and I had had quite enough surfing to last us a while!

Today the wind was back, but right on *Ella's Pink Lady*'s bow so progress wasn't great. Still, no complaints. Sydney sure looks close from this side of Tasmania which has got me really excited about being so close to finishing.

But it is also a big reminder for me to make the most of my last days out here. I always said that by halfway around the world I'd have a pretty good idea of what I want to do next, but it turns out that I was wrong. Here I am almost the whole way around the world and there's millions of things I can't wait to do next!

I've got all sorts of plans (most of which Dad isn't too thrilled about!) and there's a tonne of other sailing to look forward to. But for a while, I think re-adjusting to life on land, keeping up with some of the exciting things planned for me, finishing my book and documentary, getting my driver's licence and finishing school will be more than enough to keep me busy. I'm also desperate to do some travelling. I know that sounds a bit crazy, but I mean the sort of travelling where you stop places and meet people!

Well it's dinner time for me now. It's Easyfood lamb shanks tonight, so I better get going before they go cold.

Most of the time when I was at sea I didn't put too much thought into anything negative going on back home. But between my family and friends I'd eventually hear about the most ridiculous rumours, stories and comments. I had a laugh when I was told someone was saying I wasn't alone at sea and that *Big Wave Rider* had trailed me the whole way. Hilarious!

Right from the beginning people had claimed it wasn't me writing my blogs. Equally as hilarious but also pretty annoying was that people didn't believe a sixteen-year-old was capable of writing her own blog and knowing her own mind.

There was also some rumour about how I'd pulled into Tasmania and was spending a few days resting at a lovely little bed and breakfast. I wish!

And then, in my last few weeks at sea, a huge debate flared up about whether I'd completed enough nautical miles to claim to have circumnavigated the globe.

The article that started it all was written by a very experienced sailor, Nancy Knudsen, and first appeared on the Sail-World website. It basically said I would not take Jesse Martin's WSSRC record as the youngest person to sail solo, unassisted and non-stop around the world and quoted John Reed (the Secretary of the WSSRC and the man I wrote to in June 2009 to find out exactly what I had to do if I wanted to challenge Jesse's official WSSRC record) as saying my journey 'did not comply with the definition of around the world and bears no comparison with the achievement of Martin'.

Nancy Knudsen was right in that, on paper, I (or anyone else) would never be able to take Jesse Martin's WSSRC record as this particular record no longer exists. It was so weird that it became a story so close to me getting home. Mr Reed had as good as told me before I left that there was no point sailing exactly the same route as Jesse as the WSSRC no longer recognised age records and so would not be examining my trip. A friend and supporter, Terry Hammond, had helped me with all this in May 2009 and we had both written to John Reed and Terry had also written to Jean-Louis Fabry (the Vice-Chairman of the WSSRC) to clarify that our understanding of the rules was correct. He'd gone as far as querying which of the different formulae for calculating Great Circle distances the WSSRC used. Mr Fabry replied that the orthodromic distance (Great Circle) of the trip to be WSSRC recognised must exceed 21,600 nautical miles. After further correspondence back and forth and confirmation that the WSSRC would not ratify the voyage no matter what I did because I was under eighteen, I decided to sail a course that satisfied the criteria commonly accepted for sailing solo, unassisted and non-stop around the world.

I couldn't understand all the fuss (wasn't this old news?) and then when ABC News Online approached John Reed he told them he 'made no such statement concerning Watson'. So it seems I wasn't the only person who was confused.

I really wouldn't have cared about all this because the voyage had never really been about the record for me. It was about a personal goal and proving that it's possible for anyone to achieve their dreams. Neither of these were affected in the slightest by some official piece of paper. Then it started getting nasty. I wasn't concerned for me, but it was becoming a bit of a pain for everyone back home. People made negative comments about Andrew Fraser and suggested that I was dishonest when approaching sponsors and on my website because I had said I wanted to break Jesse Martin's record and become the youngest person to sail solo, unassisted and non-stop around the world. It was true, there was no official ratified record anymore but if I succeeded in my goal I would be much younger than Jesse Martin, David Dicks, Mike Perham or Zac Sunderland and so I would become the youngest person to circumnavigate the globe.

It seemed the point that I was being attacked on was that I hadn't sailed far enough. Yet when I compare the miles sailed on my trip to Kay Cottee's it is very similar and even a little longer, yet the WSSRC happily acknowledged her voyage as sailing solo, unassisted and non-stop around the world.

I could have let it all slide and not even mentioned it in this book but since getting back I've read a few of the articles that were going around at the time, particularly one from the *Sunday Age* that quoted Rob Kothe, the editor of Sail-World as saying: 'We don't believe she's been making her own PR decisions. We don't believe she decided her route.' There were suggestions I was not writing my own blogs and Mr Kothe went on to say, 'People think we're criticising Jessica. We're not. We're criticising her management.'

Well, he was criticising me and in my mind it was in the worst way possible. He was suggesting that I was just a puppet, that I had no voice and no will of my own.

And in the same way you'd be angry at someone attacking your family, I was annoyed that someone was also criticising the people who'd worked so hard with me to make the voyage happen.

Again, people I admire, people like Ian Kiernan, Jesse Martin and John Bertrand, spoke out for us and the blog comments from everyone were wonderful.

Thursday, 6 May 2010
Savouring every second

I don't normally bother addressing critics because some-one's always going to be saying something, no matter what I say or do. But I thought I'd have my two bobs' worth on these claims that I haven't 'officially' sailed around the world.

Call me immature but I've actually been having a bit of a giggle over the whole thing. If I haven't been sailing around the world, then it beats me what I've been doing out here all this time! Yes it's a shame that my voyage won't be recognised by a few organisations because I'm under eighteen, but it really doesn't worry me.

I mean there's millions, probably billions of people who still don't believe in global warming, so I'm more than happy to settle for a few people going against the tide and declaring that mine hasn't been an official circumnavigation. Well I think I've wasted more than enough time on the whole petty debate – so, moving on!

I've had a bit of everything with the weather over the last few days. Some sunshine, some strongish winds and a thunderstorm the other night that shot fork lightning into the water, not far from *Ella's Pink Lady*. I also pulled some of the stitching out of my repairs on the mainsail. But despite that, sore hands and a little issue with the engine I'm trying to sort out at the moment, I couldn't be in better spirits.

I'm having the time of my life slowly cruising up the coast, not pushing *Ella's Pink Lady* too hard, and looking forward to arriving on the fifteenth. I'm enjoying all the highs of solo sailing and in just a few days, I've got seeing friends and family to look forward to.

I think I can safely say that I'm now seriously excited about getting home! It's probably a good thing that I'm by myself because if there was anyone else here I'd be driving them mad with all my hyperactive energy!

Saturday, 8 May 2010
Sunshine, a ship and engine problems

I've had lots of that lovely sunshine stuff lately and today I'm over the moon to see the cabin temperature sitting on 20 degrees! It's been a while since it's been that warm.

But not everything's going as well as the weather.

The fuel system on the engine is still giving me grief, so I can't get the engine to start. This isn't the end of the world, it just means that I've got to be extra careful with power usage. If I can't get it going again, then Jesse and Mike will just have to row *Ella's Pink Lady* up to the dock after the finish line. No, only kidding, we'll work something out. It would be very nice to motor in under our own steam, so I'll keep trying.

Since I gave up on the food-bag system and went for all my favourites a while ago, I'm starting to run out of good food. I've had to start eating the stuff I'd normally leave (I know, it serves me right!), but on the upside, I've got so much spare fresh water, that I've been able to use it for washing. Other than that, the dunny has also decided not to play nicely, which is also more annoying than anything. I mean couldn't it wait just one more week before refusing to work?

Last night the AIS also picked up the first ship I've seen since under Africa, but it didn't come close and I'm pretty surprised that it's the only one I've seen.

If you've had a bit of a look at the voyage map or if you're familiar with these waters, you're probably wondering why it's taking so long to get to Sydney. If I was in any sort of rush or the weather was miserable, yes I could get in before the fifteenth. But I made the decision with my team a while back to set the fifteenth as the arrival date, so that I didn't feel any pressure trying to meet an earlier date. And the reason that we've set a date at all, rather than just letting the wind blow *Ella's Pink Lady* and me in at random, is because a lot of people needed to book flights and make arrangements.

If my estimated arrival date changed one more time, I'd have a lot of annoyed relatives! From what I've heard, planning my arrival in Sydney is turning out to be a pretty complicated business, with all sorts of different authorities involved.

If I was head-over-heels desperate to get in to shore and off *Ella's Pink Lady*, things would be different. But with the sun shining again, I'm totally excited, but not in any particular rush to get home. I'd like to make it perfectly clear that I'm not feeling any pressure from anyone back home to arrive on a particular date. Believe me, I'm far more pig-headed than that. If I wanted to push hard and come in earlier, then I would!

I enjoyed every second of those last few days. Remember how I wrote earlier about happy glasses? Well, that week I was seeing everything through 'Yay, I'm nearly home' glasses. Does that sound totally dorky, or what?! But that's exactly how it was. I felt like I had a smile on my face 24/7 and I was almost bursting with excitement at the thought of seeing everyone in only a few more days. The constant smell of diesel that was part of the engine problem and the headache it would give me couldn't dent my good mood. I was pretty exhausted after the full-on sailing towards Tasmania and so when we finally settled on arriving in Sydney on the fifteenth I was glad. It meant I could enjoy every last moment with *Ella's Pink Lady* and savour the fantastic sailing we had without worrying about missing the arrival date if something went wrong. Not to mention it gave all the people who'd sailed with me on my blog the chance to be in Sydney if they wanted. I knew there were some who had commented on the blog that they were planning to be there but I still had no idea of how many would turn up on the day. I did know that Jesse and Mike were going to sail with me once I crossed the finish line.

Monday, 10 May 2010
A working engine!

The little Yanmar engine is going again! A little delicately, but it is running with a water transfer pump rigged up in place of the fuel pump which had stopped working. It's pretty dodgy with all the mismatching hoses, but should do the job. Apart from the kick I got from actually managing to fix something, it was quite a relief as we've pretty much had no wind at all the last two days, so the batteries were lower than I'd thought.

Thanks Jim, Iain and Dad for the ideas and Bruce for the encouragement (read: threat!). Bruce knew just the right thing to say to get me fired up and to give me the incentive to get the engine going. If there's one thing I've learnt out here, it's that there's nothing that can't be fixed with enough perseverance, even if it means pulling some other part of the boat apart to do it!

So, apart from spending a lot of time lately getting covered in diesel puzzling over the engine, I've been enjoying lots of sunshine and making an extra effort with the house/boatwork so Mum doesn't have a heart attack when she sees the cabin. Actually, Mum's not like that and the cabin's never been that bad (cough cough!).

Then yesterday I saw my first blue whale of the trip (I know, I can't believe it either). Then I got a bit creeped out by something seriously big jumping out of the water all around us in the dark when the water glassed out last night. It was probably just marlin but I'd rather imagine it was something more exciting like a great white chasing dinner!

And of course yesterday was Mother's Day. I couldn't cook her breakfast in bed or make her a card like she deserves a million times over, so I've saved an extra hug for when I get in. What Mum did letting me go and helping me get to the start line while still looking after everyone else is, in my eyes, much harder than anything I've faced out here. Thanks Mum!

The problem with this lovely weather and the amazing starry nights I've been getting, is that I'm really not sure I want the voyage to end! I could go on forever like this. One quiet day after another, doing things at my own pace with little challenges and problems to keep me busy. Except, of course, there's also so, so many things I'm looking forward to when I get back home!

In one way I think sailing back through Sydney Heads is going to be as tough as it was sailing out through them. I'm told that things are going to change pretty majorly for me as well, so that's a little scary. But I'm not worried because I know that if I can find a reason to laugh while surrounded by huge waves, in the dark and after a knockdown, then I'll be able to smile through whatever comes my way.

Oh dear, I'm getting far too soppy and reflective, so I'd better finish up.

Only five more sleeps and four days left!

Thursday, 13 May 2010

So close and what I'm going to miss

My perfect conditions came to an end late on Tuesday with thunderstorms then this freezing cold southerly wind (brrrr!). Yesterday the wind was gale force but today it's eased off to 30 knots, giving us great surfing conditions with the sea standing up as it meets the east-coast current.

I've spent the day on deck watching us surf along with a grin from one seriously cold ear to the other numb one (and right now I'm paying the price with a badly wind-burnt face!).

I can't believe how fast this last week has gone. Only two more sleeps till the finish line! Have I mentioned how excited I am? It's like the day before Christmas except I don't ever remember getting this excited about Christmas. Two more sleeps till a hot shower, fresh food and . . . and . . . and . . . everything else! Mind you, I think it's going to take a fair bit longer than that for the whole 'I've just sailed around the world' thing to sink in. It's just too big to get my head around!

Sometime way back in the Atlantic, I remember I wrote about all the things I missed about home. So I thought I'd make a list of some of the things I'm going to miss out here. The first thing is pretty obvious, I'm going to miss getting up and going sailing every day. I'm going to miss being out of range of my annoying brother. I'm going to miss doing things at my own pace and singing at the top of my voice without clearing the room!

I'm going to miss the kick I get from overcoming challenges by myself, flying along in the dark. A new sunset every night and the time I always take to watch it. I'm going to miss watching the waves and sea. I know it's been nearly seven months and I'm still not bored by it. The tumbling white tops when it's windy and the glassy reflections when it's not. I'm going to miss seeing albatross circle around *Ella's Pink Lady* and beanie days for when finding a hairbrush is just too much trouble!

Bruce, Suzanne and Mick on *Big Wave Rider* are going to be meeting up with me sometime tomorrow to sail the last few miles alongside *Ella's Pink Lady* – can't wait to see them!

See you all soon!

PART THREE

Home

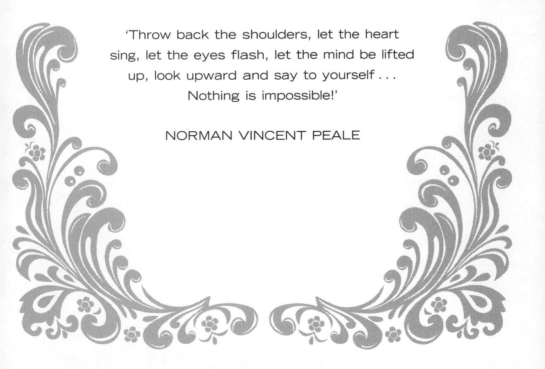

'Throw back the shoulders, let the heart
sing, let the eyes flash, let the mind be lifted
up, look upward and say to yourself . . .
Nothing is impossible!'

NORMAN VINCENT PEALE

The day before sailing into Sydney started out
like just another day out on the water. But by the end of the day,
we'd been visited by six helicopters, a plane and *Big Wave Rider*
had joined us too. So it was obvious my quiet days of sailing
were well and truly over. As the wind and sea slowly dropped off
in the evening and the heavy grey skies slowly cleared, I could
see a huge glow on the horizon and a few tiny twinkling city
lights. With *Big Wave Rider* circling around us to keep watch
for shipping, I managed a few hours' sleep, but mostly spent the
night tacking back and forth, catching up on the latest music on
the FM radio. I've never been so excited about listening to ads
and was thrilled that I actually recognised some of the songs
from before I left.

As it got light on the Saturday morning, I could make out a
thin strip of land in the distance and spent the rest of the morning
tacking into the wind towards it. The wind slowly died some
more, until sailing conditions were pretty much perfect. As we

inched closer, a trickle, then a flood of boats came out to join us. The thing that really struck me that morning was when we were 10 nautical miles from land, the wind changed. It seems like such a small thing in comparison to all the other excitement that day, but all of a sudden I could smell land. The wind suddenly felt dry and cold like it does on winter mornings with the wind blowing off the land.

The plan had been for us to pass through Sydney Heads at 11 am. The official broadcast was to begin then and the official welcome and press conference would happen not too much later. It was supposed to be all over by about 2 pm.

Great plan, but as the morning passed by things weren't going to schedule. The strong winds the day before had pushed us further north than I'd have liked and I'd also misjudged how long it would take to sail back to the finish line. Once I realised we'd be a few hours later than I'd thought I felt awful for keeping people waiting. I still had no idea how many people that would be! There was nothing I could do to get us there any faster. I pushed *Ella's Pink Lady* as hard as possible and happily tacked back and forth surrounded by a growing fleet of boats. I didn't know the pain my late arrival was causing on the harbour, in television studios and to the huge crowd.

Coming up to the finish line, boats and helicopters slowly closed in. I brought *Ella's Pink Lady* off the wind a little and as Sydney Heads slowly lined up, we were surfing along at 6 knots. Horns, noises, voices and so many people's faces overwhelmed me. After seeing only the empty ocean for so long everything was so loud and so vivid. A smile just wasn't anywhere big enough to express how I was feeling. The huge sense of relief at being back made me cry a little, but they were happy, very happy tears!

By the time we were across the line and in Sydney Harbour, I'd gone from slightly hysterical to a bit frozen up. Bruce had to yell across the water to tell me to furl in the headsail so that Jesse Martin, Mike Perham and the customs guys could board.

It was great having Jesse and Mike onboard to look after *Ella's Pink Lady* while I had my passport stamped by the customs' guy and stuffed my face with the fresh food that had been handed aboard (I couldn't help myself and let loose with a can of whipped cream and oops . . . turns out there was a live television camera pointed at me!).

I changed into a fresh set of clothes that Mum and Emily had arranged for me, babbled like a complete fool through a few more live interviews and tried to return waves to all the people on boats around us.

As the Man O'War steps came into view I could see Mum, Dad, Tom, Hannah and Emily alongside the dock. I was busting to hug everyone but as I stepped off into Mum and Dad's arms I couldn't seem to let go of *Ella's Pink Lady*. I didn't want to leave my brave little boat behind.

With Tom and Dad half walking next to me and half supporting me, we made our way up a very long pink carpet. It was the most astonishing welcome home and I felt so touched to have so many people care about what we'd achieved. I stepped off the pink carpet and carefully climbed the stairs onto a stage that looked out over a sea of people. With the white sails of the Opera House behind them and an endless blue sky above, it almost took my breath away. Channel Ten newsreader and journalist, Sandra Sully was there to meet me and then before I knew it I was standing next to Prime Minister Kevin Rudd and New South Wales Premier Kristina Keneally. They both made speeches and were lovely in their encouragement but one word stuck in my mind. Sandra then asked me a few questions before starting to wrap it all up. For the first time since stepping onto the stage my heart started racing. The Prime Minister had called me a hero and I felt compelled to say something about it but with thousands of people there, watching me, I wasn't sure I could. It would have been very easy to smile, wave one last time and step back down off the stage. I was in two minds about what to do but it was my only chance so I asked Sandra if I could say something.

The day before, when it was still just me and *Ella's Pink Lady* I'd scribbled out a few key messages I wanted to get across if I could. I wanted to share what had inspired me to take on the world.

With the crowd's encouragement, I took a deep breath and said I had to disagree with our Prime Minister (I didn't notice that apparently I almost gave Mum and Dad a heart attack, they didn't know what I was going to say but were worried I would let loose on one of my passionate rants about lowering the voting age!).

I told Mr Rudd that I wasn't a hero, I was just an ordinary girl who believed in a dream. I hope I didn't seem cheeky or ungrateful. I only spoke up because I feel so strongly that you don't have to be someone special to achieve something. And I was definitely not a hero.

I said a bit more about how it was possible for dreams to come true. Mine had! How I believe that with hard work and determination you can do anything. And then it was over.

In-between the interviews and press conferences (where someone gave me the most massive jar of Nutella) there were a few quick seconds with family and close friends and I couldn't stop looking at their faces, taking in every detail.

Finally, we headed back to Manly, where we were staying and had a quiet get-together with everyone. Being surrounded by family and friends again was wonderful and it was almost as if no time had passed since I'd last seen them.

As well as having Jesse and Mike there, David Dicks, Jon Sanders (who holds the record for the most continuous solo, non-stop circumnavigations – three!) and Brian Caldwell (the first person under twenty-one to sail solo around the world), joined us. How amazing to have all these solo navigators in the same room and even more amazing to be one of them!

At 9 pm, enough was enough and I headed back to our apartment with just the young crowd. Emily ran me the long-awaited hot bath but after that there was no way I could sleep until I had my walk on the beach. Despite being given strict instructions not to leave the apartment I dragged the others out for ice-cream and a midnight walk on the beach (rebellious teen, I know!). Actually, walk mightn't be the best way to describe it as there was far more running, chasing seagulls and splashing water involved. Eventually I crawled into my soft, dry, non-rolling bed and slept.

Everyone made sure I was well looked after, and thinking that I'd want some down time they'd made sure I didn't have any commitments for a few days. I know back in January I'd said not to make any plans for me because I was going to sleep for a few weeks but I'd changed my mind. I wasn't used to this at all. That first morning I drove everyone mad (sorry, Pam!) literally climbing the walls. There was so much to see and do and the last thing I wanted was to stay in the apartment and relax. It was incredible having achieved my goal of sailing around the world but now I'd done it I was feeling restless. I'd been working towards this one thing for years so I guess it isn't surprising I felt odd now it was all over.

I received so many cards, gifts and letters and I really enjoyed finding out how *Ella's Pink Lady* and I had helped to inspire some people to do things they hadn't dared before. I don't think I had any real idea of how many people had followed the voyage till the day we sailed into Sydney. It's the most amazing feeling to know that I've touched so many people's lives in one way or another. The media attention after I was home was bizarre. We had photographers following us pretty much everywhere we went at first but there was no way my family was going to let any of it go to my head so don't worry. I spent the first week having lots of great walks, shopping (ouch! But I love my three leather jackets) and went to three birthday parties (first mine, then Tom's, then Dad's).

I was very grateful for all the opportunities I was given to do different things including diving with the sharks at Oceanworld Manly, and Layne Beachley giving me surfing lessons also at Manly (how cool to be taught how to surf by a seven-time world champion). I also helmed one of the big Manly ferries across Sydney Harbour and climbed the Harbour Bridge. It was fantastic and I just couldn't seem to sit still because there was so much to do!

After a few weeks in Sydney I was itching to get back out on the water. A lot of people were surprised that I wanted to sail *Ella's Pink Lady* up the coast, but of course I wanted to! I couldn't wait to go sailing again and I still felt a little like I had something to finish, after all, the Sunshine Coast was where the voyage had really started for me.

Ella's Pink Lady and *Big Wave Rider* headed out together on Sunday, 31 May, for the 470 nautical mile voyage. Bruce, Murray, Tom, Mike and I planned to sail up the coast together and swap around a bit. It was a bit strange being back on *Ella's Pink Lady*, getting used to her motion and all the noises again. And it took even longer to get used to sailing with a crew. *Ella's Pink Lady* doesn't have a big cockpit, so there were a few elbows in faces during a tack or gybe before we had it sorted. There was a low pressure system off the east coast so it was a bit wet and wild for a few days but we missed the worst of it. While we were sailing, Lennox Head was hit by a mini tornado. It caused a lot of damage in one small pocket of the town and injured a dozen people so we got a few calls making sure we were okay and not near the area.

We made quick stops at Port Stephens, Trial Bay, Yamba, Peel Island and Tangalooma on Moreton Island. Everywhere we stopped people gave me a wave or a nod and at Tangalooma we were given almost royal treatment at the resort (dinner, hot showers and dolphin feeding). At Yamba we stopped in for fuel and chips and it was perfect timing because Kay Cottee was there working on her boat. I was so thrilled to finally meet her.

Stopping to raft up to *Big Wave Rider* at night for the last legs was great fun. Once we reached Queensland and more familiar waters the sun came out and we had a great few days motoring up the Broadwater and Moreton Bay, the same waters I'd learnt to sail on all that time ago. I couldn't believe how small the Broadwater looked compared to the way I remembered it. Back then it had been this huge daunting stretch of open water – now, well, I could hardly believe I'd even been nervous!

All the way up the coast I'd been thinking the welcome home to Mooloolaba was no huge emotional deal. It was great to see the familiar outline of the Glass House Mountains against a brilliant pink sunrise as the sun rose, and I was excited as a fleet of boats, with people I knew onboard, slowly gathered around us, but it wasn't until we sailed right into the bay off Mooloolaba that it sunk in. I was home! Up until this point I'd been laughing and having a great time watching the boys throw cupcakes and pancakes at *Big Wave Rider*. I don't think the police on our escort boats were particularly impressed with their childish behaviour and I definitely wasn't impressed with the mess all over *Ella's Pink Lady*!

In contrast to the Sydney welcome home, this time we were too early. Under just a scrap of headsail, to slow us down, we sailed along the beach, around the headland full of waving people, and towards the breakwaters. That was the point that it all hit me. The day I sailed into Sydney I got my head around the fact that I'd made it, I'd really sailed around the world. Since then I'd been slowly coming to terms with the way the voyage had touched so many people's lives. It was only when I saw all those people from my hometown welcoming me and *Ella's Pink Lady* that the enormity overwhelmed me. Sitting on the deck with Tom's arm around me I had a bit of a sob as it all washed over me. I couldn't believe I was looking out on the beautiful bay I'd been dreaming about for so long. It was much better than I'd remembered.

After tying up at the dock, there was an official reception, more speeches and the chance to say quick hellos to friends and supporters before eventually heading back to our house. We'd only moved in a short time before I left so I didn't have any particular attachment to the house itself. It was strange to see how everyone had settled in without me. I was almost a little jealous. More than anything it showed me how much time had passed.

Once I was home, I had a taste of what my family and team went through while I was at sea when we heard the news that Abby Sunderland had activated two emergency beacons at 41 degrees south, in the Roaring Forties, that showed she and *Wild Eyes* were in trouble. After that nothing was heard from her for more than twenty hours. When Mum woke me with the news at six in the morning I couldn't get back to sleep and spent the day on edge waiting to hear more. The waiting had me worked up so I can only imagine how her family must have felt. I always believed Abby would be okay but it doesn't matter how experienced you are (and she is very experienced), the ocean can be a very unforgiving and wild place. It was a huge relief when we heard a Qantas plane chartered by Australian search and rescue had made visual contact and then radio contact with Abby. It turned out her mast had been broken in 75-knot winds and mountainous seas which had also knocked out her communication systems.

Being at home, not knowing what was going on, gave me an appreciation for what Mum and Dad had gone through. They had that huge scare when my emergency beacon was set off during a knockdown and another when my emailed sked didn't go through and nobody heard from me for a day and a bit. I was fine but they were worried. It made me understand even more the gift they gave me in letting their daughter dream so big.

I always wondered and worried about whether I'd come back from the trip a different person. Well, I'm still just the same old me, but I've definitely changed. (Mum says I haven't, it's just that the world's looking at me in a different way.) I needn't have worried, though, because my friends and family still treat me just the same as they always have.

So what *has* changed? I'll start with the easy one, my sleeping habits. They've certainly changed . . . and not for the better. After seven months of disrupted sleep and almost two months back on land, I'm still struggling to adjust. To give you an idea of how out-of-whack my sleeping is, I'm writing this at 2 am because I am wide awake.

Then there's the fact that I don't have anything to prove to myself anymore. All that time ago I asked myself if I was tough enough to sail around the world. I've answered that and it's made me a lot more relaxed. Maybe relaxed isn't the best way of putting it, because if you asked anyone who knows me they'll tell you that I haven't been able to sit still since stepping off *Ella's Pink Lady*! I'm also more . . . confident isn't exactly the right word, but something along those lines, self-assured, maybe?

And then there's the big change! I've turned into a squealer and a giggler. A year ago you wouldn't have caught me dead squealing over a splash of cold water, now . . . !

While I'm in a bit of a reflective mood I might as well have a crack at answering that oh-so-scary 'What did I learn from spending 210 days alone at sea?' question. Well, there were little things related to equipment choices (though surprisingly few, actually) but if I have to boil it down to just one thing, it would be that I learnt not to take life, or myself, too seriously. I learnt the importance of having fun! (Not exactly original, I know.)

Since being back I've had some amazing opportunities open up to me and I'm constantly being asked, 'What's next?' Writing and finishing this book has been an adventure all of its own! It's been quite an experience reflecting on the voyage and the years of preparation beforehand. I can't believe what we all did and some of the things we went through just to get to the start line. Never once, in all those years, did I think 'Is this worth it?' or 'Why am I putting us all through this?'

I didn't realise it at the time but it's an incredible thing to have a goal you're so completely focused on that nothing is too much effort and you never stop to question it. I'm also realising how lucky I was to have people around me who felt the same. To have parents who believed in and encouraged me.

Now that the book's finished, I've got a little more time for myself. I'm looking forward to finally getting my driver's licence, working my way up to some faster sailing and racing and challenging myself with other adventures. To quote Sir Edmund Hillary, 'Once you've been there, you'll only want to go back!' More than anything, I'm looking forward to the chance to share my voyage and experiences with other people, and particularly young people. Since having so many of my own dreams come true I know how lucky I am. So many people supported me and now I want to give something back.

I don't know if you remember, but way back in the Pacific I saw that amazing shooting star and made a wish on it. I'm sure everyone assumed my wish was to successfully make it around the world. It wasn't. It wasn't anything to do with me (sorry, superstition still prevents me from actually telling you what it was!). I couldn't think of anything to wish for myself because there was nothing I wanted that I knew I couldn't get by working hard for it. How does that B.o.B song 'Airplanes' go? Something about needing a wish? I love the song but I don't need a wish. I've got the ability to dream; that's all anyone needs to make their wishes and dreams come true. You don't need a shooting star, you can do it yourself.

A GUIDE TO
Ella's Pink Lady

1. Bowsprit – used for flying code zero (a light downwind sail).
2. Forestay with furling headsail.
3. Anchor locker filled with foam as collision bulkhead.
4. Fore and aft lowers and side stays.
5. Inner forestay with staysail or storm jib at the ready.
6. Spinnaker pole (matching one on other side).
7. Mast with mainsail lashed to the boom for stormy weather conditions.
8. Handholds and jacklines for clipping and holding on (placing them on the cabin top was an idea we got from Kay Cottee's boat *First Lady*). One on each side of the cabin.
9. Halyards and reef lines running back to the cockpit.
10. Solid dodger, to provide shelter and protection. Has a 60-watt solar panel on top and a water catcher around the edge.
11. Running back stay (one on each side).
12. Wind generator.
13. Targa frame with 2 x 80-watt solar panels and VHF, AIS and Iridium aerials.
14. Life-raft in cockpit (ready if needed).
15. Sailor 250 dome for internet and satellite phone.
16. Parker (Fleming windvane).
17. Mast – with passive radar reflector, echo max and self-aligning tangs on the stays.

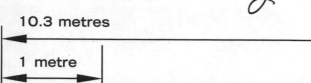

Internal guide

10.3 metres

1 metre

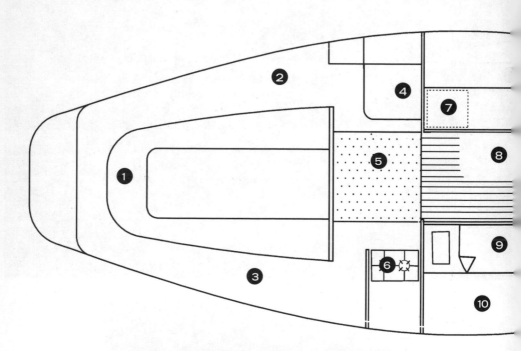

1.   Aft storage for rubbish.

2.   Sail storage.

3.   Lazarette storage.

4.   Navigation table, home of the Toughbook, chart plotter, etc. (I spent a lot of time here!).

5.   Engine.

6.   Galley, with metho stove, sink, food storage.

7.   Wet seat.

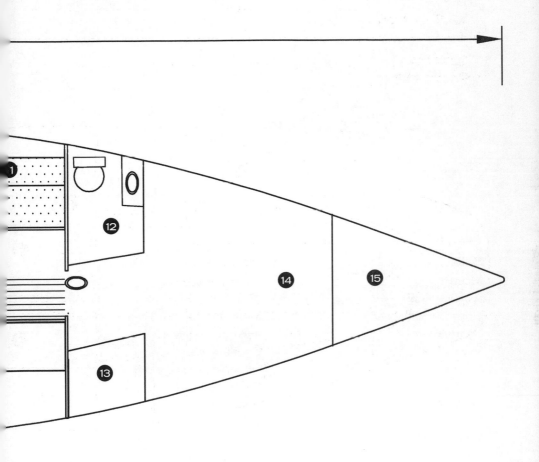

8. Box for diesel storage.

9. Bunk.

10. Water tanks (under the bunk).

11. Storage and (more) water tanks.

12. The all-important dunny and Ella Baché salon!

13. Toolkit storage.

14. Food and storage area.

15. Anchor locker filled with foam as collision bulkhead.

Equipment list

Sails
Mainsail
Spare mainsail
Heavy staysail
Light staysail
Storm jib
Tri-sail
Headsails × 2
Code zero

Sail repair kit
Sailmaker's thread
Whipping twine
Sharp punch
Sailmaker's palm
Sailmaker's needles
Double-sided tape
Heavy-duty sail repair tape
Selection of sail cloth
Heavy-duty vinyl
Rope splicing fids

Rigging
Spare spectra for emergency stays
Spare spectra halyards

Motor spares
Alternator belts × 6
Water pump belts × 4
Motor fuel filters × 3
Racor fuel filters × 3
Oil filters × 4
Oil for motor and gearbox
Coolant × 1 litre
Fuel hose
Impellers × 3
Water pump and gasket to suit
Spare alternator

Fibreglass repair kit
Epoxy resin × 2 litres
Epoxy hardener × 500 grams
Fibreglass cloth, double bias, uni, chop
    strand mat
High-strength glue powder × 84 grams
Lightweight filler powder × 92 grams
Stirring sticks 2
Brushes × 6
Coarse sandpaper
Measuring cups × 8
Paper overalls and body shield spray

Self-steering

Simrad TP32 Tillerpilot

Simrad AP24 autopilot and remote commander

Fleming self steering

General spares

Spare tiller made by Aunty Cathy

Spare washboards

Five-minute Araldite × 2, 24 millilitres

Silicone gasket sealer × 1 tube

Underwater epoxy sticks × 2

Epoxy glue × 385 grams

Polyurethane sealer × 3 tubes

Silicone sealer × 2 tubes

Tef-Gel × 1 tube

Thread locker × 1 bottle

Lanolin × 2 spray cans

Dry lubricant × 3 cans

Spare bilge pumps big and small (supplied by Johnson Pumps)

Spare wind generator and blades

Fleming self-steer vanes in a variety of sizes to suit differing conditions and spares

Winch service kit

Spare navigation lights

Spare chart plotter and GPS aerial

Spare TracPlus unit in a sealed container and spare aerial

Spare inverter

Spare blocks, jammers and shackles

Spare batteries for everything

Spare VHF aerial

Spare life jackets, harness and tethers

Service kits for life jackets

Emergency solar panel

Rubber strips

Spare ropes and lines

Huge assortment of cable ties

Large assortment of tapes

Numerous rolls of rescue tape

Assorted pieces of timber

Spare hoses and pipes and a massive assortment of hose clamps

An extensive collection of nuts, bolts and washers supplied by Coastal Fasteners (we think we had more onboard than they had in their shop in the end!)

Navigation

Simrad chart plotter with charts

Full set of Simrad instruments – wind, speed, depth.

Panasonic Toughbook laptops × 4 with Software-on-Board (SOB), including all appropriate electronic charts

Large selection of appropriate paper charts

Sextant and tables

Parallel rulers, plotter and dividers

Handheld GPS × 2

AIS receiver and transponders × 2

Broadband radar

Binoculars × 2

Publications

Cruising the NSW Coast by Alan Lucas, 5th edition

Tidal information also on Simrad NX40 chart plotter and SOB

International Regulations for Preventing Collisions at Sea

Electrical handbook

Manuals of all equipment onboard

Celestial Navigation – A Yachtmaster's Guide

Cockpit Companion

Yachting Australia Racing Rules of Sailing

Boat Owner's Mechanical and Electrical Manual by Nigel Calder

Manual for electrical installation

Software-on-Board manual for back-up computer

Yanmar engine service manual

Yanmar engine user manual

Radar manual

Course manuals for all courses completed:

- Diesel maintenance
- Marine first aid
- Sea survival
- Marine radio
- Radar operators

Communication equipment

Sailor 250 satellite communication dome for phone and internet

Iridium satellite phones × 2 with spare batteries (one stored separately in a watertight container with separate aerial)

MF/HF radio transceiver

VHF – handheld with spare batteries

VHF – handheld Simrad hard wired on mounting

VHF – fixed unit Simrad

Safety equipment

Full safety equipment detailed in Risk Management document

Full category zero safety equipment checked by David Price prior to departure

Life-raft supplied by RFD

Flares and grab-bags supplied by Pains Wessex

Para-anchor drogues with lines and bridles × 2

Series drogue with bridle

EPIRBs × 2

Personal locator beacons × 2

Echomax radar detector

Passive radar detector

Survival suit supplied by RFD

Storm boards for windows, hatches

TracPlus tracking unit with an additional spare unit and aerial packed in a water-tight container.

Jacklines

Safety ladder

Fuel and water

Diesel × 280 litres

Methylated spirits × 80 litres

Water × 375 litres

General

Mast-climbing harness with crash helmet and body armour

Torches – Dolphin-style × 4, small LED torches x 10

Fishing and knife set

Emergency hand water-maker/ desalinator (never used)

Buckets × 8

Sponges for bilges × 4

Headlights × 5

12-volt spot lights × 2

Diesel transfer pump

Water transfer pump

Don McInytre supplied many of the general bits and pieces, both from his wallet and his shed, including the essential 12-volt 'must have' hair dryer!

Electrical Spares

Extensive electrical-spare-parts kit and operating manual, complete with wiring diagrams, referenced and labelled photographs and procedures for operating and testing equipment put together by Neil Cawthorne the electrician.

Assorted wire

Battery post terminals

Connector blocks

Wire insulation stripper

Self-amalgamating tape

Electrical insulation tape

Test probe

Spare lamps

Spare fuse links, switches and circuit breakers

Cable ties

CRC spray

Inox-MX3 lubricant and corrosion inhibitor

Alternator regulator bypass kit

Pre-made short lengths of wire with various terminals fitted

Tools

Hammers × 2

Screwdriver set

Full socket set

Full spanner set, imperial and metric × 2

Shifting spanners × 6

Complete pliers set

Vice grips × 3

G-clamps × 6

Complete punch set

Hacksaws with spare blades × 2

Wood saws × 2

Battery-operated pink drill with spare battery

Hand drill

Complete drill bits set

Boltcutter

Tin snips

Wire cutters

Measuring tapes

Multimeters, basic current tester

Rivet gun and rivets

Wire crimpers

File set

Stanley knives and cutting knives

Allen keys × 3 sets

Hand oil pump

Corking Gun

Oil filter remover

Hose/pipe cutter

Mechanics extension mirror

Mechanics extension pick up tool

Alternator belt adjuster (made by Neil Cawthorne)

Electronic digital callipers

Soldering irons × 2, and solder

Assortment of shackles, circlets and split pins

Computers

Panasonic Toughbooks × 4 with cables (only the first Toughbook was ever used, the spares were not required, how tough is that!)

Multiple hard drives

Cameras

Panasonic Still FT1 Luminix

Panasonic Still FZ35

Panasonic handheld video-camera HDC-TM200 × 2

Webcam × 4

Clothes

Sea boots × 2 pairs

Complete sets of warm clothing sealed in heavy plastic bags × 6

Thick woollen socks × 12 pairs

Beanies × 4 (plus assorted selection
   throughout food packs)
Deck shoes × 1 pair
Gloves × 6 various layers
Scarves
Sarongs × 2
T-shirts × 6
Shorts × 3
Jeans × 2
Slip-on shoes and thongs
Underwear × 25
IceBreaker thermals sets × 4
Sweatshirts and jumpers × 4
Musto dry suit
Musto overalls × 2
Musto outer jackets × 2
Mid-layer Musto overalls × 2
Mid-layer Musto jackets × 2
Bodywarmers

Toiletries

Toothbrushes × 8
Toothpaste × 4 tubes
Skin wipes, toilet paper, tissues
Liquid hand soaps, hand sanitiser
Shampoo and conditioner × 5 bottles
   of each
Nail brushes × 3

Ella Baché favourites

Creme Intex-Response Cream
Masque Intex No 2 Treatment Mask
Fruit D'Eclat a la Tomate Bio
Creme de Lait Hydratante
Creme Tomate
Gommage Delicat
Hydra Brume Ressourcante – Hydra
   Replenishing Mist
Hydra Booster

Sleeping bags and linen

Mattress, 45 centimetres wide with lee
cloth to provide a snug sleeping
place with little movement. Peter
Becker and his staff from Clark
Rubber made this mattress and also
supplied some of the foam for lining
the cabin to help with insulation,
lessen the condensation and also
provide 'padding'.
Ocean Sleepwear 3-layer system
Down sleeping bag
Synthetic sleeping bag
Thermal sleeping-bag liner
Sleeping-bag liners × 3
Fitted and flat sheets (silk, cotton and
   flannelette) × 4 sets
Light blanket
Pillows with protectors × 2
Towels and facecloths × 6
Tea towels × 12

Health and first aid

We worked with Margaret Williams on
the first-aid kits. Margaret is a GP and
solo sailor who sailed solo around
Australia a few years ago. Margaret
reviewed my first-aid kit and
personalised it for me. Our local
pharmacist and offshore sailor, Suzy
Rasmussen, prepared the prescription
items and also additional medical
supplies. Suzy also put together a quick
guide for me about specific
medications, interactions and
precautions. A first-aid kit containing
basic day-to-day needs was provided
by Mark and the St John Cadets at
Dromana Secondary College. I also had
a comprehensive first-aid manual, an
air splint kit and a cervical collar.

Cleaning

Gumption
Disinfectant
Dishwashing liquid
Laundry soap
Dishcloths
Scourers
Paper towels

Cooking equipment

Gimballing methylated spirits stove
   from Peter at Arrow Caravans
Shallow and deep frypans with lids
Pressure cooker with clamps to enable
   it to be clamped onto the stove
   (donated by The Pressure Cooker
   Centre)
Egg beaters × 3
Can openers × 5
Cutlery, tongs, wooden spoon
   and egg flip
Gas lighters × 18, and matches for
   emergencies
Mixing bowls × 3
Measuring cups and spoons
Plates × 2
Bowls × 2
Thermal cups × 2

Food

The main challenges were providing
variety, dealing with no refrigeration
and ensuring the food was packaged so
that it did not deteriorate due to water
damage or chafing.

Easyfood was the mainstay of my
daily diet. Easyfoods are fully
constituted meals in plastic pouches
that have a shelf-life of about eighteen
months to two years. They only require
heating. Most were complete meals
with no need to add vegetables or
anything else. There was a great range,
from lamb chops (my favourite) to beef
ribs, beef stroganoff and various
chicken meals and curries. They are
high in energy and nutritional value,
providing a good, balanced meal that is
easy to prepare. When the weather
made it too difficult to heat and
prepare a meal, I had self-heating
freeze-dried meals (or tinned corn, ha!).
I took multivitamins throughout the
voyage.

My food was organised into sixteen
fortnightly bags with a suggested menu
on each. These bags contained the
basics with treats and Mum had
included small surprises as well.
Additional foods like butter and eggs
were stored in various compartments,
and I had a storage plan to help me
find everything. The bags themselves
were well researched for strength and
Graham from Dolphin Plastics helped
us out to find the right bag for the job.
Nick Duggan from our local IGA
helped us to source some of the more
unusual products and put the bulk of
our order together.

Lychees × 16 cans
Apricots × 16 cans
Pears × 16 cans
Plums × 16 cans
Mango × 48 cans
Mandarin × 48 cans
Pineapple × 32 cans
Assorted packets of stewed fruit: apple,
   rhubarb, etc.

Assorted dried fruit: mango, pineapple, pear, cranberries, apricots, prunes and banana chips
Assorted fruit puddings
Sultanas × 72 small boxes

Baby potatoes × 64 cans
Asparagus × 16 cans
Corn kernels × 24 cans
Baby corn × 10 cans
Chinese stir-fry vegetables × 16 cans
Water chestnuts × 10 cans (nice and crunchy)
Carrots × 24 cans
Beans × 10 cans
Peas × 10 cans
Capsicum × 16 cans
Tomatoes × 30 cans
Beetroot × 18 cans
Mushrooms × 16 cans
Dried mushroom × 10 packets (repackaged into individual serves)
Assortment of dried peas and carrots
Deb Potato (dried) × 36 packets

Cocktail onions × 48 jars
Stuffed olives × 24 jars
Dill cucumbers × 10 jars
Tinned mussels × 10 cans
Tinned oysters × 10 cans
Tinned pâté × 6 cans
Tinned camembert × 4
Sesame bars and muesli bars
Assorted crackers
Pringles × 64 packets
Popcorn × 12 packets
Salt and pepper × 4 packets of each
Assorted nuts
Whittaker's chocolate bars × 280 (all donated in the very early days when the voyage was first made public.)

Assorted custard mixes and dessert mixes
Assorted mueslis and Weet-Bix (repackaged into individual serves)
Porridge × 60 individual serves
Assorted Cup-a-Soups × 150 serves
Chocolate biscuits × 24 packets
An assortment of other biscuits × 24 packets

Cheese: sticks, processed blocks, jars of cream cheese, wedges and parmesan cheese
Mayonnaise
Reduced cream × 36 tins
Long-life cream × 90 tins
Powdered yoghurt (repackaged into individual serves)
Cans of butter × 24 (donated by Ballantyne Foods in Melbourne)
Milk powder to make 200 litres
Dried whole-egg powder

Assorted juice poppers × 250
Powdered cordial, sachets and jars

Flour
Baking powder
Baking soda
Vanilla essence
Cocoa
Desiccated coconut
Sugar: white, raw and brown
Assorted cake and muffin mixes
Icing sugar
Golden syrup
Assorted cake decorations (chocolate sprinkles, etc.)
Chocolate melts, chips, marshmallows, cooking chocolate
Yeast
Bread mixes × 66

Soy sauce
Oyster sauce
Tabasco sauce
Tomato sauce
BBQ sauce
Olive oil
Brown and white vinegar

Couscous (repackaged into individual
　serves)
Noodles, various
Pasta (repackaged into individual
　serves)
Rice, regular, instant, plain, brown and
　flavoured
Assorted beans for sprouting
Dried garlic
Dried onion
Dried bacon bits
Assorted dried herbs and spices

Tinned pies × 20
Assorted tinned casserole mince, dried
　mince, Spam and tinned hotdogs
Salmon, tuna and sardines × 36 cans
Taco flavouring × 24 sachets
Taco shells (repackaged into 20
　individual serves)
Vol-au-vents × 10 serves

Vegemite × 3 jars
Peanut butter × 3 jars
Honey × 3 jars
Marmalade × 3 jars
Jam × 3 jars
Nutella × 6 jars
Tea, assortment of flavours
Coffee, instant, plunger and individual
　serves
Milo

Chocolate drinks
Flavoured milk straws

Plastic wrap × 3 rolls
Baking paper × 2 rolls
Foil × 3 rolls
Assorted zip-lock bags

Entertainment

Two dry bags of assorted books from
　Hachette Australia, biographies,
　adventure and general light reading
Some of my old favourites from my
　book collection
Stereo: radio and CD player
A huge selection of music from friends
　and family. Everyone donated their
　favourites. It was great because it
　reminded me of the different people
　and provided heaps of variety.
DVDs
Audio books and podcasts
Wool and crochet hooks
Stationery, including notebooks,
　scissors, pens, pencils and rubbers,
　drawing supplies, Velcro dots, Blu
　Tack and glue.
Schoolwork (although this is
　inappropriately in the entertainment
　section!)
Crew! The assorted crew were gathered
　from my bedroom and some also
　arrived in the last few weeks to sign
　on, leaving their dry beds and
　comfortable homes to become
　mouldy and damp but nevertheless
　have the adventure of their lives!
　Thank you to their previous owners
　for allowing them to come!

Glossary

aft – Towards the rear of the boat.

AIS (Automatic Identification System) alarm – An instrument with an alarm that sounds when another ship is within a set range, used to help avoid collisions.

autopilot – Powered device used to steer the boat.

backstay – Wire supporting the mast, running from the top of the mast to the stern.

bilge – The lowest inside area of the hull in which water collects.

bilge pump – A pump to remove water from the bilge.

boom – A pole at 90 degrees to the mast, which can move from side to side, and holds the bottom of the mainsail.

bow – The front-most part of the boat.

broad reach – Sailing with the wind aft of the beam.

bulkhead – A structure that divides the hull into compartments.

buoy – An anchored, floating structure used as a marker.

chainplate – A metal fitting that secures the stays of the mast to the deck.

close-hauled – Sailing as close to the wind as possible.

close reach – Sailing at about 80 degrees into the wind and waves.

cockpit – Area at the aft of the boat where the boat is handled from.

code zero – A big sail flown from the bowsprit in light down-wind conditions.

companionway – The entrance to the boat's cabin from the cockpit.

docking – Tying up the boat at a marina or wharf.

dodger – Cover over front of cockpit, either soft or hard.

drogue – Small parachute deployed off the stern and used to slow the boat down in rough weather.

EPIRB (Emergency Position Indicating Radio Beacons) – Distress radio beacon.

fenders – Used to protect the boat when docking.

forestay – Wire supporting the mast, running from the top of the mast to the bow.

furl – To wrap a sail around a furler.

furler – Used to pull the headsail in and out.

galley – The boat's kitchen.

gybe – To change direction passing the stern through the wind.

halyard – Lines or ropes used for hauling sails up the mast.

hanks – Metal clips attaching the sail to the forestay.

heading – The boat's intended course.

headsail – The front sail flown from the bow.

headsail sheets – Lines or ropes that allow you to control the headsail.

heel – The tilting of the boat as it sails.

HF radio – A high frequency marine radio used for long-range communication.

hull – The main body of the boat between the deck and the keel.

iron topsail – Slang for engine.

jack lines – Lines running down the deck that are used to attach the safety tether to.

jury rig – An emergency sailing rig made from whatever material is available.

keel – The lowest part, or 'fin', of the boat that helps stabilise the boat.

knockdown – When a boat is capsized by the action of wind or seas to the point where the mast touches the water.

knot – A measurement of speed. One knot equals one nautical mile per hour.

lee cloth – Attached to the bunk to stop you falling out while asleep.

log book – A book used to record position, weather, etc.

LOL – Laugh out loud.

luff or luff up – When the front part of the sail flaps as the boat points too closely into the wind.

mainsail – The principal and largest sail.

mainsheet – The sheet and tackle used to control the mainsail.

multihull or catamaran – A boat with more than one hull.

nautical mile – A measurement of distance. One nautical mile equals 1.852 kilometres.

OMG (Oh my god!) – An exclamation.

pitch – The motion of the boat rolling fore and aft.

PLB (Personal Locating Beacon) – A small personal distress signal.

pulpit – A metal railing surrounding the bow for safety.

pushpit – A metal railing surrounding the stern for safety.

radar reflector – To make the boat look like a bigger target to radars.

reaching – When the boat is taking the wind side-on.

reef/reefing – To reduce the area of the sail in strong winds, making it less powerful.

rigging – A general term to cover all the ropes and wires that support the mast and control the sails.

Roaring Forties – The geographical location between 40 degrees south and 50 degrees south, named for the prevailing and extreme winds.

rudder – Used to steer the boat.

sextant – An instrument used to determine your position using the stars or sun.

shifter – A monkey wrench or adjustable spanner.

sked – A slang term for a scheduled radio talk.

skiff – A small light boat.

spinnaker pole – The alloy pole used to pole out headsails.

stanchion – A vertical post at the deck's edge that forms part of the safety railing surrounding the boat.

stay – Wires that hold up the mast.

staysail – The small sail between the mast and the headsail.

stern – The back-most part of the boat.

storm boards – Emergency boards used to cover a porthole if the glass should break.

storm jib – A small, strong sail attached in the staysail position and used in heavy winds.

tack – To change course by passing the bow through the wind.

tangs – Where the stays attach to the mast.

targa – A frame on the stern of the boat that holds solar panels, aerials and the wind generator.

tether – A safety line from sailor to the boat.

tiller – Used to hand-steer by controlling the rudder.

toe rail – A low partition around the edges of the deck.

trim – To adjust the sails.

vang – Light tackle used to adjust the angle of the boom and flatten the sail.

VHF radio – Very high frequency marine radio used for short-range communication.

washboards – Boards that close off the cabin to keep out water.

winch – A device used to control sheets, halyards or ropes.

windvane – A mechanism that uses the wind to automatically steer the boat.

windward – Into, or towards, the wind.

Recommended reading

My favourite sailing and adventure books

Aebi, Tanya, *Maiden Voyage*, Ballantine Books, New York, 1991.

Castrission, James, *Crossing the Ditch*, HarperCollins Publishers, Sydney, 2009.

Cottee, Kay, *First Lady*, Pan Books, Sydney, 1989.

Dicks, David and Ayris, Cyril, *Dave the Brave*, Cyril Ayris Freelance, West Perth, 1997.

Graham, Robin Lee and Gill, Derek L. T., *Dove*, HarperCollins Publishers, New York, 1991.

Hamilton, Bethany, *Soul Surfer*, Pocket Books, New York, 2004.

MacArthur, Ellen, *Taking on the World*, Michael Joseph, London, 2002.

Martin, Jesse, *Lionheart*, Allen & Unwin, Sydney, 2000.

Moitessier, Bernard and Rodamor, William, *The Long Way* (*La Longue Route: seul entre mers et ciels*), Adlard Coles Nautical Books, St Albans, 1974.

Morpurgo, Michael, *Alone on a Wide Wide Sea*, HarperCollins Publishers, London, 2006.

Nichols, Peter, *A Voyage for Madmen*, HarperCollins Publishers, New York, 2001.

Perham, Mike, *Sailing the Dream*, Bantam Press, London, 2010.

Ransome, Arthur, *Swallows and Amazons*, Jonathon Cape, London, 1930.

Slocum, Joshua, *Sailing Alone Around the World*, Penguin Books Ltd, New York, 1999.

Acknowledgements

I might have been out there alone but in no way did I achieve this by myself. The voyage might have started out as a personal dream but sharing it with so many amazing people during the preparation and actual voyage has been one of the best parts. While at sea you must have noticed I referred to 'us' and 'we' – I wasn't just talking about *Ella's Pink Lady*, Parker and myself but every one of you who was thinking of me out there and who helped in some way. It was your voyage too! I hope you think of it that way.

Firstly then, in no particular order:

Thanks Mum, my first supporter, and Dad for letting me go. I'm only just starting to realise how hard that must have been.

Emily, Tom and Hannah (and of course Elliott and Fraser, Hannah's guinea pigs), thanks for putting up with me, and for treating me just the same as always.

Thanks Bruce and Suzanne Arms for the trillions of hours of effort that went into getting me around the world, and thanks Bruce for sharing the dream and for being a mate.

Thanks Bob McDavitt for always having one eye on my weather conditions and for all the time that went into my forecasts.

Don McIntyre, for believing in me from the beginning and for the great advice.

Frase for going way above and beyond! That's all I need to say.

Thanks Scott Young, Liz Harrod and everyone at 5 Oceans Media for being part of the team.

To the Fredrics, thank you for putting up with such chaotic friends!

Neil Cawthorne, thanks not just for all the work and the sturdy electrical system but for always being completely honest. I'm sure it made the voyage safer.

Thanks David Lanbourne and Bucky Smith for not just the rig and sails that got me around the world but for committing them before I had a boat to put them on.

Thanks to the refit team for all the hours, for making *Ella's Pink Lady* what she is and for all the fun we had: Adrienne, Gilly, Jack, John Stout, John O'Dea, Les Arms, Ian Coward, Rod and Brenda Cran, Pat and Judy Gannon, Mick Tilden, Francois Jouannon, Steven Lys, Murray and Hayden Sharpe, Richard Taylor, Damien Williams, Jim Williams, Granddad Chisholm, Graeme Adin and Ed Zehr.

Thanks John Bankard, Chris Wilks, Chris Bone, Jim Hawke, Ricki Colson and Martin Chadwick for the support early on and for helping me get the experience I needed.

Acknowledgements

Thanks Aunty Cathy, Uncle Campbell, Aunty Vivienne, Uncle Andrew, Uncle Neville and Aunty Wendy for helping out in the early days.

Joe Akacich (Black Joe), Graham Eaton (Scooter), Dean Leigh-Smith and everyone at AME and the Gold Coast City Marina – thanks a million for putting us back together and for the support right when we needed it. You guys have hearts of gold!

Thanks Jesse Martin and Mike Perham for getting us through the madness of Sydney Harbour after the finish line. Jesse, thanks for being you! Mike, thanks for all the unintelligent conversations. They never failed to make me smile, and for understanding.

Arrow Caravans, Aussie Soles, Bayside Crane Hire, Best Cranes, Bill Woods, Coastal Fasteners, Dan Farmer, David Dicks, David Price, Dick Smith, Fiona Harper, Gary Cobb, Gary Slater, ISO Flex, James and Justin (*Crossing the Ditch*), Layne Beachley, Karen and Steve Chellingworth, Kerry Hughes, Dr Jarrod Meerkin at Body Composition Australia, Minards Diesel, Offshore Marine Training, Pearl Street, Storks Boating Services, Jason Mineff from Linemaster Marine, Dr Margaret Williams, Melinda Taylor, Nick Duggan, Rivergate Marina and Shipyard, Suzy Rasmussen, Graeme and Wendy from Sunsport Marine, Hamish Allen, Barry Colston, Pete Goss, John Ashby, Ross Cameron, Peter Becker, Michael Hogan, Lisa Fraser . . . Thanks!

Thanks Vanessa Radnidge, my publisher aka decoder! It's been great to work with you, thanks so much for all the overtime. I'm still in awe of your ability to understand my handwriting and spelling! Thanks also to Emma Noble for her publicity skills, and to Kate Stevens for the editing, not a job I envy! Christa Moffitt for the cover and internal layouts, and to Simon Paterson and Samantha Collins for typesetting so beautifully and quickly!

And to everyone at Hachette – including Malcolm Edwards, Fiona Hazard, Matt Hoy, Matt Richell, Jodie Mann, Anne Macpherson, Dianne Murdoch, Isabel Staas, Jacquie Brown, Katrina Collett, Clare Meldrum, Dannielle Williams, Heather Young, Brendan Fredericks, Pam Dunne and Roberta Ivers – for your support from the beginning. The first time I met the Hachette team and saw your enthusiasm for books and the voyage all my doubts about writing a book disappeared. Again, part of the team that got me around the world!

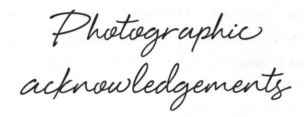

Photographic acknowledgements

I had so many photographs to choose from, it was really hard to decide which ones to put in. All the photographs in *True Spirit* are from the voyage and our family collection except where credited. The photograph of me and *Ella's Pink Lady* on page 341 is courtesy of Suzanne Arms.

Particular thanks to:
Ben Upton – Echo Imaging
www.echoimaging.com.au

Domenic Genua and Paul Ruston
Sydney International Boat Show
www.sydneyboatshow.com.au

Howard Wright/IMAGE Professional Photography
www.imagephoto.com.au

Newspix

News Limited photographers were there to capture some of the milestones of the trip. It was thanks to them that Mum and Dad were able to see me near Cape Horn and again off Cape Leeuwin. Newspix photos appear on the front, back and inside covers and also in picture section two, page 7 (top inset) and picture section three, page 8 (bottom left).

www.newspix.com.au

Steven Chee

www.stevenchee.com

Bureau of Meteorology

The weather map on page 307 appears courtesy of the Australian Bureau of Meteorology. MSLP Analysis of Indian Ocean Region, National Meteorological and Oceanographic Centre, copyright Commonwealth of Australia, reproduced by permission.

List of sponsors

There is no way I could have attempted my voyage without the generous support of all my sponsors.

Ella Baché became my major sponsor and *Ella's Pink Lady* and I couldn't have been happier. This company was the perfect fit for my pink S&S 34.

One HD were brilliant right from the start.

I'd like to thank all my sponsors for standing by me.

Australian Maritime Enterprises
Bainbridge International
Bias Boating
Bob McDavitt (New Zealand Meteorological Ambassador)
BWR Multihulls
Coastal Fasteners
David Lambourne Yacht Rigging
Easyfood
Ella Baché
Events New South Wales

Fibreglass International (FGI)

5 Oceans Media

Fleming Mechanical Self Steering

Fresh Promotions

Gold Coast City Marina and Shipyard

Hachette Australia

Hella Marine

Icebreaker

International Yachtpaint

Iridium

Jeppesen Marine

Johnson Pump

McIntyre Adventure

McMurdo Emergency Location Beacons

Mooloolaba Marina

Musto

News Limited

OceansWatch International

One HD

P&W Marine Engineers

Pains Wessex Australia

Panasonic

Pearl Street

Profurl

Red Lid Advertising and Design

Rescue Tape Australia

RFD

Rutland Windcharger

SatCom Global

Simrad

Sunshine Sailing Australia
Sydney City Marina
TracPlus
Trimworx
Ullman Sails
Whittaker's
Yanmar

You can watch
Jessica & Ella's Pink Lady
take on the world in her DVD

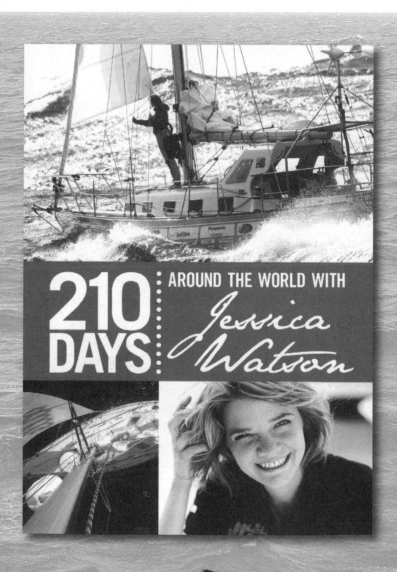

You can listen to the music that was
the soundtrack to Jessica's voyage

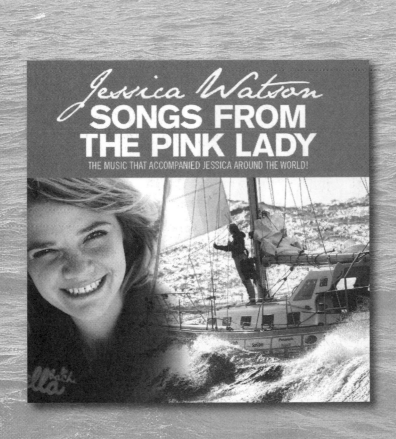